A Global View of Business Insolvency Systems

A Global View of Business Insolvency Systems

Jay Lawrence Westbrook
(Editor and Senior Author)

Charles D. Booth
Christoph G. Paulus
Harry Rajak

With a foreword by Anne-Marie Leroy, Senior Vice President
and General Counsel of the World Bank Group

THE WORLD BANK
Washington, D.C.

MARTINUS
NIJHOFF
PUBLISHERS

A co-publication of The World Bank and Brill

LEIDEN • BOSTON
2010

This book is printed on acid-free paper.

Library of Congress Cataloging-in-Publication Data

A global view of business insolvency systems / edited by Jay Lawrence Westbrook.
  p. cm.
 ISBN 978-0-8213-8103-8 (pbk. : alk. paper)
  1. Bankruptcy. 2. Corporate reorganizations. 3. Debtor and creditor. I. Westbrook, Jay
Lawrence.

  K1375.G58 2009
  346.07'8–dc22

                                                                          2009039585

ISBN   978-90-04-18025-3 (Hardback)
ISBN   978-0-8213-8103-8 (Paperback)

CONTENTS

ABOUT THE AUTHORS

CHARLES D. BOOTH is a Professor of Law and the Director of the Institute of Asian-Pacific Business Law at the Richardson School of Law at the University of Hawaii. He taught law for 16 ½ years at the University of Hong Kong, where he also headed the Asian Institute of International Financial Law. He has served as a consultant for the World Bank, the ADB, the OECD, the International Republican Institute, and the ABA-UNDP International Legal Resource Center on many Asian insolvency and commercial law reform projects. He is also a co-director of the Hong Kong Institute of Certified Public Accountants Diploma in Insolvency Course and heads the insolvency portion of an ADB law reform project for Vanuatu.

CHRISTOPH G. PAULUS is Professor of Law at the Humboldt University at Berlin, Germany—teaching i.a. national and international insolvency law. As an expert in this area, he has published several books and numerous articles. He has worked extensively as a Consultant to the World Bank and the International Monetary Fund in Washington D.C.

PROFESSOR HARRY RAJAK, formerly Dean of the Sussex Law School, has been a visiting law professor at the Hebrew University, University of Connecticut and Bonn University. He was a member of a Thyssen Foundation funded study on Groups of Companies in Europe, a study by the Wirtschaftsuniversität, Vienna of the Insolvency Laws of 8 central and eastern European countries, and has advised on reform of insolvency law in South Africa.

JAY L. WESTBROOK is Benno C. Schmidt Chair of Business Law at The University of Texas School of Law. He teaches bankruptcy, secured finance, and international business law and litigation. He served as the United States Reporter, American Law Institute Transnational Insolvency Project and as Co-chair, U.S. Delegation to the UNCITRAL conference that produced the Model Law on Cross-Border Insolvency. He is President of the International Academy of Commercial and Consumer Law and a director of the International Insolvency Institute. He also serves as a consultant to the International Monetary Fund and the World

Bank. Publications include *The Fragile Middle Class: Americans in Debt* (Yale University Press 2000) (co-author); *The Law of Debtors and Creditors* (Aspen 6th ed. 2009) (co-author); and *A Global Solution to Multinational Default*, 98 Mich. L. Rev. 2276 (2000).

FOREWORD

As General Counsel of the World Bank Group, it is both a pleasure and an honor to write a short introduction to "A Global View of Business Insolvency Systems".

Credit is one of the major driving forces of the world economy, and particularly in an adverse economic climate, its ready availability enhances predictability and commercial confidence. Properly designed insolvency and creditor rights laws play an important role in economic development, by facilitating the provision of credit in the first place, by encouraging the preservation of distressed but viable enterprises, and by ensuring that the assets of irremediably failing businesses are redeployed to more promising uses.

In the aftermath of the Asian financial crisis, the international community in 1999 mandated the World Bank to identify internationally recognized best practices in the design of insolvency laws and the due protection of creditor rights. The Bank was also entrusted with the responsibility of assessing the effectiveness of domestic systems through the compilation of Reports on the Observance of Standards and Codes. This is the origin of the Bank's *Principles for Effective Insolvency and Creditor Rights Systems*, approved in 2001 and revised in 2005, developed in conjunction with partner organizations, international experts, and the international community. These Principles, together with the Recommendations of the UNCITRAL Legislative Guide on Insolvency Law, form the basis of the Bank's work in this area.

The current global financial crisis infuses this work with particular urgency, as the Bank contributes efforts to stabilize and develop financial systems. Alongside the formulation of standards of international best practice and the assessment of municipal insolvency regimes, the Bank renders technical assistance to client countries, helps build capacity, and disseminates knowledge.

The present work by Professors Westbrook, Booth, Paulus and Rajak fits perfectly within this broad strategy, and forms an integral part of the Bank's insolvency and creditor rights initiative. The book takes a systematic approach to a variety of topics related to credit and insolvency regulation. The functional analysis starts with the study of debt enforcement, continues with an examination of general corporate insol-

vency legislation, corporate rehabilitation proceedings, informal workouts, employee rights, judicial and administrative institutions, and the
considerations key to cross-border insolvency proceedings. In relation to
each of these topics, the authors' primary objective is to illustrate policy
options with examples taken from a variety of jurisdictions. The authors
draw on a diverse range of legal systems to uncover the principles underlying bankruptcy policy. They regard insolvency and creditor rights as a
particularly complex area, in which legislative choices must be peculiarly
sensitive to local legal traditions and the social and economic environment of the jurisdiction.

The synergetic efforts of this premier team of international bankruptcy
scholars lift this exercise to the level of an academic *tour de force*. It goes
without saying that not all of the views they express would be universally
accepted. The views are, however, always well structured and clearly
articulated, and they constitute a valuable and weighty contribution to
the scholarly and policy debates in this arena.

While the views expressed in the book are the authors' and not necessarily those of the World Bank, it is important to highlight the affin-
ity in broad terms of the authors' approach to the Bank's own efforts in
this arena. The Bank is, and must be, guided by a deep understanding
of the fact that a "one-size-fits-all" approach would be particularly undesirable here. The Bank has carried out assessments of creditor rights and
insolvency systems in almost fifty jurisdictions across four continents. Its
approach emphasizes, not the prescription that all system adopt particular doctrines or policy choices, but rather the overall functionality of the
system. An effective system can function with a variety of legal institutions and techniques, provided that the legislative, regulatory and institutional choices are internally coherent, mutually supportive, and appropriate to the country's economic and social situation. Attempts to transplant
rules drawn from one or a family of legal systems without due assessment
of the broad features of the intended recipient's general system or without an adequate understanding of its social, cultural and economic environment are liable to prove inefficacious, or worse, counterproductive.
Real reforms are preceded by appropriate diagnostic efforts and consci-
entious research, and are driven by a conscious intent to find the appropriate solutions in the specific context of the jurisdiction to the specific
problems there.

The Bank's support for this book, which started under the leadership
of Gordon Johnson at the early stages of its insolvency and creditor rights
initiative, is an indication of the Bank's commitment to scholarly research

as the basis for ground-breaking legal work. The same commitment is also demonstrated by the fact that two leading insolvency academics, José Garrido and Riz Mokal, have just assumed the responsibility to lead and reinforce the Bank's insolvency and creditor rights initiative.

It is apt to recall that in ancient Greek, the word "*crisis*" means "*decision*". In a time of global financial crisis, policymakers need to take particularly complex *critical* decisions in the field of insolvency and creditor rights. I hope that this work will assist and offer guidance to those seeking to assess the appropriateness and impact of legislative reforms, and will stimulate academic debate on insolvency regulation.

Anne-Marie Leroy
General Counsel and Legal Vice-President
The World Bank Group

CHAPTER ONE

INTRODUCTION

We live in a time in which insolvency laws are being rewritten all over the world for the first time in a century. As investment and employment have become more global, there has been a sharp rise in interest in the application of insolvency procedures as part of the overall scheme of commercial and corporate law. There is also a growing need for lawyers and judges to gain an understanding of the insolvency procedures to be found in other jurisdictions where a multinational company may have assets and operations.

The purpose of this book is to provide a coherent overview of the insolvency systems found around the world. Its intended audience includes academics, judges, lawyers, and policymakers. Its focus is on businesses rather than natural persons.[1] We hope to give the reader a sense of some of the principal approaches to managing the general default of a business debtor. We will discuss the nature of the costs and benefits arising from the various policy choices legislators have made. In the process, we will emphasize the close interrelationship among various elements of an insolvency regime so that these elements can be viewed as part of an overall system and not just as a series of policy decisions about particular rules, such as the method of initiation of an insolvency case or the balance struck in setting the boundaries of an avoidance power. As we identify these points, we want to avoid either generalizations too abstract to be useful or a mass of confusing detail.

We will also avoid the easy labels so often used in this field, like describing a system as "pro-debtor" or "pro-creditor." There are some useful generalizations to make, but the reality of insolvency systems is that they have multiple policy goals and those goals are often in tension with each other. We identify both the policies and the tensions, discussing the various compromises that have been adopted under various legal

---

[1] We do not exclude natural persons in business from this study, but we focus primarily upon businesses that are corporations or other types of legal entities.

regimes. We pay somewhat less attention to traditional bromides such as "equality of distribution" as goals of insolvency and more to the costs and benefits that seem to us to reflect the judgments that legislators have actually made. In that connection, we often refer to three fundamental goals of any insolvency law—transparency, predictability, and efficiency:

a. Transparency in the enforcement process is important. Transparency typically includes a system of indexing judgments and judgment liens (for example, by recording judgments in land records), an accessible and inexpensive method of registering security interests, and effective notice of insolvency proceedings. These elements are important for the credit-granting process as well as for enforcement and management of a general default of a business.

b. Closely related to transparency is predictability. Lack of predictability in the legal system when enforcing the rights of creditors inevitably leads to inflation of credit costs to compensate for the resulting uncertainty. Predictability lowers those costs, so we will be concerned with its presence or absence. Generally, a system will be more predictable and fair if it is simple and clear.

c. Efficiency is easily understood as a concept while hard to measure in reality. We will be interested to understand it with regard to the needs and rights of both debtors and creditors.

Although these desiderata are universally applicable, each jurisdiction must also address issues of fairness and social justice as they are understood in that society. The insolvency laws of a country are closely linked with its other laws and will inevitably reflect its fundamental values.

While this book will be useful to law reformers, we would refer the reader to the UNCITRAL Guide, the World Bank Principles, and the American Law Institute Principles for suggested reforms. Our task is to provide a large-scale map of the insolvency field worldwide so that lawyers, judges, and academics can understand the traditional patterns and the emerging ones. They can then slot into the conceptual array the particular systems of interest to them.

The organization of the book reflects our view of insolvency laws as complete systems, including not only the "insolvency" or "bankruptcy" code of a jurisdiction but also closely related laws and the institutional framework in which those laws are applied. Thus we begin with an overview of the collection of particular debts outside of insolvency through enforcement of judgments or security interests against debtor assets. Then we proceed to the core of the work—business insolvency law—a collective response to a debtor's general default.[2]

We first address traditional liquidation provisions, proceeding more or less chronologically through the stages of a liquidation case, from eligibility for filing through distribution. The next subject is the process variously called in English reorganization, rehabilitation, or rescue. Such a process always involves an attempt to preserve the going-concern value of the assets of a business and at least some of its job opportunities and often includes an attempt to rehabilitate the company itself. Closely related is the emerging phenomenon of out-of-court workouts, with or without a visit to the insolvency court after the deal is struck. We also devote a chapter to employee rights because of their unique and important impact on insolvency systems. We then consider the institutions—typically courts assisted by official administrators and court-appointed private trustees—within which the insolvency laws operate. In that connection, we also consider the important role of regulation of those professionals (lawyers, accountants, and others) who perform key roles in the administration of insolvency laws in many countries. Finally, we survey cross-border insolvency, an increasingly important facet of globalization.

In our discussions, we mention some theoretical works, but our focus for the most part is descriptive and analytical rather than theoretical. Having said that, it will be helpful to state some fundamental propositions about insolvency that reflect our views and, we believe, the views of most experts and policymakers around the world. We start with the fact that insolvency is a collective proceeding, by contrast with the enforcement of individual creditor rights in the judgment enforcement process. In some rough sense, the individual enforcement system deals with recalcitrant debtors and the insolvency system deals with incapable debtors. However, the individual enforcement system also serves the function of identifying incapable debtors by forcing them into insolvency proceedings. The security system straddles the enforcement and insolvency systems. It is a super enforcement system for the individual creditor, superior in many countries to the judgment enforcement system, but it also represents the highest and best priority within an insolvency

---

[2] We do not address certain aspects of remedies. For example, we do not consider imprisonment or other physically coercive measures of enforcement nor methods of "shaming" debtors into payment. *See, e.g.,* James Q. Whitman, *The Moral Menace of Roman Law and the Making of Commerce: Some Dutch Evidence,* 105 YALE L.J. 1841 (1996).

proceeding in most jurisdictions. The secured party's special status following a debtor's insolvency arises either as a result of special treatment within the insolvency proceeding or, better still from the secured creditor's viewpoint, by freedom to enforce its rights without restraint by the collective system. These characteristics emphasize that these three elements—individual enforcement, security, and insolvency—are intimately intertwined yet quite distinct in form and function.

We begin each chapter with an overview of the various systems or approaches used around the world so that the discussion of each specific problem and solution can be understood in the system's context. While we are not in the business of advising the reader as to what approaches are better than others, we do try to note costs and benefits in various approaches, leaving it to reform institutions and policymakers to weigh them in the balance.

We try to avoid the United States pattern of massive footnoting in favor of an English-language bibliography. For practitioners and judges, the odd citation to a Dutch provision here and a Mexican provision there is not likely to be of much help in a concrete case. We do not claim to have done a global survey of laws or to report anything close to the full range of variations found in insolvency laws around the world, but we have drawn deeply on sources that describe the laws of many different jurisdictions and have included many of those sources in the bibliography. It goes without saying that we do not hold ourselves out as experts in laws outside of the jurisdictions where we teach, but we frequently mention a rule from a particular jurisdiction that exemplifies the point being made. Readers of course must go to national sources and local legal experts as to any specific legal question.

The terminology of insolvency law varies even within a single language. For example, most of the world uses in English the term "insolvency proceeding" to refer to a legal proceeding related to the financial distress of a business. The usage sometimes refers only to a liquidation proceeding but increasingly seems to include reorganization or rescue as well. In North America and a few other jurisdictions, the term "bankruptcy proceeding" is often used for a proceeding involving a distressed business and it too is used both narrowly and broadly. We generally use "insolvency" rather than "bankruptcy."

The four authors bring to the subject different perspectives formed by nationality and academic focus. One of the two American authors has worked intensively with Latin American and Canadian experts in insolvency law and extensively with experts from all over the world. The other taught for many years in Hong Kong and writes frequently about Asian insolvency laws and trends. The English author writes about British and Commonwealth insolvency laws and has edited commentaries in which a number of European authors analyze the insolvency systems in their home countries. The German author is a leading expert in civil law insolvency systems and has served as a consultant on insolvency matters for the International Monetary Fund and the World Bank. We hope that these varying perspectives come together to provide a well-rounded summation of the principal systems found around the world.

Insolvency law is often misunderstood as a sort of legal mortuary when in fact it is a hospital where the assets and the expertise of a business injured by management mistakes or the vagaries of the free market are recapitalized or rechanneled to renewed productivity and social benefit. The insolvency process is uniquely intertwined with many other aspects of a country's laws. It is also the ultimate scale in that the rights of entrepreneurs, workers, and creditors must be properly balanced if an economy is to reach its maximum potential. Those characteristics make its study both important and intellectually rewarding.

Charles Booth
University of Hawaii

Christoph Paulus
Humboldt Universität-Berlin

Harry Rajak
University of Sussex

Jay Lawrence Westbrook
University of Texas-Austin

CHAPTER TWO

SYSTEMS FOR THE ENFORCEMENT OF DEBT

2.0. *Overview*

In general, the most important method of enforcing monetary obligations in most countries is through the seizure and sale of the debtor's property. A secured creditor obtains an interest in the debtor's property at the start of the transaction by getting a security interest to secure payment of the debt. Upon default, that interest can be enforced either through private, self-help action (in some jurisdictions) or through a public official, such as a policeman or sheriff, often under court order. Unlike a secured creditor, an unsecured creditor must first obtain a judgment in court and then obtain enforcement of that order by an official under court order or through an official administrative debt-collection procedure. Both methods generally permit a debtor an opportunity to show that the procedure should be prevented or undone for a valid legal reason (for example, that the debt has already been paid).

Although the emphasis in this work is upon insolvency systems, enforcement of debt outside of insolvency is also highly important. Indeed, a debt-enforcement system and an insolvency system should be understood as part of one overall system. They should be designed to work smoothly and effectively together. An example is the close relationship between individual debt enforcement and the initiation of an insolvency proceeding. In an efficient system of enforcement of security interests and judgments obtained by unsecured creditors, a creditor's decision to enforce its[1] interest is fully credible. A debtor who is able to pay will do so because the debtor must either pay or lose its property. A debtor who cannot pay will be forced into an insolvency proceeding with the result that the debtor's affairs will be placed before the court for the protection of all creditors.

---

[1] Debtors and creditors may, of course, be men or women or legal entities. We use the neuter form of the pronoun here because this discussion is largely concerned with commercial debtors, a high proportion of which are entities.

The inability of a creditor to enforce a security interest against a debtor in a timely fashion—or at all—can skew the insolvency remedy. For example, where a debtor can withstand a creditor's attempts at security enforcement, the debtor has increased leverage. This often leaves little reason for a debtor to enter into negotiations with a creditor to restructure or reorganize. Eventually, the creditor might have no other option but to file a liquidation petition against the debtor to force the debtor to the table. But by that time the going concern value of the enterprise might well have been lost, leaving no more than the liquidation value of the assets. The debt enforcement system—both judgment enforcement and the enforcement of security—should reinforce itself. A lack of synergy between debt collection laws and insolvency laws is exampled in the various insolvency systems of Asia, wherein reform of the insolvency laws came well before reform in secured credit laws, thus failing to ensure that the two systems properly meshed.[2]

These examples also illustrate the process of balancing the rights of debtors and creditors—entrepreneurs, investors, suppliers, customers, and lenders. An efficient enforcement mechanism can produce one of two good results, either the collection of the debt or the filing of an insolvency proceeding by the debtor, the party with the best information about its financial condition and the need for such a proceeding. Forcing the debtor to the choice puts that decision in the hands of the party with the relevant information and provides strong incentives to make the correct decision. On the other side of the coin, the availability of a reorganization procedure to help a debtor who is unable to pay immediately but is arguably viable in the long term reduces the risks that might otherwise exist in giving the creditor an enforcement mechanism that operates with summary procedures and with minimum delay.

Secured and unsecured credit each play important roles in most developed economies, although a few systems (for example, the British and

---

[2] Secured transaction law reform and insolvency law reform are most effective if they go hand in hand and if changes are promulgated according to a time schedule. Nevertheless, it is not uncommon for calls for insolvency law reform to arise only after the onset of financial crisis and for the reform of secured transaction laws to follow years later, if at all. Unfortunately, this has been the trend in Asia after the onset of the 1997 Asian Financial Crisis. The initial waves of law reform focused primarily on insolvency law independently of secured transactions. Only in the last few years have some of these countries commenced the reform of secured transactions laws that will enable them to gain the benefits of the combined law reform synergy.

German systems) depend much more upon secured credit law as the lynch pin of their systems than do others. The balance drawn between secured and unsecured credit is a defining characteristic of a commercial-law system.

While debt enforcement has a strong and necessary relationship to insolvency proceedings, it has its own important and independent role to play in an economic system. Insolvency proceedings are not effective tools for debt collection as such. A collective proceeding is too cumbersome and expensive, and too dangerous to the survival of a debtor's business, to be useful for the purpose of forcing payment of a particular debt. Thus this chapter begins by examining systems for the collection of unsecured debt. It should be noted that in every jurisdiction there are intersections between the enforcement of debt and the criminal law. In some jurisdictions, nonpayment of debt is treated directly as a criminal matter, while in others criminal charges, or contempt of court, may arise from related events, such as violation of a court order to turn over certain assets to creditors. For the most part, this book does not address these criminal-law consequences.[3]

In this chapter the discussion of secured credit focuses upon its use as a mechanism for enforcement of a particular debt. It also serves as a powerful priority position in an insolvency proceeding in many insolvency systems. We will discuss that aspect of secured credit in the insolvency chapters.

2.1. Enforcement of Unsecured Rights

There are numerous questions of court or administrative procedure that are closely related to the processes discussed below. Obviously, the procedures that must be followed in seizing and selling the debtor's property, including the method for initiating action by the appropriate official, the notice required to be given to the debtor and others, and similar questions, are a function of local procedural law and vary greatly from one country to the next. The discussion therefore presents approaches to the process that vary as a function of the details of local procedures.

---

[3] Certain other methods of debt collection are also not discussed.

2.1.1. *Enforcement of Unsecured Debt in General*

The process for an unsecured creditor necessarily begins with obtaining a judgment of a court (or similar authority) determining that the creditor is owed a fixed sum of money.[4] In many jurisdictions, the process of enforcing a judgment is carried out by a bailiff or other official attached to the judicial system and under its supervision. The official is given a court order that directs seizure and sale of property to pay the judgment and is required to follow specified steps in carrying out that order. (For example, the official may be required to attempt to satisfy the judgment by seizing and selling the debtor's movables before proceeding against the debtor's immovables.) In other countries, there is a government office devoted to debt collection and its officials carry out the necessary steps.[5]

Once a creditor has obtained a judgment of a court against a debtor (and thus has become a "judgment creditor"), some systems provide a time of "grace" (i.e., delay) in enforcement. This grace period may permit the debtor to appeal the judgment to a higher authority or to pay the creditor the amount the court has found owing. In the case of an appeal by the debtor, the time for enforcement may be extended until the appeal is heard, although in many systems such a further delay requires the posting of a bond or guarantee of a specified sort in favor of the judgment creditor. The effect of such a requirement is to ensure that the creditor will be paid quickly and in full if the appeal is unsuccessful.

Most systems require that a judgment be served on the debtor at the start of the grace period. There may be special rules for "default" judgments, where the debtor fails to defend against the creditor's suit, especially in consumer cases. The enforcement of a default judgment may require giving the debtor a separate grace period to appear and provide an excuse for the failure to appear originally before the judgment is entered. After that opportunity, however, the judgment is fully enforceable.

---

[4] Of course, court judgments may involve many others forms of relief, but those are not within the scope of this book.

[5] Switzerland is an excellent example of a country with an established debt collection office (Betreibungsamt). *See* Christoph Stäubli and Nicole Battistini-Kohler, *Swiss Insolvency and Restructuring Law—A Short Overview and Some Issues of Debate in Corporate Restructurings in Switzerland*, 15 J. BANKR. L. & PRAC. 5, at Art. 5, III(B) (Oct. 2006). *See generally*, Stephen V. Berti, SWISS DEBT ENFORCEMENT AND BANKRUPTCY LAW (1997).

2.1.2. *Types of Property Seizable*

Unless the grace period has been extended or the judgment paid by the debtor, the judgment becomes enforceable against the debtor's property. In most modern systems, procedures exist for the enforcement of judgments against every form of property known to the economy in question. Thus a creditor can enforce against both immovables and movables. Amongst movables, the creditor can enforce against tangible property, securities, debts owed to the debtor (for example, bank accounts, accounts owed by customers, or wages owed by an employer), patents and other intellectual property, and so on. In general, the methods of enforcement are by seizure and sale of the property by a public official, by transfer of title of the property to the creditor by a court, and by recordation of the judgment in a registry. When the property is held by a third party, or consists of a debt owed to the debtor by a third party, enforcement may be by an order directed to the third party, as discussed below.

There are some limitations in every system. For example, few systems have devices for present enforcement against property the debtor will come to own in the future. In some systems, however, it is possible by recording a judgment in a public office to acquire an interest in immovables or even movables in which the debtor acquires an interest in the future.[6] An order to an employer to pay over certain amounts from the debtor's wages may be enforceable in the future on each day of payment of wages. In general, however, enforcement must be against interests the debtor holds at the time of enforcement.

2.1.3. *Exempt Property*

When the debtor is a natural person, there are often a variety of special protections, including the exemption of certain property from the judgment-enforcement process. Such property may include the debtor's residence or patrimony and certain necessary movables, such as tools of the debtor's trade or a method of transportation like an automobile

---

[6] *See, e.g., In re Hilde,* 120 F.3d 950 (9th Cir. 1997). California and Florida are two jurisdictions in the United States that permit recording of a judgment against all a debtor's movable property. *See* Elizabeth Warren and Jay Lawrence Westbrook, THE LAW OF DEBTORS AND CREDITORS 36–37 (5th ed., 2006).

or horse. Typically, such exempted property is defined with reference to both a category (e.g., tools of the trade) and a limitation of value per category or item (up to a value of so many currency units). There may be a total combined value limitation for all exempted property as well. Because of value limitations, such systems typically have procedures by which a debtor can designate which property is to be exempt within an exempt category of property, either before or during the enforcement process.

2.1.4. *Enforcement Process*

The enforcement of the judgment is usually done by a non-judicial official, often one connected with the court that gave the judgment. Most systems rely on the judgment creditor, formally or informally, to locate the debtor's property and advise the official where to seize it. However, a number of jurisdictions, including Germany, have procedures designed to require the debtor to appear in court and provide information about assets. In the United States, for example, such procedures go further to require the debtor to turn over certain assets or suffer imprisonment for failure to do so. (Note that the imprisonment is not for failure to pay the debt but for failure to turn over an identified, specific asset.)

There are a host of varying rules about the official's entitlement to seize property of the debtor and the official's liability if the wrong property is seized (e.g., property really belonging to another person). Some jurisdictions, like France, permit the court to transfer the title to the property to the creditor, giving the creditor the right to dispose of the property as its owner. Others require the official to offer the property in a public sale and then to pay the proceeds of the sale to those entitled to them, including the creditor. There are various rules governing such sales. These rules are designed to avoid collusive bidding and to obtain the maximum value for the asset sold.[7] They include requirements for advertising the sale, requirements for assuring that the winning bidder can and will pay the amount bid, and legal rules assuring that a buyer will obtain title completely free and clear of competing claims. This last point is of special importance. If a buyer takes the property subject to the debtor's oppor-

---

[7] A good example can be seen in a United Kingdom decision, *American Express Banking Corporation v. Hurley* [1985] 3 All E.R. 564, [1986] B.C.L.C. 52.

tunity to buy back the property within some period of time or subject to lawsuits from various claimants for the property, then the assets will bring much lower prices because of the perceived risk of loss to the buyer. The modern trend is to give the debtor a reasonable opportunity to buy prior to or at the time of the sale, but not later. As to disputes from rival claimants to the property, they are left to be settled in the determination of the proper distribution of the proceeds of sale, without tainting the good title of the buyer at the sale.

2.1.5. *Third Parties*

If the property is under the control of a third party—as with wages, a bank account, a securities account with a stockbroker, and so on—there are generally special procedures required that "freeze" the property but give the debtor and the third party an opportunity to resist enforcement before it is finally ordered. Thus the third party may be ordered to hold the property pending further court order while the parties resolve any disputes about it. Often a similar procedure is used where intangible property is represented by a registry as, for example, a patent right or a share ownership not represented by a physical certificate. In that case, the third party would be the administrator of the registry, such as the patent office or the corporate office maintaining the share register. A typical procedure would serve the third party and the debtor with the judgment and require the third party to disclose any property of the debtor it holds or any amount it owes to the debtor. The order would also forbid any disposition of the property. Once the debtor and the third party have responded, the court would rule on any disputes and then order the property turned over to a public official for sale or directly to the creditor. Ordinarily, if the property is cash or the equivalent (as with seizure of a bank account), the cash would be paid directly to the creditor in partial or complete satisfaction of the debt.

2.1.6. *Priorities*

It goes without saying that a debtor that is the subject of an enforcement action is highly likely to have other unpaid creditors, so that there may be a creditor race to seize the debtor's assets. That fact gives rise to a need for legal rules to determine priorities in the property or its proceeds as among judgment creditors. Priority rules will also be needed *vis à vis* other persons with interests in the property, notably secured creditors and tax authorities. Concerns that exist in this area are similar to those involving priorities of secured creditors, where they are discussed.[8]

In establishing a system of priorities among judgment creditors, it is also important to integrate that system with the secured credit priorities. This point is often overlooked, even in sophisticated legal systems, because the two laws—judgment enforcement and secured credit enforcement—are often located in different parts of the statute books. For example, the judgment enforcement statute may say that the priority of a creditor in a movable "relates back" to the creditor's filing with the court for enforcement, regardless of the actual date of seizure of the property. A secured credit law may say that a secured creditor's priority arises upon registration of its interest, regardless of the actual date of the loan. One law or both should say which of these priorities overrides the other in case of a conflict between a judgment creditor and a secured creditor, but this is not always done.

Once such a system of priorities has been established, it becomes more important to establish a registry of judgments and judgment liens, with indices, so that creditors can learn about rights already accrued against debtors. Such a registry should be part of the registry that includes security interests or the two should be linked. Given modern capabilities, it may be more practical and useful to simply link various registries so that one search will encompass them all. The United States is, unfortunately, an example of a jurisdiction that does not have such a capability in official form. Private credit services in effect provide the cross-registry searches but necessarily without the priority effects that could be established in an official system.

It should be noted that the question of priority between secured creditors and employees has been particularly contentious in many jurisdictions, especially upon the commencement of insolvency proceedings.

2.1.7. *Provisional Remedies*

Virtually all modern systems of judgment enforcement provide provisional remedies designed to protect a creditor against the risk that assets will no longer be available by the time a judgment is obtained. Their mechanisms are generally mirror images of the post-judgment meth-

---

[8] *See infra* 2.2.8.

ods described above, with the added problem of protecting defendants whose liability has not yet been established in court. Obviously, seizing someone's property before a court has ruled risks a denial of due process and natural justice. The most common safeguard is the requirement that the creditor provide a sufficient guarantee from which the defendant can be compensated if the creditor is unsuccessful in the lawsuit. In some systems it is possible for the defendant to respond to a seizure of property in the same way, substituting a guarantee for the property seized and thus obtaining its release. Another important safeguard that is sometimes found is the requirement that the creditor provide some evidence that there is an unusual risk of debtor flight or concealment of assets along with some evidence that the creditor has a valid claim on the merits of the lawsuit. The defendant may have an opportunity for a rapid hearing before the court, even after seizure, to rebut the creditor's evidence in either respect.

Many systems also provide for a provisional remedy of public recordation when there is a dispute involving real estate. A party may be permitted to make an entry in a public land record that will put all potential buyers and lenders on notice of the party's asserted interest in the real estate.

The procedural remedies for successful parties may include orders requiring the defendant to perform some specific obligations, but those types of provisions are beyond the scope of this book.

2.1.8. Cross-Border Enforcement of Judgments

There are many different approaches to the recognition and enforcement of foreign judgments around the world. Some countries, such as the United States, are very friendly to the enforcement of judgments from other countries. Others, such as China, are said to present many difficulties to such enforcement.[9] Because the topic is too large for treatment here, we refer the reader to other works focusing on those issues.[10]

---

[9] *See* Arthur Anyuan Yuan, *Enforcing and Collecting Money Judgments in China from a U.S. Judgment Creditor's Perspective*, 36 GEO. WASH. INT. L. REV. 757 (2004).

[10] *See, e.g.*, Gary B. Born, INTERNATIONAL CIVIL LITIGATION IN UNITED STATES COURTS 935–978 (3d ed. 1996); Eberhard Braun, COMMENTARY ON THE GERMAN INSOLVENCY CODE 592 (2006).

2.2. *Secured Credit Systems*[11]

Secured credit serves an important role in every developed economy, but its importance and the legal rules governing it vary greatly among jurisdictions.[12] Our discussion is only introductory.[13] Therefore this section does not provide a full description of various systems but discusses their principal features and their relationship to insolvency systems.

This section of this chapter is limited in two other ways. Most of this section is devoted to systems of secured credit in movables. It is so limited for reasons discussed at the end of the section. The second limitation arises from the fact that the focus of this book is insolvency law *per se*. Security interests in movables are of central importance in many insolvency systems but are often studied as if they were a separate subject. In large part, the reason is that they straddle two worlds: individual debt collection that works side by side with the execution procedures just discussed; and the collective default management system that is an insolvency regime.[14] In this section, we focus primarily on their role in individual debt collection. We will refer to their role in collective proceedings in the text devoted to that subject.[15]

Countries have made and will continue to make different decisions about where to draw the balance between secured and unsecured credit. Some, for example, may conclude that giving considerable power to a secured creditor is essential to produce a sufficient flow of credit to start-up companies. Others may differ, believing that too-strong secured

---

[11] For an extraordinary summary, *see* Ulrich Drobnig, *Present and Future of Real and Personal Security*, 2003 EUROPEAN REV. PRIV. LAW 623. *See generally*, Symposium, *Harmonised Modernization of the Law Governing Secured Transactions*, 8 UNIF. L. REV. 320 (2002). Eva-Maria Kieninger offers a set of 15 "cases," fact situations with commentary applying to each set of facts the laws of various European countries, a useful comparative device. SECURITY RIGHTS IN MOVABLE PROPERTY IN EUROPEAN PRIVATE LAW (Eva-Maria Kieninger ed., 2004).

[12] For one example of the importance of security in movables in enhancing the availability of commercial credit, see Nuria de la Peña & Heywood W. Fleisig, *Romania: Law on Security Interests in Personal Property and Commentaries*, 29 REV. OF CENTRAL AND EAST EUROPEAN LAW, 133 (2004).

[13] For a truly extraordinary comparative study of security interests in many jurisdictions, see Philip R. Wood, Comparative Law of Securities and Guarantees (London 1995). Another important source is the UNCITRAL, LEGISLATIVE GUIDE ON INSOLVENCY LAW (2005). Other excellent sources are listed in the Bibliography.

[14] Jay Lawrence Westbrook, *The Control of Wealth in Bankruptcy*, 82 TEX. L. REV. 795, 855–861 (2004).

[15] *See infra* 3.5.4, 3.10.7.

creditors stifle entrepreneurship. To some limited extent, the discussion that follows may implicate those questions. For example, a country like England that favors strong secured creditors may permit very broad general liens and creditor management of many defaults, while a country like France with a less favorable view of secured credit may disfavor general liens and insist upon more court involvement in enforcement.[16] Other jurisdictions, like the United States, may be in between, permitting broad liens and self-help enforcement but requiring substantial court involvement once an insolvency case has been opened.

The discussion in this section is limited to security interests in movables granted by a debtor by contract, along with the property right arising from a retention of title to goods by a seller, a lessor, or any other person who gives possession to a debtor but retains title to the goods. All these types of interests arise from contractual relationships wherein one party has an interest in property whose possession or title is held by another party. This section does not include any priorities ("privileges"), special or general, that arise by operation of law without contractual agreement, except insofar as it discusses the relationship between legal priorities of that sort and contractual creditor interests.

With all the risks attendant upon generalization, one might say that there are four principal categories among modern systems of secured credit: those derived from the systems in Germany, England, North America,[17] and France.[18] Overall, these systems run roughly in order from the German, the most favorable to secured creditors, to the French, the least favorable. Most of these systems permit security interests over most types of property and most transactions, although the French system is more constrained. Most of them require publicity concerning security interests, with Germany a notable exception. Many countries, including Spain and the United States, cover vendor's liens while permitting leases to partly escape the secured credit system; others, including France, include leases but exempt vendor's liens. The English and North

---

[16] Note that the United Kingdom has recently adopted some major changes in its system of secured credit. *See infra* 4.2.1.

[17] "North America" here refers only to the common secured-credit law systems in Canada and the United States, which are similar but which are quite different from the Mexican system. The Personal Property Security Acts found in the Canadian provinces are similar to, although not identical with, Article 9 of the Uniform Commercial Code as adopted in all of the states of the United States.

[18] The Islamic approach is *sui generis* and is discussed at 2.2.6.

American systems give broad play to private enforcement of security interests, while most other systems do not. A valuable example of recent reform is Mexico.

Because the modern systems share so many common characteristics, a summary description of any of them must amount to: (i) identification of its difference in key respects from general trends; and (ii) its choice as to the features that divide principal systems. Note once again that the discussion that follows is devoted to the secured-credit systems in exemplary countries as such, rather than their relationship to insolvency. Thus, for example, the discussion ignores the fact that the United States is very secured-creditor friendly under Article 9 but more balanced among the various interests involved when the insolvency system is also taken into account, while the British system is very favorable to secured creditors with or without consideration of insolvency proceedings.

The German system is dominated by security interests that for the most part do not have to be disclosed.[19] The result is that practically all commercial actors must assume that any property of the debtor may be subject to a security interest. To be more precise, the courts have imposed a duty to investigate the existence of a security interest.[20] Most German secured credit law is based on case law rather than statute. Security over tangibles derives in significant part from the concept of a vendor's lien on property sold. A "security transfer" gives ownership in trust to a lender, with the lien "extended" and "enhanced" to cover much of the debtor's tangible property.[21] "Extension" and "expansion" can be obtained as to vendor's transactions as well. Secured parties generally prevail over competitors for collateral, but an insolvency administrator may be entitled to liquidate the collateral and to receive from the proceeds a substantial fee for its administration and liquidation. Enforcement is solely through court action.[22]

British security law distinguishes between fixed and floating charges, although both have to be filed in a public registry to be effective.[23] Fixed

---

[19] *See generally*, Burkhard Jakel, *Outlines of Security Interests Under German Law*, *in* Bridge & Stevens, CROSS-BORDER SECURITY AND INSOLVENCY (2001); Tibor Tajti, COMPARATIVE SECURED TRANSACTIONS LAW (2002).

[20] Bundergerichtshof (Supreme Court), 28 Juristenzeitung 27 (1973).

[21] Tajti, *supra* note 19, at 277–279.

[22] Tajti, *supra* note 19, at 285–289.

[23] *See generally*, Roy Goode, PRINCIPLES OF CORPORATE INSOLVENCY LAW (3d ed., 2005).

charges are liens on specific assets while floating charges are potential liens on most, if not all, of the debtor's property. The key differences are: (a) those who deal with the debtor in the ordinary course of business take free of the interest created by a floating charge; (b) the floating charge is subject to a "carve out" in favor of unsecured creditors; and (c) the floating charge holder has a very favorable enforcement mechanism in the form of an administrative receiver. The receiver, generally an accountant and always a qualified insolvency practitioner, is appointed by the secured party. The receiver generally acts in the interests of the secured party, although formally the receiver is the company's agent.

In the United States, secured credit law is found in the Uniform Commercial Code, Article 9, revised with effect from 2001 in all the American states. The Personal Property Securities Acts ("PPSAs") in Canada (and now in New Zealand as well) were based upon Article 9 but represent a substantial modernization in comparison with the 1962 and 1972 versions of the United States statute. They are now in effect in all of the Canadian provinces in one form or another. Article 9 and the PPSAs are often joined in discussion as the North American approach, even now when the approach has spread to the South Pacific. The most important characteristic of the North American system is unity. It brings together to a unique extent all of the types of collateral and transactions likely to be important in a modern secured credit regime.

The characteristic differences of the North American system are in coverage and enforcement. In its near universality of coverage, it is like the British system but may go even further under the revised Article 9 in covering a huge range of transactions. On the other hand, the North American system does not contemplate management of a business and sale of the collateral by a receiver appointed by the secured party, even where the creditor has a general lien, so its enforcement system varies greatly from the British approach. The North American secured creditor is benefited by a system of self-help repossession and sale, avoiding the need for judicial enforcement, unlike many other systems.

The French system is much less favorable to secured creditors and much more complex. There are special rules for various forms of property, such as intellectual property and inventory. There is a general business lien—the *nantissement du fonds de commerce*, or enterprise mortgage—but it specifically excludes inventory and immovables. A security interest must be perfected by registration or possession, except in the case of a vendor's lien. On the other hand, leases must be registered. The French system includes a large number of privileges imposed by law and some of them are superior in priority to security interests. Enforcement for both possessory and non-possessory security interests is by sale after notification to the debtor.

Finally, Mexico presents an instance of a new reformed regime that combines traditional and foreign elements.[24] It has retained possessory security interests similar to the Spanish (and French) systems, but has added a nonpossessory security device similar to the security interests created under the North American system. It must be registered to be effective. Vendor's liens, however, remain free of a registration require-ment. Mexico also retains a "guaranty trust" device that substitutes an Anglo-American-style trust for a security interest device, although the reform has made this method closer to the new nonpossessory security interest in effect. It also permits a modified form of self-help in enforce-ment.

These five examples present a cross-section of the principal systems found around the world. It is probably correct to say that the North American system is currently the most influential in the reform of older regimes, but it is not uncommon for reform efforts to include elements of more than one existing system. Some aspects of international reform efforts are mentioned below.[25]

One last general observation should be made: we do not discuss "struc-tural security," which we may define as organizational arrangements that use legal entities, especially the corporate form, to isolate pools of assets in favor of certain creditors with much the same economic consequences as arise from security interests. For example, a lender might insist that a debtor corporation create a finance subsidiary and place the debtor's principal financial assets (such as accounts) in that subsidiary. The lender then lends to the subsidiary that "upstreams" the loan proceeds to the debtor parent. The lender is the only creditor of the subsidiary (which has promised not to incur any other debts) and thus has sole access to the pool of the debtor's financial assets held by the subsidiary, much the same result as if the lender had taken a security interest in those assets. Of course, the lender might take a security interest as well. Structural secu-

---

[24] *See generally,* Am. Law Inst., International Statement of Mexican Bank-ruptcy Law (2003) [hereinafter "Mexican Statement"]. Another post-Cold War example of reform is Hungary, which has a system that includes elements of the United States and the United Kingdom systems along with some unique local features. Tajti, *supra* note 19, at 293.

[25] *See infra* 8.2.

rity is generally much less important than secured credit and we do not attempt to include it in this brief survey of secured credit.

2.2.1. *Personal Guarantees*[26]

In many civil law countries, guarantees are treated as a form of security ("personal" security rather than "real" security), while in common law countries guarantees are treated as a distinct form of personal obligation. The reason for thinking of them as security is that they make all of the nonexempt assets of the guarantor (the person giving the guarantee) potentially available to satisfy the guaranteed obligation. However, the guarantee by itself does not necessarily create any priority for the creditor in any of the guarantor's property as a real security right would.

In outline, there are five types of personal security: 1. Suretyship; 2. Independent Guarantee; 3. Standby Letter of Credit; 4. Comfort Letter; 5. Codebtorship with Security Function.

With traditional Suretyship, the guarantor can be sued (that is, can be the subject of a legal action to collect the debt) only after demand against the "original" or "primary" debtor and in some systems only after legal judgment has been obtained against the primary debtor and enforcement has failed. In other words, the guarantor's liability is contingent on a prior demand having first been made on the primary debtor. The guarantor would be entitled to assert in defense any defenses the primary debtor would have had on the primary obligation[27] and also certain "suretyship" defenses, such as the creditor's failure to pursue all remedies against the primary debtor. A new form is "suretyship on first demand" that may mean the creditor may take action against the guarantor without first seeking payment against the primary debtor and the guarantor must pay regardless of defenses, but the guarantor may then sue the creditor for return of its money and in that legal action may assert the defenses of a surety.

An Independent Guarantee differs from Suretyship in that the creditor may take action against the guarantor without first seeking payment against the primary debtor and the guarantor has none of the suretyship

---

[26] This subject is succinctly but comprehensively discussed in Drobnig, *supra* at note 11.

[27] *Akzessorietät* is the term for this parallelism of the defenses of the primary debtor and the surety in Germany, where it has considerable importance.

defenses except fraud. Some jurisdictions find it difficult to recognize this form of guarantee because of a lack of legal "causa" to support the guarantee obligation.

A Standby Letter of Credit serves many of the functions of an Independent Guarantee. The condition of collection is often presentation of a document showing a failure of performance by the primary debtor under another contract. The bank, as issuer of the letter, is similar to a guarantor, but the transaction is treated as largely separate from the obligation guaranteed, subject to the wording of the condition that triggers the credit and subject to possible exceptions in case of fraud. These letters often state that they are governed by the Uniform Customs and Practices 600.

A Comfort Letter is often used by a parent company to give assurance of a subsidiary's performance. It may amount to a guarantee of some kind, depending on the interpretation of its language.

In the case of a Codebtorship with Security Function, the guarantor is in the same legal position as the primary debtor in every respect as against the creditor, so that the creditor has two primary debtors. The guarantor may have some rights of reimbursement as against the other debtor.

In any of these relationships:

a. The guarantor may or may not grant to the creditor security rights in its assets to secure its obligation to the creditor.
b. The guarantor may or may not be a professional in the business of assuming such obligations, like an insurance company, and may or may not be compensated for giving the guarantee.
c. Especially where the guarantor is not a professional guarantor and is not compensated for its guarantee, there may be special requirements to make the guarantee enforceable, including required warnings or required execution before a notary.
d. Guarantees in a consumer context may be heavily regulated or forbidden altogether.[28]

2.2.2. Security Interests Generally

Because most systems of debt enforcement depend upon seizing and selling the debtor's property, the key difference between unsecured and secured credit is that the secured creditor gets an enforceable interest in

---

[28] *See, e.g.,* Ulrich Drobnig, *Recent Legislative Trends in the Field of Personal Security*, 2 EUR. BUS. ORGAN. L. REV. 511 (2001).

the debtor's property at the beginning of the transaction, rather than by a legal action after default. Because the secured party wants to be able to seize and sell the property securing its debt ("the collateral"), it must have rights superior to those of the debtor once a default by the debtor has occurred. Because it wants to be entitled to the proceeds of that sale, it must have a priority (or privilege) over third persons who may claim some right in that property, including other secured or privileged creditors, buyers of the property, and an insolvency administrator.[29] Thus the secured party requires three enforceable rights: to seize, to sell, and to obtain priority in the proceeds of sale. It must obtain those rights first against the debtor and then against third parties. Enforceability against the debtor may be called "attachment" and enforceability against third parties may be called "perfection."[30]

It should be noted that the availability of the collateral is only assured if the secured creditor is protected against those who have acquired interests prior to default. Examples would be other secured parties or buyers of the collateral. For a secured credit law to be effective, it must ensure that a secured party can obtain a priority superior to that of these competitors or its rights may be of little value following default. A system that gives that priority in turn effectively restrains the debtor's capacity to transfer property without the secured party's approval, a result that may be called "asset constraint."[31] Where the collateral consists of most of the debtor's assets, or of the key assets necessary to its business, the result of the secured party's priority and default rights may be effective control of the business by the secured party.[32]

On the other hand, two types of debtor protection are often considered necessary. Debtors need protection against improper seizure of their property and against fraud or manipulation in the process of sale.

Equally important, third parties need notice of the secured party's interest in the collateral. That notice is crucial to provide stability and certainty in the marketplace, ensuring: (i) that purchasers can take ownership of property, confident that they are not subject to a secured party's

---

[29] Note that in the German system priority arises less frequently as an issue because there is not generally permitted a second assignment of a movable. Tajti, *supra* note 19, at 284.

[30] These are United States terms found in Article 9 but they have gained widespread use in English-language commentaries generally.

[31] Westbrook, *supra* note 14, at 841.

[32] *Id.*

priority; and (ii) that other creditors, secured or unsecured, know of the existence of any security interest and can price their credits accordingly. Thus the required notice accomplishes the general purposes of transparency in any market but is especially important here because it relates to specific legal rights in specific property.

The goals of a modern system of secured credit are to satisfy the needs set forth in the prior two paragraphs as efficiently and inexpensively as possible.[33] Each of these goals is addressed in different ways in various legal systems around the world. One of the reasons for the variation is the tension or conflict among these goals.[34] Because of the great variety of secured credit systems, it is difficult to generalize about them. However, certain patterns are discernible. Two are especially important: the requirement of publicity and the control of assets after default.

Most countries, both common law and civil law, have some form of publicity for at least some security interests in movables, but there is enormous variation in the extent of such systems and the approaches used to provide public notice. By way of example, most security interests in the United Kingdom must be registered to be enforceable, while in Germany most security interests are not registered but are fully enforceable. The consequences of the two approaches ripple throughout the secured credit and insolvency systems of each country. Thus there is actually a judicial presumption in Germany that a debtor's assets are subject to security interests, illustrating that the system of unregistered interests requires a prudent creditor to assume that a business's assets will be subject to priority claims by others.

A second pattern relates to control of assets, especially after default. Most legal regimes put post-default control in the hands of courts or administrative agencies that use public officers to enforce security rights. However, private enforcement is found in a number of countries, most of them common law jurisdictions. In the common law countries other than the United States there has been a longstanding use of the "floating

---

[33] See, for example, the European Bank for Reconstruction and Development's "Ten Core Principles," which accompanied its 1994 Model Law on Secured Transactions, discussed in SECURITY RIGHTS IN MOVABLE PROPERTY IN EUROPEAN PRIVATE LAW, *supra* note 11, at 102–104.

See also Jacob S. Ziegel, *The EBRD Model Law on Secured Transactions—Some Canadian Observations*, in FESTSCHRIFT FÜR ULRICH DROBNIG ZUM SIEBZIGSTEN GEBURTSTAG 209 (Jürgen Basedow ed., 1998).

[34] For example, in some countries, like Germany, where the bank lenders are especially strong, there is a concern that strong forms of security might create an imbalance between lenders and borrowers.

charge" that has unique characteristics. Without attempting to describe them in detail, the key points are two. First, the floating charge permits the secured party to obtain a blanket security interest covering all of the debtor's assets, although it permits free use of those assets prior to default. Second, default gives the secured party the power to appoint a private receiver to operate and then sell the assets for the benefit of the secured party, but under a legal doctrine that largely insulates the secured party from liability for any misstep by the receiver. The result is a system that operates largely outside of court supervision and outside the insolvency laws. Recent amendments to those laws in the United Kingdom have, however, greatly reduced the power of the secured creditor to make such appointments,[35] a point discussed below.[36] It should be noted that these systems also permit a creditor to obtain a "fixed" charge or lien on specific assets. That charge has certain advantages over a floating charge. In particular, the fixed charge is not subject to the claims of preferential creditors. Yet only a floating charge gives control of the enterprise to a receiver after default. As a result, a secured creditor may often choose to obtain both fixed and floating charges. Thus the English banker's saying, "The fixed charge for priority; the floating charge for control."

The intensity of the competition between preferential and secured creditors over certain assets, coupled with acute and opportunistic drafting of security instruments by lawyers acting for secured creditors, led to an attempt by secured creditors to have the bankrupt's book debts or receivables classified as an asset that could be included within the property that constituted a fixed security. Receivables are often the most valuable of a debtor's movable assets, and by shifting this category of asset from a floating to a fixed security, this device permitted secured creditors to leapfrog above preferential creditors. It was upheld in 1979 in *Siebe Gorman & Co Ltd. v. Barclays Bank Ltd.*, but in 2005 it was decisively rejected by the House of Lords in *National Westminster Bank plc.v Spectrum Plus Ltd.*, so that this important category of security remains subject to preferential claims.[37]

The receivership system is one approach to the problem of control of assets following default, but the use of private enforcement is not limited to the receivership method. In some countries—notably the United

---

[35] Section 250, Enterprise Act 2002—applicable to Great Britain (i.e. England, Scotland, and Wales but not Northern Ireland, § 280(2) Enterprise Act 2002).

[36] *See infra* 4.2.1.

[37] *See infra* 3.7.1.

States—"self-help" repossession and sale is permitted after default as long as there is no risk of a "breach of the peace." Thus the whole process of taking possession of collateral, selling it, and applying the proceeds may be accomplished without court intervention or supervision.

One of the reasons that characterization of legal regimes as "pro-debtor" or "pro-creditor" is often misleading is that such characterizations often focus only on the secured credit law or only on the insolvency law of a jurisdiction, whereas the actual position of creditors requires viewing both of them as part of a single system, along with the debt-enforcement law. Thus the Bankruptcy Code of the United States, which governs insolvency cases, is often called "pro-debtor" with some justification. But Article 9 of the American Uniform Commercial Code is strongly protective of secured creditors, providing a balance not obvious if only one or the other is observed.

2.2.3. *Title Retention*

2.2.3.1. *Generally*

The largest difference among systems of secured credit is the extent to which title-retention systems are included or excluded from the system. Most countries have the legal concept of title retention, where the owner of goods contracts to give to another (the debtor) the right to possess and use the goods but with the understanding that the owner retains title (ownership) to the goods. The two most common examples of title retention are found in the sale of goods and the lease of goods. The seller of goods often retains title until the full price of the goods has been paid. Similarly, the owner-lessor of goods retains title to goods and will have the right to reclaim them at the earlier of (i) default under the lease by the debtor or (ii) the end of the lease. Both arrangements have much in common with a security interest, including the fact that the party extending credit is entitled upon default under the contract to obtain the return of the specific goods, not merely to sue for monetary damages. That difference is, of course, crucial in insolvency cases, where unsecured creditors often get little or nothing.

The broader concept, which includes title retention, is title finance. It includes devices that are like title retention in the use of title to the property as a way of gaining many of the advantages associated with security interests, but often with fewer of the detriments. In title finance the financier has title or ownership of the asset as opposed to a mortgage or security interest. Apart from hire, purchase, and finance leases, other examples are trade finance forms, including retention of title; discounting, factoring, or forfeiting of commercial receivables; sale and leaseback; sale and repurchase ("repo agreements"—commonly used for investment securities and important in financial markets); and stock borrowings. Perhaps one might include in this bracket securitizations of receivables and repackagings of debt securities, of which there are many variations.

In essence, title finance often has the commercial effect of security. Indeed, many of the techniques are designed to avoid the obstacles of pledge laws. The attitude of jurisdictions toward title finance has ranged from enthusiasm to hostility. Some jurisdictions encourage the escape from the cage of mortgages and hence support form over substance. Others, like the United States and German systems, seek to rebolt the gate: they recharacterize a title transaction as security with the result that it often fails for noncompliance with a pledge rule or is reintroduced into the regime covering security interests (such as Article 9 of the United States Uniform Commercial Code). Some legal systems protect one form (such as seller's retention of title to goods) but not others.

Reservations of title have longstanding importance in continental Europe. A reservation or retention of title clause is generally found in an agreement between a buyer and seller and provides that the seller transferring property thereunder retains ownership of such property until satisfaction of the conditions in the agreement, such as payment in full. By agreement, the reservation may extend to the proceeds of the goods if sold, to the extent traceable. On the other hand, some civil law systems are hostile to this device.[38]

Retention of title devices are not confined to sellers but also may be used by lenders or other providers of financing for the sale of property. Retention of title effectively provides a security for payment of the purchase price. The well-recognized effect of such clauses is to confer upon the holder of the reservation of title a prior right or security interest in the goods in question. These clauses protect sellers against the rights of other secured creditors holding security interests, as well as against preferential rights granted as a matter of law. Retention of title devices often do not require registration or notice and hence may operate as a hidden interest when such clauses may be enforced without notice or registration to any

---

[38] Boris Kozolchyk, LA CONTRATACIÓN COMERCIAL EN EL DERECHO COMPARADO 404 (2006); Boris Kozolchyk, *Law and the Credit Structure in Latin America*, 7 VA. J. INT'L L. 1, 10, n. 15 (Apr. 1967).

other party. However, some jurisdictions (for example, Portugal, Spain, and Switzerland) require registration for the title retention to be effective. Indonesia uses a fiduciary transfer under which the creditor receives title in trust until the debt is paid.

There are various consequences of maintaining a separate legal regime for title retention, but the most important is that such interests are often free of the requirement for registration or some other form of publicity. As a result, these devices create serious potential problems in the market place, although those problems may be mitigated in some instances by transparency in practice. Another major difference is the strength of the device, with variation in rules as to when the right is lost (when the transferee buyer or lessee takes possession of the property, when the transferee resells, or at a still later point) and whether it extends to the proceeds of the sale of the property.[39]

The central point of interest is not whether title finance is similar to security—it often is—but the role of this safety valve. If a device is established and widely used to escape incompatible pledge and mort-gage restrictions, it should probably be governed by rules that address the problems discussed in this chapter with respect to security inter-ests. If devices of this sort are permitted, a title retention system that requires some form of public registration, at least for collateral values over a stated amount, avoids most of the serious cost disadvantages men-tioned in the discussion.[40] Those costs may also be minimized in systems where retention is narrowly confined to include only purchase-money situations rather than the grant of security interests over property already owned.

Although the concept of title retention is found in many countries, there is great variation in the extent that title-retention interests are treated as security interests. In North America and Germany, for exam-ple, all title retention by sellers is governed by the rules that govern secu-rity interests, while in France title retention by sellers is kept almost entirely separate from the secured credit system and governed by very different rules. On the other hand, in North America title retention by lessors is kept separate, while in France lease title retention is subject to registration requirements similar to those for security interests.[41]

---

[39] See infra 2.2.8.6.
[40] See infra 2.2.8.
[41] It is possible in France to register a title retention as a lease. This is done to gain some procedural advantages in insolvency.

In some countries, notably Germany, the title-retention concept has been carried well beyond the simple model of a "conditional" sale or lease of goods and permits by agreement a number of financing devices. In North America and elsewhere, the lease form of title retention has similarly been expanded to be a general-purpose financing arrangement.

2.2.3.2. *Ambiguity of Interests*

In legal systems where title-finance systems are not integrated into a secured-transactions law, the title-finance approach may provide a creditor with legal advantages over the secured-transaction approach. For example, the title-finance transaction may give the creditor an even greater power to reclaim goods in an insolvency proceeding (as in France) or permit the debtor and creditor to avoid registering the transaction under circumstances where registration would be required for a secured transaction. Where there are such advantages, parties will naturally attempt to obtain them by structuring their transactions as title retentions. If they do so without changing the economics of the transaction, it may be that the transaction is economically a secured transaction that merely bears the form of a title-finance. For example, the sale-leaseback, where a debtor "sells" an existing asset to a creditor and then leases it back is usually a secured transaction restructured as a lease to gain various advantages given to lease transactions over secured transactions. Especially if the advantages include avoiding publicity by registration, their widespread use can greatly reduce the efficiency-enhancing effects of transparency in a registry system because creditors do not know whether hidden interests have been granted to others.

This situation is also a problem with intangibles. If an assignment of intangibles for security differs in its legal effects, including a registration requirement, from an outright sale of intangibles, parties will naturally try to give transactions the form that provides the most legal advantage, even if the economic substance of the transaction is of the other type.

It is important to note that this problem does not arise merely because parties try to disguise transactions. It also arises because often the parties do not clearly state the nature of their bargain. For example, those who deal in accounts receivable routinely lend against the security of accounts and also buy accounts from their customers. Their contracts may not make clear which of the two is being done in a particular case. The variation in terms from contract to contract (for example, as to any obligation of the assignor/borrower to repurchase doubtful debts) may make it difficult to determine the nature of the transaction. Finally, this problem can arise where the parties are genuinely trying to achieve an economic result that provides some of the characteristics of a security interest and some of the characteristics of another sort of transaction. The law does not generally recognize this "in-between" state but will see the transaction as being either a security interest or not.

One approach to this problem is to authorize judges to review carefully such transactions and to "recharacterize" them if they appear to adopt a form different from their real economic basis. Thus in the United States, for example, Article 9 of the Uniform Commercial Code authorizes judges to determine if a transaction called a lease (that does not require registration under Article 9) is really a secured transaction economically. If it is, and has not been registered, then it is likely to be unenforceable in insolvency. However, that system also permits lessors to register leases in order to protect against the risk of such a recharacterization.

Other systems have other approaches. The German civil law code, for example, gives lawyers and judges the right to characterize any transactions on the basis of the parties' bona fide intentions.[42] Moreover, the BGB prescribes that judges must recharacterize a void transaction into a valid one if the void transaction fulfills all the requirements of a valid one; thus, a void suretyship might be interpreted as a valid guarantee.

Conversely, some jurisdictions in the United States have adopted "true sale" statutes that require the courts to recognize a transaction as a sale, not the grant of a security interest, if the parties call it that, regardless of its economic realities. It is not clear if the federal bankruptcy courts in the United States will accept these state statutes in the context of insolvency.

Recharacterization without protection for the creditor (such as permissive registration) has the disadvantage of increasing to some degree the risk of otherwise useful transactions (for example, leases). However, mere acceptance of the form followed by the parties may greatly reduce efficiency and increase the cost of credit, as indicated above, because of uncertainty created by a lack of transparency. For these reasons, some prefer a different approach: imposing certain secured-transactions rules —especially the requirement of publicity—on all transactions that are similar to secured transactions. The Canadian requirement for the registration of leases is an example.

---

[42] *See* Bürgerliches Gesetzbuch [BGB] [Civil Code] §§ 133, 140, 157.

2.2.4. *Obtaining a Valid Security Interest*

Turning to the specific goals of a secured credit system, the first—obtaining an enforceable interest against the debtor—is achieved, by definition, through a contract between debtor and creditor. What is permitted and what is required in this contract may vary. Some of the problems presented by this first goal have been resolved similarly in most systems, while there are substantial differences as to others. To begin with the commonly agreed points, three types of liens that were often not permitted in the past are included in virtually all modern systems: non-possessory security interests, security for future (after-incurred) credits, and security in future (after-acquired) collateral. Naturally, there remain differences in detail.[43]

2.2.5. *Types of Liens Permitted*

Possessory security interests are the traditional sort. Possession of collateral solves a number of potential problems in a secured credit system. It provides evidence of the agreement to grant the possessing creditor an interest, it eliminates the need to seize the collateral to sell it after default, and it provides effective notice to third parties that the debtor-owner no longer owns the collateral free of other interests. The difficulty is that the creditor's possession denies the debtor the use of the collateral. Especially in a business context, the creditor's possession of the collateral that the debtor needs to run its business and generate the funds for payment would be self-defeating. Further, most systems permit security interests in intangible property—like accounts receivable, intellectual property, and investment securities in electronic form—all of which are impossible to "possess." Thus every system has found some way to permit the enforcement of non-possessory security interests. Some systems have moved fully and openly to a system not dependent on possession, while others have used various fictitious or constructive concepts to try to bring non-possessory interests within the framework of a possessory system.

When a system departs from a requirement of possession, whether completely or partially, it must then solve the problems that possession

---

[43] *See generally*, Kieninger, *Evaluation: A common core? Convergences, subsisting differences and possible ways for harmonization*, in SECURITY RIGHTS IN MOVABLE PROPERTY IN EUROPEAN PRIVATE LAW, *supra* note 11, at 647.

previously solved. To achieve the goals of a modern system, it must specify the formality necessary to create and evidence the granting of the interest to the creditor (such as a writing), it must provide a mechanism for gaining control of the collateral and realizing its value, and it must provide a method for notice to the commercial community that the debtor holds the collateral subject to the creditor's interest. While there is wide variation in the extent to which modern systems have solved these problems and the methods they have used, the non-possessory security interest is commonplace today. At a conceptual level, systems vary depending on the extent to which they continue to rely on analogies to possessory systems in order to formulate non-possessory security interests, as opposed to adopting a new conceptual framework in which possession is simply another method by which a security interest may be made enforceable against third parties.

Most modern systems also permit coverage of future credits and future collateral.[44] The first refers to a method for making the arrangements for security only once, at the start of a credit relationship, while providing that the collateral will secure both credit extended at that time and credit extended in the future. It is especially important for modern "revolving" loans or lines of credit, where the credit rises and falls as credit is extended, the debtor makes some payment, and then new credit is granted. Similarly, modern systems facilitate security interests in property acquired by the debtor after the initial grant of security. These are essential as to inventory, where goods are being sold and new goods are being bought constantly, but they are also very helpful as to other types of collateral. In one way or another, these devices permit any outstanding credit to be secured by all the property of a specified type (or all property) owned by the debtor at any given time, including property acquired after the initial grant of security.

It should also be noted that one of the major advantages of a security interest is that in some jurisdictions such an interest can be granted in property that is exempt or otherwise protected from seizure in the debt enforcement process. Thus the secured creditor may have access to property that is unavailable to an unsecured creditor even after default.

---

[44] Where a system does not do so, there is pressure on lawyers and judges to develop alternative measures that in turn weaken the existing registration system. *See, e.g.,* J.O. Fabunmi, *Contract Registration and Perfection*, 14 LESOTHO L.J. 175, 183 (2001–2004) (Nigeria).

2.2.6. *Constraints on Secured Transactions*

On the other hand, modern systems vary considerably as to other aspects of this first goal, obtaining an interest enforceable against the debtor. The three largest variations among legal systems are the formal requirements for such a contract, the extent of the lien that may be obtained, and the exclusion of certain types of or transactions from the secured credit system.

Some systems impose fairly extensive formal requirements. For example, some jurisdictions (e.g., France) require that the contract be signed before a public official, a notary, and set forth a specific description of the collateral. Other systems, such as the North American system, have minimal formalities, requiring only a writing signed by both parties containing a general description of the collateral and waiving even the writing requirement where the creditor takes possession.

There is also considerable variation in the coverage that a security interest may have and the ease with which a broad coverage may be obtained. In the United Kingdom and in some other common-law countries, the "floating charge" routinely covers all or substantially all of the debtor's assets. In the United States, the "blanket" lien or "dominant security interest" may be equally broad, although in practice it is less common. By contrast, a number of civil law systems have no single lien so broad. Even the so-called "enterprise mortgage" in France specifically excludes the inventory of the enterprise. (For differences between the "floating charge" and other general liens as to management of default, see Section 2.2.2.)

The third area of substantial variation is in the exclusion from some systems of some types of collateral. It goes without saying that things excluded from commercial transactions (for example, sale of parts of the human body) are excluded from secured financing as well. Many systems provide for specialized methods of security for certain types of collateral, such as ships. Beyond that, however, many exclusions are merely historical accidents. That is, certain legal systems have simply failed to adopt the necessary rules to permit the grant of security interests in certain kinds of collateral. In other instances, exclusion may represent a policy decision. One very modern example of deliberate exclusion is the repurchase agreement, whereby a party buys a security at a certain price and the other party promises to buy it back within a certain time at a certain, higher price. Often the economic purpose and effect of the agreement is the same as secured financing, but because these agreements are common in international finance, most modern systems exempt them from the secured credit regime. In some countries, religious or cultural constraints may be important. For example, in Saudi Arabia and some other Muslim countries obtaining financial protection akin to a security interest must be through mechanisms that are Sharia-compliant.[45]

A closely related point is the problem of anti-assignment clauses in debt contracts. If a potential borrower and its customer sign a contract with such a clause, then the debt to the borrower arising from that contract may not be assignable for security, thus reducing the assets available for secured financing. Some jurisdictions have rendered such clauses unenforceable as they relate to debts[46] while enforcing them as to other types of performance.

One other form of attempted constraint on the grant of security interests is the "negative pledge" clause. The clause is often found in credit agreements, whether secured or unsecured. The debtor: (a) promises to refrain from granting security to any other creditor; or (b) promises that if it grants security to another creditor, it will grant a pro rata ("equal and ratable") security interest to the other party to the credit agreement containing the clause. In at least some countries, including the United States, such agreements are of limited practical value because they are difficult to enforce.[47] For example, in some Commonwealth jurisdictions where negative pledge clauses or other restrictive clauses are included in floating charges, issues may arise as to whether subsequent fixed charge holders had actual knowledge of the restrictive clauses.[48]

2.2.7. Enforcement

All modern systems provide for the achievement of the second goal of secured credit, a mechanism for enforcement of a security interest by seizure and sale. One of the most persistent defects in security systems is

---

[45] Michael J.T. McMillan, et al., *Shari'ah-Compliant Equivalents to Western Mortgage-Based Financings: Structures and Primary and Secondary Markets*, THE COMMON CORE OF EUROPEAN LAW: LAWS OF MORTGAGE (forthcoming).

[46] That is, debts may be assignable despite a contractual agreement that the creditor may not assign the debt. For example, this is the case in the United States. UCC §§ 9–406 – 9–408.

[47] *See* Grant Gilmore, SECURITY INTERESTS IN PERSONAL PROPERTY 1017 (1965). (United States); Tajti, *supra* note 19, at 272 (Germany).

[48] Gerard McCormack, *Reforming the Law of Security Interests: National and International Perspectives*, SING. J.L.S. 1, 20 (July 2003).

the difficulty and expense of enforcement through judicial methods.[49] This factor often results in creditors using only those security devices that permit non-judicial enforcement and a lack of available credit where such devices are not applicable.[50] Denying secured creditors self-help remedies can lead to substantial delays in the recovery of debts. For example, in Thailand where secured creditors are required either to reach agreement with the debtor or to commence judicial action, recovery can typically take as long as two years.[51] Indeed, it was estimated in 2002 that the backlog of 65,000 claims by secured creditors would take at least 7 years to process.[52] Delays of this magnitude can embolden debtors and make them feel recovery proof.

Many systems provide summary methods for judicial assistance in this process, so that the debtor by granting the security interest has, in effect, agreed to waive some or all of the formalities and protections of the litigation process as to the seizure of the collateral.

Some systems go further and permit private enforcement of various sorts. The two most notable are self-help repossession and receivership. Self-help repossession is seizure of the collateral by the creditor or its agents without judicial intervention. In North America, for example, creditors are allowed to repossess collateral in this way as long as no "breach of the peace" (violence or the threat of violence) occurs. Recent regulations in India permit banks and other institutional lenders to exercise this power with no court involvement except through debtor recourse to special Debt Recovery Tribunals.[53] Many jurisdictions will not permit this form of seizure, reserving that function to the state through the courts or an administrative debt-collection office. The new Mexican law represents an apparent attempt to take a first step toward private enforcement, although there will be disagreement as to its likely results. Regardless of the method, most modern systems permit relatively inexpensive and swift seizure, balanced by rights given the debtor to regain the property and even collect damages if the creditor acted

---

[49] On the other hand, countries like Switzerland seem to have efficient public enforcement. *See* Peter Straub, *Remedies under Security Interests (Switzerland)* at 219, in Ian Fletcher & Odd Swarting, REMEDIES UNDER SECURITY INTERESTS (2002).

[50] *See, e.g., id.*

[51] Lampros Vassiliou, *Legal Issues: Thailand, Siam Premier Guide to Restructuring in Asia*, at 127 (2000) at http://www.adb.org/Documents/Reports/Restructuring_Asia/Thailand.pdf.

[52] Thailand Economic Monitor, p. 35 (May 2002).

[53] Aparna Viswanathan, *Banking and Financial Law Reform in India: Will It Improve Lenders' Rights and Recovery?* [2003] J. INT. B. L. Rev. 257.

wrongfully in initiating the seizure. Some systems represent a middle ground, permitting enforcement by professional bailiffs without court involvement under some circumstances, such as enforcement of security documents satisfying a high level of formalities, including notarization.[54]

All modern systems have rules governing the sale of seized collateral. Some require sale under judicial supervision, while others permit a secured party to conduct auctions or even privately negotiated sales, subject to rules designed to ensure that procedures are followed that are likely to attract the most buyers and the highest price. Thus rules may permit private sales as well as auctions but often with a requirement of adequate notice to the debtor and adequate attempts to advertise the sale and attract buyers, a requirement called under the United States provisions "commercial reasonableness." Using such methods assumes appropriate and workable sanctions when the sale rules are violated, thus providing incentives for conformity. In the United States system, for example, the creditor risks losing its right to sue for any part of the debt that is not recovered from the sale.[55]

Receiverships are found in the United Kingdom and some other common law jurisdictions that permit a secured creditor upon default by the debtor to appoint a private receiver under a floating charge to take possession of the debtor's business and its assets for the purpose of selling the business as a going concern or selling the assets individually. In effect, many of the functions performed by insolvency administrators in other jurisdictions are instead carried out by the receiver appointed by the secured party.[56] Here, too, a commercial reasonableness doctrine may be said to apply. While the receiver's primary duty is to the secured creditor at whose instance the appointment was made, the receiver also has duties to others who might have an interest in the estate. Thus a receiver will be liable to make good any loss to the estate where he fails to observe appropriate commercial standards when disposing of the debtor's assets or otherwise in acting negligently causes a loss to the estate.[57]

---

[54] The Slovak Republic is an example. These methods, however, are often limited to circumstances in that the debtor cooperates. In Indonesia, sale is by the State Auction office.

[55] *See* White & Summers, UNIFORM COMMERCIAL CODE (5th ed.) at § 25–13.

[56] *See infra* 5.5.1.

[57] *Standard Chartered Bank* v. *Walker* [1982] 1 WLR 1410; *American Express International Banking Corporation* v. *Hurley* [1986] BCLC 52; *Knight* v. *Lawrence* [1993] BCLC 215.

2.2.8. *Priority*

The third goal of the secured creditor, to obtain priority in the proceeds of sale over others who have claims to the debtor's assets, creates three categories of issues: publicity (registration), the primacy of the secured creditor's priority (whether subject to subordination in favor of other priorities or privileges), and the rule for establishing priority (by date or category).

2.2.8.1. *Publicity*

The existence of any priority in a debtor's assets or a specific asset of a debtor necessarily creates a problem of publicity. The credit market, like all markets, operates most efficiently when it is the most transparent. Information about a debtor's finances is central to the pricing of credits for that debtor. No datum is more important than the existence of priorities for certain creditors in the assets of the debtor because in case of default the value of those assets will be lost to creditors not enjoying an equal or superior priority in them. Therefore, in principle there should be public disclosure of any such priority. (The fact of having taken the correct steps for publicizing the secured party's interest in particular collateral is often called in English "perfection" and the secured party who has completed those steps is often said to be "perfected.") The most common method of publicity is registration in a public office.

Nonetheless, no legal system is perfectly successful in requiring publicity concerning all priorities (privileges) in a debtor's assets. Even those systems that maximize such publicity and impose significant sanctions for failure to publicize have some exceptions for some priorities. Yet there are great differences of degree in various systems as to the amount of publicity concerning security interests, title retention, and other priorities. Some require most such interests to be disclosed to the market, while others produce very little disclosure.

The usefulness of a registration system depends greatly on the sanction for failure to register or otherwise publicize the existence of a security interest. Many systems make proper registration a condition of priority over third parties, but some do not.[58]

---

[58] For example, the new perfection law in Japan imposes this sanction for security interests (actually assignment of title as security) in claims but not for security interests in other movables.

2.2.8.2. *Exemptions*

The most important single reason for incomplete disclosure is the exemption of title-finance interests. Thus, for example, the North American system requires registration of most security interests under pain of forfeiture or subordination of the interest for non-compliance, yet an increasingly important category of financing, lease title-retention, does not require registration in the United States and Ontario.[59] A similar rule for title retention is found in Spain. In the United States, the effects of this exclusion are mitigated in practice by precautionary filings by many lessors. Conversely, the French system exempts vendor's liens from registration but requires registration of many leases. In Germany, there is a greater effect than in the other countries mentioned because the availability of the title-retention device for various types of modern financing means non-disclosure is so widespread as to leave the market with little meaningful information about priority interests in a debtor's assets. And in the United Kingdom, at least three institutions—setoff, the unpaid vendor's lien, and the resulting trust—that emerge from the general principles of equity enable a position akin to that of secured creditor to be established, despite the absence of registration or any other form of publicity.[60]

2.2.8.3. *Registration*

Aside from the extent of a registration requirement, there are three main variations among registration systems: detailed or general; officially reviewed or merely filed as submitted; and multiple registries or centralized registries.

Some systems (for example, the French) require detailed information to be filed with a public official, often including the security contract itself. These systems typically insist upon a fairly detailed and specific description of the collateral and the credit being extended. They may require refiling for future extensions of credit. Other systems (for

---

[59] The other Canadian provinces with PPSAs have adopted the rule that all commercial leases over one year in length must be registered under the PPSA.

[60] *London & Cheshire Insurance Co Ltd v. Laplagrene Property Co Ltd* [1971] Ch. 499; *National Westminster Bank Ltd. v. Halesowen Presswork and Assemblies Ltd.* [1972] AC 785; *Barclays Bank Ltd. Quistclose Investments Ltd* [1970] AC 567.

example, the Spanish and the North American) require only a brief notice, including items like the debtor's name and address, the creditor's name and address, and a general description of the collateral, often by category or type. The assumption underlying the second approach is that the third party searching the public record for this information needs only to be alerted to a possible problem so the debtor or creditor can be contacted for fuller information. The second system provides less information, at least initially, but is inexpensive to administer. The first system is more likely to lead to invalidation of security interests for technical and formal reasons, making their value less predictable.[61] On the other hand, the second system presumes a commercial culture in which accurate information will be readily provided by the secured party in response to a third-party inquiry.

To some extent, the two approaches just outlined for the content of a registration overlap with the adoption of two different roles for the registering public agency. In some systems, the agency conducts a content review of each filing by a secured party and refuses to accept the filing unless it provides properly the information required. This approach is supported by the view that third parties should be able to rely on a degree of control exercised by the responsible public agencies and that commerce will function more smoothly with that confidence. This "content review" approach may be more common where detailed content is required.

The other approach is to accept any filing that appears conforming, with little review by the agency. In this sort of system, the sanction for failure to provide proper information is post hoc, in that the filing may later be considered wholly or partially invalid because of the defect, with a consequent loss of priority. This second approach has the great advantage that the registry does not require a large number of employees and elaborate rules, so that its functioning is cheap and fast. The secured party has a substantial incentive to make the filing accurate, lest it be held later to be invalid, while any problem as to the content of the registration will have to be reviewed only in the small minority of cases where the debtor defaults. Such an inexpensive system may be especially attractive to countries in the development process that might otherwise find it difficult to support a comprehensive registry. The second approach also lends itself to an electronic registration system, which is much cheaper

---

[61] Substantive review by the filing office may lead to refusals to file and therefore delays and backlogs, rendering sales difficult.

and faster than paper records and easier to set up and maintain. On the other hand, a system with substantive review may be thought desirable where parties do not have ready access to legal advice and therefore the official review in effect assists them in filing forms that are legally correct and enforceable.

The third question about registries is the degree of centralization. Ideally, there would be one registry covering all possible contractual interests (security interests and title retention interests) and legal privileges (priorities by operation of law). The OHADA treaty is an example of one centralized registry, although admittedly in the context of exclusion of various types of property and transactions from the coverage of the treaty.[62] With one registry, a party dealing with a debtor (purchaser or creditor) could easily and cheaply determine all interests other persons might have in the debtor's property. Unfortunately, no country has yet achieved this ideal. There remain considerable differences of degree among countries, with some having unified the registration process much more than others.

The most important division is between movables and immovables (personal and real property). Even modern systems generally have separate registries for security in land, although with a variety of rules about movables that are associated with land, such as machinery installed in a building ("fixtures"). Hawaii is the only state in the United States with a single statewide recording office for immovables and movable property (i.e., real estate and Uniform Commercial Code Article 9). Within the category of movables, few countries have reached the ideal of a single registry, but some countries still have many separate registries (or other systems of publicity), while others have reduced the number of registries to a few. Multiple registries may arise from having different registries for different types of collateral, different types of transactions, or different types of industries (for example, farm products or commercial inventory). It is not uncommon for legal privileges (priorities as a matter of law) to be unregistered or to use a different registry. Multiple registries may also arise, especially in federal states, from having registries administered at the local or provincial level of government rather than at the national level. Such is the situation in the United States where the Uniform Commercial Code registries are administered at the state level but the transfer of copyrights are the administered at the federal level in the United States

---

[62] *L'Organisation pour l'Harmonisation en Afrique du Droit des Affaires* (OHADA Treaty), Oct. 17, 1993, *available at* http://www.ohada.com/traite.php. *See infra* 8.2.6.

Copyright Office. This, in turn, has led to debate as to whether the federal filing is exclusive or whether a filing may be made in either the United States Copyright Office or by a U.C.C. filing.[63]

It seems clear that developed economies will move in the direction of electronic registries that tend to favor less detailed notice and minimal agency review, although an electronic registry does not require those attributes. The key point is that electronic registration solves most of the problems of multiple registries because it permits on-line searches of all registries and the use of internet links among registries.

The search logic of the electronic system is also of great significance. As the search logic of computers improves, the need to search under a permutation of names (that is especially problematic for individuals) will likely ease. For countries setting up new systems, a possible improvement in the process to lead to greater accuracy in searches could be to search by identification number and not by name.[64]

2.2.8.4. *Other Methods of Publicity*

Although registries are the most common solution to the problem of publicity for priorities for non-possessory interests and privileges, three other approaches are employed. A common approach is title registration. In many countries, some kinds of assets are considered so uniquely valuable and vulnerable to misappropriation or fraud that a separate title certificate is assigned to each such asset, and transfers in such assets are recorded in a public file.[65] Ships, airplanes, and motor vehicles are common examples. Where such a system exists and is intended to cover comprehensively all the possible interests in an asset, it is common that registration of security interests and other interests would be accomplished through the title system.

In the case of security assignments of debts, some legal systems require that formal notice of the security assignment be given to the person obligated to the debtor on the debt. For example, if a store offered its accounts

---

[63] *See, e.g., National Peregrine, Inc. v. Capitol Federal Savings and Loan Association of Denver (In re Peregrine Entertainment, Limited)*, 116 B.R. 194 (C.D. Cal. 1990) (finding that receivables generated by a copyright must be filed in the federal system).

[64] On the other hand, the revisions to Article 9 of the Uniform Commercial Code in the United States had unintended consequences, because computers are so literal minded. Meghan M. Sercombe, *Good Technology And Bad Law: How Computerization Threatens Notice Filing Under Revised Article 9*, 84 Tex. L. Rev. 1065 (2006).

[65] Tajti, *supra* note 19, at 276.

receivable as security, the persons obligated on the account would have
to be notified before the assignment would be effective against them
or other third parties, such as subsequent assignees. The customers are
sometimes called the "account debtors" to distinguish them from the
debtor-borrower, the store in our example.[66] In some systems, the notice
must be given by an official in a prescribed form. Obviously, notice to the
account debtor is necessary before the account debtor is legally responsible to pay the assignee (secured party) rather than the original party with
whom the account debtor contracted. However, in some systems failure
to give this notice has more serious consequences than the risk of a payment to the wrong party. At the most extreme, the notice is a condition
of validity of the assignment. In other words, the notice is a constitutive element in the creation of the security; without notice to the account
debtor, the assignment has no effect, although there is no reason that the
secured party's debtor should escape its contract because its customer
was not notified.

In other systems, the notice is necessary to provide publicity concerning the assignment in addition to, or even in substitution for, public registration. However, notice to an account debtor does not fulfill any effective public notice function. Furthermore, such notice is impractical in
the case of bulk assignments and security over ongoing streams of receivables. The notice requirement is incompatible with the concept of security over classes of assets and security over future property that do not
lend themselves to individual specification.

For these reasons, there is a definite trend toward elimination of notice
to the account debtor, except for the limited purpose of directing the
account debtor to pay to the assignee (secured party) when appropriate under the assignment/security contract with the debtor. Notice to
the account debtor does not feature as a constitutive element of a security assignment in the UNCITRAL Draft Convention on Assignment of
Receivables Financing or in the draft chapter on assignment in the forthcoming part III of the Principles of European Contract Law prepared by

---

[66] The UN Secured Credit Guide includes this discussion at ¶ 26:
"Finally, the debtors of the receivables may be notified that their receivables have been
the subject of factoring (notification factoring), or they may not be so notified (non-
notification factoring). When notice is given to the customers, it is often accomplished
by requiring the assignor to make a note on the invoices that the assignor sends to its
customers."

the Commission on European Contract Law.[67] A number of civil law systems likewise have begun to adapt their laws in this regard.

Finally, some countries have a rule of publicity based on notice in newspapers or official publications. On the whole, this approach has been viewed as seriously flawed and it is not used in modern legal systems. It requires a constant monitoring of the publications that are used. Often those publications are not well-indexed, given their serial nature, so that a person seeking financial information at a given time as to a transaction with a new seller or potential borrower has no efficient or reliable way of determining what interests may exist in the other party's assets. This approach also does not lend itself to transactions on a national scale and may well become more of a "legal fiction" of notice than an effective notice mechanism. On the other hand, posting on an official website may be the wave of the future, at least where the relevant technology is widely available.

2.2.8.5. *Extent of Priority*

The second major issue as to priority for secured parties is the extent of that priority. That is, do security interests receive an unqualified preference in the proceeds of the sale of the collateral over all other parties? Some systems come close to giving such a complete priority, while others permit a number of other interests and privileges to come ahead of a secured party's priority. In the North American system for movables, for example, only the costs of sale of the collateral and certain taxes come ahead of a secured party's priority. On the other hand, in the English system, despite its favoring of secured credit, some privileges come before a secured party's "floating charge" priority, including insolvency expenses, although holders of "fixed charges" (security interests on particular items of collateral) receive a more absolute priority.[68] Hence, the attempts by

---

[67] The Principles are available in English at http://frontpage.cbs.dk/law/commission_ on_european_contract_law/Skabelon/pecl_engelsk.htm; See also United Nations Convention on the Assignment of Receivables in International Trade, Sales No. E.04.V.14 2004, http://www.uncitral.org/uncitral/en/uncitral_texts/payments/2001Convention_ receivables.html.

[68] The amendments to the British system have abolished the "Crown priority" in favor of setting aside a certain portion of the proceeds of sale for unsecured creditors. *See, e.g.*, Andrew McKnight, *The Reform of Corporate Insolvency Law in Great Britain*, [2002] J.I.B.L. 324. There is a similar "carve out" in German law but it supports administrative costs. Braun, *supra* note 10, at 128, at § 39. A number of civil code regimes give a priority to administrative costs to some extent.

creditors in Commonwealth systems over the past few decades to have their charges construed as fixed charges and thereby come ahead of the preferential creditors.[69] In France and Mexico, and in many countries that have similar legal traditions, employees have a "super-priority" that overrides security interests.[70]

The subordination of the priority of a security interest to privileges like taxes or employee claims in many jurisdictions exemplifies a "categorical" priority, that is, one that is given to a certain category of debt regardless of the date it arose or was registered. The other major method of determining priority among security interests and between security interests and other priorities is by date, with the oldest priority ordinarily being given first place. Within a rule of priority-by-date, there is variation as to what date is crucial for priority purposes. For some priorities, the crucial date is the date when the debt arose or became secured, while as to others it is the date on which it was registered or otherwise publicized. In some systems, there is an interaction between the two events—creation and registration of the priority—so that registration is essential to priority, but once registration is achieved, the priority-granting date "relates back" to the date the debt arose or became secured. There is sometimes an interaction between the categorical approach and the chronological. For example, priority might go to the debt first registered, but in case of registration on the same day, a debt in one category (for example, taxes) might have priority over other debts.[71] Conversely, priority within a category might be determined by date. Finally, some systems (for example, the Spanish) traditionally gave a priority to interests publicly created in a particular form.[72]

---

[69] See infra 3.7.2 and n. 142.

[70] See infra 3.4.1.2, referencing the debate in China on this issue.

[71] In many systems, certain privileges or liens, sometimes called "conservative privileges," that arise from transactions that enhance the property in question, take priority over security interests and other priorities that arose earlier in time. These liens themselves may rank in reverse chronological order, last in time first in priority. For example, France and the United States provide a "retention right" (not to be confused with title retention), or "possessory lien," that is given to certain providers of services such as lawyers, accountants, or mechanics.

[72] Another right of secured creditors, one that is both more and less than a priority, is the right of separation from an insolvency proceeding See, e.g., Stacey Steele, *Insolvency Law in Japan*, in INSOLVENCY LAW IN EAST ASIA 50–51 (Roman Tomasic ed., 2006); Braun, *supra* note 10, at 136–140.

2.2.8.6. *Proceeds*

In a modern economy, collateral of one type is constantly transformed into another. In an ordinary sale of goods, for example, inventory becomes accounts receivable or instruments, then cash, then the cash goes to the purchase of the next batch of inventory. It is characteristic of highly developed systems of secured credit that they extend the secured party's interest to the new type of collateral arising from the original collateral. That process can be viewed as value-tracing through the transformations of collateral.[73] Thus the security interest in inventory becomes a security interest in the resulting accounts receivable, and so on. Systems vary greatly in the extent to which they extend the security interest to "proceeds" and whether the extension is automatic. The German and North American systems are perhaps the most expansive in this regard.

The extension of security interests in proceeds makes security interests much more effective, but it also raises a number of legal problems. One legal problem is publicity. The new type of collateral that represents proceeds of the original collateral may be subject to different publicity rules. If, for example, the original collateral was an airplane subject to a certificate of title system and the proceeds of its sale is a promissory note, the method of publicity for the first (notation on the certificate) will be different than the method for the second (probably possession or registration). If the secured party is required to re-publicize (re-perfect), then it must closely watch the debtor's business. If not, then a later party will not be alerted by the publicity represented by the title notation.

A second major problem is conflict in priorities between the secured party with the priority interest in the original collateral and the one with the priority interest in the new collateral. A typical example is a bank account, in that both the bank (as lender) and the debtor's inventory supplier (on the basis of a proceeds claim) may have an interest. The solutions to these and many other proceeds problems are complex.

To explore these solutions is beyond the scope of this chapter. Because, as noted earlier, the German system creates a general commercial expectation that there will be unpublicized security interests, the addition of proceeds interests without publicity is not necessarily a serious burden. Parties have made commercial adjustments to the system, although there may be different views as to the efficiency of the required adjustments.

---

[73] Lynn M. LoPucki & Elizabeth Warren, SECURED CREDIT: A SYSTEMS APPROACH (5th ed., 2006), p. 162.

By contrast, the North American systems have elaborate rules governing publicity and priority in proceeds. Using the example introduced in the last paragraph, under the Revised Article 9 in the United States the bank would ordinarily prevail as to the money in the account, unless the supplier had taken steps to get a disclosed interest in the account itself. A price paid for this sophistication, however, is the complexity that it produces.

2.2.9. *Setoff (Offset)*

In many legal systems there is a right to set off mutual debts. That is, if A owes $ 100 to B and B owes $ 75 to A, A may satisfy its debt to B by paying the net amount, $ 25, to B. In English this right is called indifferently "setoff" or "offset," with no difference in meaning. The economic effect of a right of setoff is much the same as a security interest.[74] In the foregoing example, the debt that B owes to A is "paid" by the offset just as if A had a security interest in an asset of B worth $ 75. Instead of A receiving, say, 10 % of its debt in a insolvency distribution, A is allowed to cancel $ 75 of a debt that A would otherwise have to pay to B, a customer account that is ordinarily an asset of B in an insolvency proceeding. Therefore the right of setoff is often treated in insolvency as if it were a security interest, although registration is not required. It is not uncommon for the right of setoff to enjoy priority over a security interest in the debt held by the debtor. The setoff right is most valuable in insolvency and is discussed further in that part of this book.[75]

2.2.10. *Cross-Border*

Internationally, there have been a few initiatives to develop cross-border systems of secured credit, although these efforts are in the early stages.[76]

---

[74] *See, e.g.,* Afredo L. Rovira, Alehandro I. Lubinski, & Gonzalo Rovira, *Security Interests Under Argentine Law* at 25 (*derecho de retención*). This article makes the point that property other than a debt can be retained if it relates to a claim against the debtor.

[75] *See infra* 3.9.9.

[76] *See, e.g.,* Nicola Yeomans, *UNCITRAL Convention on Assignment of Receivables: Toward a Uniform International Law of Bulk Assignments?* [2005] J. INT. BUS. L. REV. 411; Christel Bourbon-Seclet, *Cross-Border Security Interests in Movable Property: An Attempt at Rationalising the International Patchwork: Part 1*, [2005] J. INT. BUS. L. REV. 419; Roy Goode, *The Protection of Interests in Movables in Transnational Commercial Law*, 3 UNIF. L. REV. 453 (1998). *See generally* UNCITRAL, LEGISLATIVE GUIDE (2005).

Aside from these efforts, courts are required to apply choice-of-law rules to determine which laws control as to transnational security interests when the collateral is in more than one country. The traditional rule is that the place of location of the collateral ("situs") is controlling and that is the rule in most countries.[77] However, Article 9 in the United States has adopted a rule of the debtor's state of incorporation as a substitute in most domestic transactions involving intangible collateral like accounts. In part, this change was a response to the difficulty of "locating" modern intangible collateral like accounts and intellectual property. Most legal systems have fictional "locations" for such collateral (for example, the place where an account is to be paid) as a method of applying the traditional situs rule. These questions are underdeveloped and in the process of reexamination in many countries, so it is not possible to state very much detail about their resolution. Some legal systems permit the parties to choose the applicable law.[78]

Perhaps the most odd choice-of-law rule is found in the revision of Article 9 of the Uniform Commercial Code in the United States. For debtor corporations organized under the laws of a country other than the United States, perfection for non-possessory security interests requires registration in the jurisdiction of the debtor's place of business or chief executive office, subject to an ex post determination by a United States judge that the jurisdiction of registration has a system that has roughly the same consequences that would apply under United States law.[79]

2.2.11. *Consolidation of Laws*

In many jurisdictions, there are a number of different laws governing secured transactions and related transactions like title retention, leasing, and legal privileges. In others, the laws have been consolidated to some extent. One of the greatest intellectual and practical accomplishments of Article 9 in the United States was the integration of most types of secured transactions into one law, with variations in methods of publicity (perfection) and other details, but with a single set of concepts and priority rules. The latest revision has gone even further in bringing more types of collateral and transactions into the coverage of Article 9,

---

[77] For example, see the EU Insolvency Regulation, Article 6.

[78] Nigel J. Howcroft and Hugh Gillespie, *Remedies under Security Interests* (Bermuda), in Fletcher & Swarting.

[79] UCC 9–307(b)–(c).

although important categories of economically similar transactions (like leases) remain outside its operation. Cutting against the approach of Article 9 are the problems that arise when laws are made exceedingly detailed and complex, a problem that has been especially serious in common law countries.

Going against the consolidation trend is the emergence of special laws concerning certain types of financial collateral. A leading example is the European Union Directive on Collateral.[80]

2.2.12. *International Initiatives*

There are several international initiatives relating to secured credit. Particularly noteworthy are those of the European Bank for Reconstruction and Development, which offers a Model Law based substantially on Article 9,[81] and UNCITRAL, which has proposed a Model Law on the assignment of receivables internationally.

2.2.13. *Immovables (Real Estate)*

Mortgages on immovables are an important potential source of commercial credit, although as an economy develops they tend to become less important as compared with security interests in movables. These liens will not receive extended discussion in this work for two reasons. First, in a number of countries the entire system of land ownership and registration has serious defects, making impossible an effective system for notice and enforcement of liens on immovables.[82] The second reason is that countries with workable systems of land ownership have systems that are highly variable from country to country and are closely tied to local real property laws and their particular histories. In most of those coun-

---

[80] EU Directives: Directive 2002/47/EC (financial collateral arrangements) and Directive 2009/44/EC amending Directive 98/26/EC (settlement finality). *Cf. France Eases Restrictions on Collateral and Netting*, INT'L FIN. L. REV. (June 2005).

See, e.g., Nuria de la Peña & Heywood W. Fleisig, Romania: *Law on Security Interests in Personal Property and Commentaries*, 29 REV. CENTR. & E. EUR. LAW 133 (2004).

[81] *See* Tajti, *supra* note 19, at 293. *See generally* Frederique Dahan and John Simpson, *The European Bank for Reconstruction and Development's Secured Transaction Project: A Model Law and Ten Core Principles for a Modern Secured Transaction Law in Countries of Central and Eastern Europe (and elsewhere)*, in Kieninger.

[82] *See, e.g.*, Tajti, *supra* note 19, at n. 1249 (Serbia). *See generally*, Hernando de Soto, THE MYSTERY OF CAPITAL (2000).

tries the systems of security in immovables work reasonably well, subject to broader institutional problems of judicial or administrative expense, delay, or influence.[83]

Two points that should be considered nonetheless are non-judicial enforcement and the modernization of procedures generally. There are systems that use trusts or separate corporate entities to permit creditors to take ownership of an immovable, or to sell it, upon a debtor's default, without incurring the expense and delay of a judicial proceeding. One example is found in the "Deed of Trust" system in a number of jurisdictions within the United States;[84] another example is the procedure for enforcement of mortgages in Turkey when there is acknowledgement of default by the debtor.[85] Mexico also has a trust system often used for liens on immovables.[86] On the other hand, enforcement procedures in some countries are burdened with old-fashioned, inefficient procedures, especially with regard to the mechanics of sales and the debtor's right to reclaim the property. Time and money can often be saved with more modern procedures that still provide ample protection for debtor's rights.

2.2.14. Theoretical Debates

Although in this book we avoid purely theoretical discussions for the most part, we should offer at least a glance at the longstanding and extensive debates concerning secured credit in the academic literature in the United States.[87] The debate seems to have been sustained by a sense, not often articulated, that there should be some justification for giving certain creditors enormous advantages over others. For more than a decade the debate centered on the efficiency *vel non* of permitting secured credit. It began with a question: if interest rates were lowered (good) by secured creditors because of their lowered risks, why would not that benefit be canceled by interest rate increases by unsecured creditors whose risk was increased by the grant of security? Various

---

[83] Philip R. Wood, COMPARATIVE LAW OF SECURITY INTERESTS AND TITLE FINANCE, 264–266, 554–555 (2007).

[84] Restatement of the Law—Property Restatement (Third) of Property: Mortgages § 3.3. *See* Bender et al., MODERN REAL ESTATE FINANCE AND LAND TRANSFER 100–104 (3d ed. 2006).

[85] *Id.* at 431.

[86] *See* ALI Mexican Statement App. E, 179.

[87] For a sampling, see the authorities collected in Westbrook, *supra* note 14, at n. 8.

reasons were advanced, including claims that unseured creditors relied upon the "monitoring" of the debtor by the secured creditor, that the grant of secured credit was a "signal" that the debtor was financially sound, and that secured creditors (especially banks) would give the debtor good advice and could make sure the debtor took it. None of the justifications has won general acceptance.

More recently, the focus has been on the control that secured creditors exercise over a debtor in financial distress, partly or wholly replacing the role of the insolvency administrator. It is generally agreed that control by secured creditors has increased, at least in the case of large companies where management has been separated from ownership, but there remains a fierce contention as to whether this development is to be cheered or deplored.

CHAPTER THREE

CORPORATE INSOLVENCY LEGISLATION

3.0. *Introduction*

This chapter introduces insolvency legislation and policy generally, but with an emphasis on liquidation. Rehabilitation is discussed more fully in Chapter 4. The choice between the two types of proceedings is one of the issues that often must be considered prior to the commencement of a formal proceeding. The other two are valuation of the business and the liability of directors. We start with those three and then turn to the procedure.

3.1. *The Liquidation/Rehabilitation Dynamic*

The choice between liquidation and rehabilitation is complex and dynamic, changing with evolving circumstances as a proceeding continues. For that reason, it is important that there be readily usable procedures for choosing liquidation or rehabilitation and for converting from one to the other.

Some countries adopt a unitary approach (e.g., France, Germany, Mexico) that establishes an interim period for review of the business prospects before deciding on whether to liquidate or rehabilitate the business. In countries that do not adopt the unitary approach, it is particularly important that the court and participants have the ability to request a conversion of the proceeding where, in retrospect or based on a change in the financial circumstances of the enterprise, it becomes apparent that rehabilitation can or cannot be achieved. As discussed under the provisions on rehabilitation below, conversion to liquidation might be appropriate even after a restructuring plan has been approved if approval for the plan has been procured by fraud or the enterprise is unable to perform its restructured obligations under the plan. Typically, proponents of conversion will be those with a financial stake in the outcome of the proceeding (e.g., creditors, management, unions, etc.).

3.2. *Valuation*

Valuation issues are fundamental in insolvency cases. They are especially important in reorganizations because a central point of the proceeding is to avoid selling the property of the business, which means its value must be estimated for various purposes. Prior to commencement of a formal proceeding, valuation may be important to determine insolvency on a balance-sheet basis, *inter alia*, to determine possible liability of directors and officers and to permit a formal proceeding to be opened. It may also be important to permit sale of the business as a going concern as part of an out-of-court workout. In the Western countries valuation is generally done by independent experts hired by individual creditors, by creditors committees, or by management.

Once a case has been commenced, valuation is often immediately important to determine the position of secured creditors pending proposal of a reorganization plan and for evaluation of a plan when one is proposed. In the United States, until the mid-1980s it was common for creditor committees in larger cases to hire accountants to assess the value of a distribution proposed in a plan of reorganization. In the mid-1980s investment bankers started to get involved in the process, and once one official committee hired one, it was only a short time before almost all did in the larger cases. It is also common for the debtor in possession in large cases to hire an investment banker of its own. The upshot of this hiring of experts is that in the United States creditors have come as close as they can get to full assessment of the risks and values involved in a proposed plan of reorganization. (Of course, this better assessment often comes at a high cost, including delay.) On the other hand, in a typical reorganization, a full-blown valuation of the company usually will not be necessary unless a cram-down[1] is proposed. In smaller cases, where less expensive approaches are necessary, accountants and uninvolved bankers are often employed. In real estate cases, the relevant expert is typically a specialist in real estate appraisal.

---

[1] *See infra* 4.5.3.

3.3. *Director and Officer Liability*

3.3.1. *Comparative Legislative Survey*

3.3.1.1. *Background: Common Law/Case Law Approach*

Over the years, various case law approaches have developed in many common law systems regarding when directors may be held liable for actions that lead a company into insolvency. In a recent paper, one commentator discusses the development of the following common law principles in England:[2]

1. The imposition on directors of duties of good faith and the practice of care and skill;
2. The assurance that a limited liability company's capital would be available to creditors by requiring that dividends be payable out of profits and by prohibiting companies from purchasing their own shares or issuing shares at a discount; and
3. The development of the *ultra vires* doctrine, by which a court could declare actions outside a company's object clause to be void (including misfeasance, breach of fiduciary duty, or unlawful conduct).

Similar principles have developed in other common law jurisdictions. Other principles include holding directors personally liable under arguments based on the "piercing of the corporate veil" and imposing a duty to creditors when a company is insolvent or in "the zone of insolvency."[3]

Over the years some of these common law principles have been codified in the companies or corporate law of common law jurisdictions. For example, in Canada creditors and shareholders rely on corporate law oppression remedy provisions in attempts to pierce the corporate veil.[4] In some jurisdictions, directors can also be held personally liable for unpaid wages owed to workers.

---

[2] Harry Rajak, *Director and Officer Liability in the Zone of Insolvency: A Comparative Analysis*, II POTCHEFSTROOM ELEC. L. J. 32 (2008).

[3] This duty has been expanding in a number of jurisdictions despite academic criticism. *See generally*, Henry Hu & Jay Lawrence Westbrook, *Abolition of the Corporate Duty to Creditors*, 107 COLUM. L. REV. 1321 (2007).

[4] Janis Sarra, *The Oppression Remedy: The Peoples' Choice*, in ANNUAL REVIEW OF INSOLVENCY LAW 133 (Janis P. Sarra, ed., 2005).

However, it must be noted that, although these principles will often be applicable in insolvency situations, the principles themselves are broader than that and also apply to non-insolvency situations. The primary difficulties with the common law approach are that it requires litigation, it is expensive, and many of the principles require burdens of proof that are difficult to meet, with the result that cases are infrequently commenced.

3.3.1.2. *Specific Insolvency Law Statutory Provisions*

In many jurisdictions in which the company law has English origins, the legislator has supplemented the case law approaches described above with corporate insolvency law provisions prohibiting fraudulent trading and, to an increasing extent, wrongful/insolvent trading. Examples can be found in the United Kingdom, Australia, Hong Kong, New Zealand, Singapore, and South Africa. These provisions are triggered by the winding up of a company.

3.3.1.2.1. *Fraudulent Trading*
This provision provides for both civil and criminal liability against any person who was knowingly party to the carrying on of business where it appears that any business of the company has been carried on with intent to defraud creditors of the company or creditors of any other person or for any fraudulent purpose. Of course, in particular jurisdictions there are differences in application. For example, in England and Australia, the provision may be used only by the liquidator; in Hong Kong, the official receiver or any contributor or creditor may also bring suit. In South Africa, creditors may also bring suit.

The scope of the potential target of the provision is broad. Of course, directors will be the main target but other potential targets might include shadow directors, creditors, or holding companies. As the standard of proof is very high (requiring proof of dishonesty), the provision is rarely used. Moreover, in those cases in which civil recovery is sought, the potential defendants may have little or no resources. Forcing them into an insolvency proceeding will be of little benefit to the insolvent company's creditors.

The South African provision extends the scope of this provision to also cover persons who carried on the business of the company "recklessly," which has been interpreted by the courts to mean with gross negligence.

3.3.1.2.2. *Wrongful/Insolvent Trading*

Because fraudulent trading is notoriously difficult and expensive to prove, several countries (e.g., the United Kingdom, Australia, New Zealand) have enacted wrongful or insolvent trading provisions that apply where a company incurs a debt at a time when it is unable to pay its debts as they fall due. In some jurisdictions, the provision applies only against directors (e.g., Australia); in others, to other specified individuals (e.g., as proposed in Hong Kong, to directors, shadow directors, and senior management). Unlike fraudulent trading provisions, these provisions provide only for civil liability and do not require proving the dishonesty of a director. Where a company has gone into insolvent liquidation and the liquidator believes that it has engaged in insolvent trading, the liquidator may apply to the court for an order declaring that a responsible person or former responsible person is liable for insolvent trading.

There are subtle and sometimes quite significant distinctions in the legislation of different countries,[5] but there is sufficient similarity in the underlying principles to enable certain useful generalizations to be drawn. The conduct of the responsible person or persons—that is to say, directors and other officers of the company—must be such as to fall below that of a reasonable person. It must also—under the United Kingdom regime—have contributed to the insolvent liquidation of the company and—under the Australian regime—have caused the incurring of a debt at a time when the company was either already insolvent or would become insolvent as a result of that further debt. The insolvent liquidation of the company is not a necessary condition for the invoking of this provision in all jurisdictions, but given the circumstances, it is highly unlikely that this provision would be invoked except where the company has, in fact, gone into insolvent liquidation.

The conduct of the defendants will be judged by reference to a particular point in time identified by the court in its post hoc analysis of the circumstances. Under the United Kingdom provisions, that point is the time a reasonable person in the position of the defendant directors or officers would or ought to have known that the company could not avoid insolvent liquidation and would, therefore, have taken all possible steps to minimize the loss to creditors. Under the Australian legislation,

---

[5] *See* Andrew Keay & Michael Murray, *Making Company Directors Liable: A Comparative Analysis of Wrongful Trading in the United Kingdom and Insolvent Trading in Australia* (2005), 14 INTERNATIONAL INSOLVENCY REVIEW 27–55.

that point is the time when reasonable grounds exist for suspecting that the company is insolvent or would become insolvent if a further debt were incurred. A strict rule prevails in Germany, where the director of a GmbH has the duty to check constantly whether or not the company is insolvent. If so, the director has the duty to seek a company filing within three weeks.

These provisions also include some defenses for a responsible person: for example, that he took every step that ought to have been taken to minimize the potential loss to the company's creditors after the time he became aware (or ought to have become aware) of the unavoidability of insolvency. An additional defense recently proposed in Hong Kong (the provision has not yet been enacted), that only applies to senior managers, provides that a senior manager will not be liable if, before the company incurred debt whilst trading in insolvent circumstances, he issued a "warning notice" in the proper form to the company's board of directors.

3.3.1.2.3. Directors' Disqualification and Overall Risk of Liability of Directors

Here a sample of statutory provisions may be helpful:

(1) Several jurisdictions (e.g., the United Kingdom, Hong Kong) have enacted statutory directors' disqualification regimes, pursuant to which, when companies are wound up, directors may be disqualified from serving as corporate directors if they are found to be unfit. These regimes are as effective as the overall corporate and regulatory culture of which they are part. For example, although the provisions in the United Kingdom and Hong Kong are almost identical, the United Kingdom provisions have been far more frequently applied than those in Hong Kong.

The relevant law in the United Kingdom is the Company Directors Disqualification Act 1986. It provides that where the court has made a disqualification order against a director or the director has given a disqualification undertaking to the Secretary of State that has been accepted, the director risks going to prison or exposing himself to personal liability if he contravenes the order or undertaking. The order or undertaking is interpreted substantively—the director cannot simply act as if he is no longer a director, such as by changing his job description. He also cannot give instructions for others to manage the company. In addition to being prevented from acting as a director, an individual subject to an order or undertaking may also not act as a receiver of a company's property or be concerned with, or take part in, the promotion, formation or management of a company.[6]

Part of the law's success in the United Kingdom is tied to the adverse consequences that result from being disqualified, including the public shaming of a director, especially when a former director's name is posted on a website of disqualified directors, the Disqualified Directors Register, that is maintained by the Companies House.[7] To date, over 2,800 directors have been disqualified.

The INSOL International "Directors in the Twilight Zone" project categorizes countries by how they treat a director acting in the "Twilight Zone" period when a company is in financial difficulty but it is not clear whether an insolvency case or workout will occur. The initial INSOL survey in 2001 covered 13 jurisdictions and the 2005 survey was expanded to 19 jurisdictions. The Overview to the 2005 INSOL study ranks common law jurisdictions that adopt the "knowingly negligent" liability standard (e.g., England, Australia, New Zealand) as medium risk jurisdictions for directors.[8]

(2) United States—The United States has not enacted fraudulent trading or wrongful/insolvent trading provisions. It relies on common law doctrines and state corporate laws.[9] In the United States directors are not infrequently forced to accept disqualification from public companies through enforcement actions by the Securities and Exchange Commission. Directors in the United States are rarely held personally liable for continuing to trade while a company is insolvent, and the application of the "business judgment rule" works to the directors' advantage. However, class actions against directors are becoming increasingly common. The "Directors in the Twilight Zone" project categorizes the United States as a low risk jurisdiction for directors.

---

[6] These issues and others are set out in a pamphlet issued by The Insolvency Service. The Insolvency Service, *Company Directors Disqualification Act 1986 and Disqualified Directors: Effect of disqualification orders and disqualification undertakings*, that may be found at http://www.insolvency.gov.uk/pdfs/guidanceleafletspdf/cddadd.pdf.

[7] *See* http://www.companieshouse.gov.uk/ddir/.

[8] Philip Wood, "Overview," *Directors in the Twilight Zone II* 6 (INSOL 2005).

[9] *See generally*, Hu & Westbrook, *supra* note 3.

(3) Civil law jurisdictions

Germany—Contrary to the "vague" wrongful trading approach of many Commonwealth jurisdictions, Germany instead opts for more explicit triggers. For example, directors in Germany are subject to criminal and civil liability if they violate any "protection status" that provides for the protection of others. They are also subject to criminal and civil liability if they fail to petition for the commencement of insolvency proceedings in a timely fashion. They are also liable to the company for any payments made after a company has become illiquid or the discovery of overindebtedness.

France—Directors in France are subject to "draconian personal liability" for their serious business mistakes that lead to the insolvency of their company.[10] Engaging in risky ventures, borrowing imprudently, or engaging in similar actions leads to the personal liability of directors, and it is not uncommon for the insolvency of a company to lead to the personal bankruptcy of the directors. Article L.624–5 of the French Commercial Code sets forth a list of actions by a director that may lead to the personal liability or personal bankruptcy of a director. The "Directors in the Twilight Zone" project categorizes France as a high risk jurisdiction for directors.

3.3.2. Relationship Between Director and Officer Liability and Corporate Governance

It is clear that addressing directors' wrongful behavior solely at the insolvency stage is almost always too late to help creditors. This point has clearly been proved by the massive corporate failures in the United States of Enron and Worldcom. In both cases, poor corporate governance procedures were at the heart of the problem. Such procedures lie outside the scope of this book, but it is clear that when such procedures are not followed, the risk of insolvency dramatically increases. By the time fraudulent or wrongful trading provisions or directors' disqualification regimes are applied against directors of insolvent companies, the wrongful behavior has already been committed. Although some of these provisions will provide for the application of criminal and/or civil penalties, it is the exception rather than the rule that the offending directors and officers are able to compensate creditors in full for the harm caused them.

---

[10] Wood, *supra* note 8, at 6.

Rather, the effect of fraudulent and wrongful trading (or directors' disqualification) provisions is the fact that rational directors will attempt to avoid the application of such provisions by seeking assistance or filing for bankruptcy protection rather than by engaging in the offending behavior.

To prevent such wrongful behavior (and, in turn, to prevent many bankruptcies from occurring), the best safeguards are strong corporate governance and the efficient and effective enforcement of creditors' rights.[11] However, it must be borne in mind that effective corporate governance procedures are more effective when they are part and parcel of a strong corporate governance culture. In countries with such a strong culture, such as the United States, related factors include the active participation of shareholders on corporate boards, the requirement that companies publicize adverse corporate news in a timely and efficient fashion, and the publication by leading magazines and newspapers of the attendance record of directors and of the correlation of directors' pay to corporate performance. Class actions can also have a beneficial effect on corporate governance.

A strong corporate governance culture is often less likely to take hold in jurisdictions in which most companies are closely held—i.e., family controlled—and less responsive to outside, public pressure. Closely held companies are often reluctant to disclose adverse corporate news. In such jurisdictions, it is necessary for the government and banks to jointly push for effective corporate governance. At present, the global flow of capital is another factor that leads to increased awareness of corporate governance by such companies, because international capital is more likely to flow to companies dedicated to effective corporate governance.

Overall, throughout Asia historically there has been less transparency and less willingness by banks and financial institutions to disclose bad news to the market than in the West. Consider, for example, the reaction to Russia's default on its international bond obligations in 1998. While United States banks and investment banks were quick to disclose their expected losses from the default, such disclosure was quite rare in Asia, a result of less comprehensive disclosure laws and a more secretive Asian approach to disclosure. For example, it has been reported that Japan's banks apparently have objected to the promulgation of regulations requiring banks to disclose the extent of their losses on derivatives.

---

[11] *See infra* 3.6.

In the aftermath of the 1997 Asian financial crisis many called for the reform of corporate governance procedures in Asia. Although some changes have been made over the last decade, for the most part the changes have not been dramatic. For example, after the collapse of Enron an article in the *Asian Wall Street Journal* compared the situation in the United States with that in Asia and concluded that "Enronitis" is a problem in the United States because Americans had wrongly thought that there was transparency; in contrast, in Asia, Enronitis was not much of a problem because people already assumed that there was little or no transparency.[12]

However, at least in relation to disclosure, the gap has been narrowing, as is evidenced by the responses to the recent sub-prime crisis in the United States. Global capital now demands more, and quicker, disclosure. More recently, it has not only been banks in the United States that have disclosed (and later revised upwards) their expected losses on investments related to the sub-prime crisis; banks in Europe and Asia have also been disclosing (and revising) their expected losses on investments related to the sub-prime crisis.

This discussion is necessarily limited to those aspects of special importance in and near insolvency but effective corporate governance throughout the life of a corporation is of great importance to any commercial law system. Notably, the World Bank has been active in assessing the effectiveness of domestic corporate governance systems around the world and is furthering its efforts in collaboration with the OECD through the Global Corporate Governance Forum.[13]

3.4. *Scope and Commencement of Insolvency Cases*

3.4.1. *Scope of Application*

Reform legislation increasingly adopts the consensus that formal insolvency legislation should apply broadly to as many types of enterprises and corporate enterprises as possible, with a few narrow exceptions for certain entities.

---

[12] *See* Sarah McBride & Phillip Day, *Asia Looks Immune to "Enronitis"—Region's Investors Long Ago Learned not to Expect Transparency*, ASIAN WALL ST. J., Feb. 8, 2002.
[13] *See* http://www.worldbank.org/ifa and http://www.worldbank.org/gcgf.

3.4.1.1. *Financial Institutions, Insurance Companies, Regulated Industries, and Other Groups*

There is an ongoing debate among law reformers as to how best to handle the insolvency of financial institutions and insurance companies. However, at the outset it should be noted that it would be better to refer to "regulated" industries and sectors rather than only to financial entities and insurance companies. Other groups that might need special treatment include stockbrokers, commodity brokers, companies wound up by securities or market regulators, railroads, and utilities (e.g., electric power and water companies). The special problem of foreign regulated-industry debtors is not addressed here.

The first approach is to handle the insolvencies under separate legislation. The United States adopts this approach for the liquidation and reorganization of banks and insurance companies. This is a sensible approach for the United States given that: (1) the United States Bankruptcy Code is a federal piece of legislation that permits commencement by creditors for insolvency-related reasons and not by regulators for non-insolvency reasons; (2) there are more banks and financial services companies (as well as insurance companies, stockbrokers, and commodity brokers) in the United States than in most other countries; and (3) the regulation of financial services and insurance operations in the United States is quite complicated and involves an overlap between state and federal law. Given these factors, it would arguably be more complicated and, perhaps, even unworkable for banks and insurance companies to be subject to the United States Bankruptcy Code.

Other jurisdictions have separate legislation for reorganization and liquidation and exempt regulated industries from one but not the other. Hong Kong is a case in point, with certain defined regulated industries (that are not exempt from the liquidation provisions in the Companies Ordinance) exempted from the proposed Provisional Supervision legislation. It is anticipated that the regulatory authorities for those industries will amend the relevant non-insolvency legislation to cover the reorganization of entities subject to the regulators' control.

A second approach is to handle the insolvency of the regulated industry under the generally applicable insolvency law as supplemented by special rules within the insolvency law. The United States adopts this approach, with special rules applicable to the reorganization of railroads (handled pursuant to a special subchapter IV of Chapter 11 of the United States Bankruptcy Code) and to the liquidation of stockbrokers and commodity brokers (governed by a special subchapter IV of Chapter 7 of the United States Bankruptcy Code).

A third approach is to allow ordinary insolvency law provisions to apply to regulated industries, as supplemented by additional provisions in separate legislation applying to the regulated industry. Aspects of this approach can be found in those jurisdictions that have adopted the original English approach of incorporating corporate insolvency law into company law. Although England has hived off its insolvency law from its company law, many other jurisdictions have not yet done so. Hong Kong is a case in point. In such jurisdictions, since there is not a separate piece of insolvency legislation, statutory provisions that set out the grounds for commencing the liquidation of a company include insolvency-related grounds upon which creditors may rely, along with the regulatory grounds that the government may rely on for winding up a company that have nothing at all to do with insolvency. Other pieces of legislation set out more detailed commencement procedures and other criteria for liquidations commenced by the State against companies in such regulated areas as banking, insurance, and stock broking. Such petitions are called "public interest" petitions.

In such jurisdictions, "public interest" petitions are handled under the usual insolvency provisions, as amended or supplemented by the relevant provisions in other legislation that pertains to the relevant industry. However, for the most part, the normal winding-up provisions in the company law will apply to the companies that are the subject of the public interest petition. Problems can occur under this approach, as is the case in Hong Kong, in that the Companies Ordinance fails to cross-reference the additional provisions that supplement or replace the provisions in the Companies Ordinance in the case of a winding up on a public interest petition.[14] In other jurisdictions, all of the relevant provisions are either included in a separate ordinance for the regulated sector or are grouped in one chapter in the insolvency part of the Companies Ordinance setting forth special rules for these types of cases (as in the United States in its treatment of the reorganizations of railroads).

As noted above, England has enacted a separate piece of insolvency legislation. Section 422 of the Insolvency Act provides that the Secretary of State may make an order setting forth that provisions relating to

---

[14] *See* Charles D. Booth, *When Government Intervenes: Winding Up Fraudulent Companies in Hong Kong*, 29 HONG KONG L.J. 368 (1999).

liquidation and corporate rescue that are contained in the Insolvency Act are to apply to banks. The Secretary of State did so in 1989 and the Banks Administration Proceedings Order (1989) provides that the administration procedures in the Insolvency Act are applicable to banks.

A fourth approach for addressing the restructuring of regulated industries is to establish a separate administrative institution to liquidate or otherwise dispose of non-performing assets. This approach was followed by the United States in the establishment of the Resolution Trust Corporation in the aftermath of the Savings & Loan crisis in 1989. This has also served as the model in the aftermath of the 1997 Asian financial crisis in many jurisdictions in that the financial sectors were reeling from the high levels of non-performing loans ("NPLs"). Asset management companies ("AMCs") were established to assist with restructuring and the disposal of NPLs in an orderly process. For example, the Indonesian Bank Restructuring Agency ("IBRA") was established in Indonesia, the Pengurusan Danaharta Nasional Bhd ("Danaharta") in Malaysia, and the Thai Asset Management Company ("TAMC") in Thailand. For the most part, these entities were created as part of emergency measures and have been or are now in the process of being wound down.[15] More recently, China has also adopted this model—but rather than establishing a single, centralized AMC, China instead set up four AMCs that were each linked to one of the four largest state-owned banks.[16]

Which of these approaches is followed depends on the interaction between the insolvency law and the regulated industry, the regulatory framework for the regulated industry, and the history of the regulation and administration of such regulated industries in the given jurisdiction.

3.4.1.2. *State-Owned Enterprises*

As a general rule, it is best for State-Owned Enterprises ("SOEs") to also be subject to the applicable insolvency law. Exceptions are sometimes necessary, however, in those jurisdictions in the midst of transition from centralized, government-run economies to more market-oriented economies. Of course, the debate in such countries often focuses on the point in time when the SOEs should be made subject to the insolvency

---

[15] Douglas W. Arner, Charles D. Booth, Berry F.C. Hsu, Paul Lejot, Qiao Liu & Frederick Pretorius, *Property Rights, Collateral and Creditor Rights in East Asia*, in EAST ASIAN FINANCE: SELECTED ISSUES Part III.B, 38–39 (Ismail Dalla ed., World Bank, 2006).

[16] *Id.* at 39–40.

law. Making SOEs comply with insolvency prematurely can lead to dramatic increases in the unemployment rate as well as a significant knock-on or domino effect on the financial sector that will, in turn, be forced to write off high levels of NPLs.

It is not surprising that difficulties arise in these periods of transition from the many conflicts of interest inherent in dealing with the administration of SOEs. Power struggles often arise. An insolvency law that attempts to assert jurisdiction over all SOEs will often be opposed by government authorities that have been responsible for supervising particular SOEs, often for many years. In countries with SOEs it is not unusual for the relevant state authority to have to give permission for an SOE to file an insolvency proceeding. Thus, such authorities will try to retain their influence over the SOEs subject to their control by lobbying for the exemption of SOEs from the new insolvency law. Of course, as the number of exemptions increases, the effect of the new insolvency law will diminish for it is often the case that the entities most in need of the new insolvency law are the oldest or largest and, in many cases, the most inefficient SOEs. Whether or not the exemptions can be kept to a minimum is a political issue far removed from insolvency law.

China, for example, has been dealing with this very issue. One of the most significant areas of debate regarding the new Chinese insolvency law was whether to apply the new law to SOEs. At an early stage it was clear that there was a split in the drafting committee about how best to proceed. However, during the years that the debate was ongoing, the Chinese government commenced an ambitious scheme to close or otherwise deal with those SOEs in most need of assistance. In essence, during this period China established a bifurcated insolvency system with many of the SOE insolvencies being handled under government policy decrees and regulations and all other insolvencies being commenced under the applicable insolvency laws.[17] The new PRC Enterprise Insolvency Law came into operation on June 1, 2007. The goal of the Chinese government is eventually to subject all SOEs to the new law, which will no longer be administered subject to State Council regulations. However, it might well be premature to proclaim the end of policy bankruptcies in China. Article 133 of the new law provides that the insolvency of SOEs shall be handled within the time limit and to the extent stipulated in regulations

---

[17] *See* Charles D. Booth, *Drafting Bankruptcy Laws in Socialist Market Economies: Recent Developments in China and Vietnam*, 18(1) COLUM. J. ASIAN L. 93, 106–108 (2004).

issued by the State Council. In January 2006, the State Council issued opinions exempting roughly 2,000 SOEs from the new law through 2009. Only time will tell whether China's dual track system will come to an end in 2009 or whether further extensions will continue to be made.

3.4.2. Defining Insolvency

The test for defining insolvency is a crucial aspect of an effective insolvency system because that concept serves a number of important functions. Perhaps most important is determining a debtor's eligibility for an insolvency proceeding, which in most systems requires a showing of insolvency. The problems with definitions based on balance-sheet tests ("overindebtedness") are legion: in countries with strict balance-sheet tests, it is at times impossible to force a debtor company into an insolvency proceeding over the company's opposition. Given the subjectivity and myriad difficulties involved in determining balance-sheet values and the fact that this information is under the control of the debtor, this should not be surprising. Thailand is an excellent case in point. It historically has adopted the balance-sheet test. The Thai judicial decision in Thai Petrochemicals (TPI) after the onset of the Asian financial crisis—in which the court relied on a novel interpretation of the balance-sheet test and ordered the debtor company to be wound up—was proclaimed at the time as the most important commercial case in Thai history because it was the first time that a court had ordered a company in Thailand to be wound up over the company's opposition.[18]

A cash flow, or liquidity, test is much easier to administer and fairer to creditors because it puts the definitional factors within the control of creditors—every creditor is able to seek repayment and if repayment is not forthcoming (with a few exceptions, such as *bona fide* dispute), there may exist a presumption that the debtor is insolvent. A debtor is obligated to pay its debts when they become due and the failure to do so should trigger an insolvency proceeding. Under this approach, the creditors will not have to fight with the debtor over access to "confidential" data and valuation experts will not have to be called to testify on whether or not an enterprise's assets exceed its debts. Common liquidity tests include a finding that the debtor is "generally not paying" its debts (United States)

---

[18] Of course, in retrospect it is clear that the debate over the propriety of winding up the company was but the first stage of the battle waged by TPI's management to retain control over the company.

or is "unable to pay its debts as they become due" (the traditional "equity" test in common law countries). Several civil law countries use cessation of payments as the test.[19]

3.4.3. *Commencement Criteria*

Ideally, the commencement criteria for insolvencies should make access to the laws convenient, inexpensive, and quick. Unfortunately, criteria are too often ambiguous or include requirements that restrict access or are cumbersome. These sorts of requirements will often lead to litigation at the outset of insolvency cases and make for an inefficient system.

Insofar as a system depends on voluntary filings by debtors, insolvency tests may be questioned as a necessary criterion for access. If debtors are prepared to concede that they need legal protection because of their financial condition, or imminent financial failure, it is not clear that the delay and expense associated with an insolvency test produces a corresponding benefit. The United States is a notable example of a system that imposes no requirement of insolvency in voluntary cases, where the filing of a voluntary petition is equivalent to the opening of an insolvency proceeding that might be either a liquidation or a reorganization.[20] That system relies on dismissal for "bad faith" filing as a protection against abuse of the system. However, most systems require a showing of insolvency for both voluntary and involuntary filings, Mexico's new law being a recent example.[21]

For either voluntary or involuntary filings, delays often destroy value for the debtor and its creditors and make it more likely that a proposed rescue will result in a liquidation. Similarly, inconvenient and expensive procedures will also deter creditors from filing for an insolvency proceeding. The fewer hurdles there are, the greater the likelihood of a case going forward in a timely fashion.

A factor that increases access to an insolvency proceeding is the adoption of bright-line tests (for example, whether the debtor paid a debt when due) rather than inquiries into a debtor's intention or desire or alleged misconduct (for example, whether the debtor committed an "act

---

[19] European Principles § 1.2. Tests often vary for voluntary and involuntary petitions.

[20] Because the United States Chapter 11 regime may be used to save value for equity owners as well as creditors, an insolvency requirement would obviously be at cross-purposes with one important function of its insolvency law.

[21] ALI Mexican Statement at 26–27. *See also* UNCITRAL, Legislative Guide on Insolvency Law 45–48 (2005).

of bankruptcy"). Although factors that set out subjective elements may arguably lead to greater exactitude in determining which debtors should be made bankrupt, this exactitude comes at a great cost because the determination of such issues will inevitability lead to contested proceedings and result in delay, uncertainty, and greater expense. In contrast, although bright-line tests may lead to over- or under-inclusiveness in a given case, this may be compensated for by the ease of administration that flows from the adoption of such tests.

It is in this area that the criteria for access overlap with the definition of insolvency. An insolvency test based on liquidity or cash flow provides for much more efficient access than does a test based on balance-sheet considerations even though it risks bankrupting a debtor with assets exceeding liabilities. But too loose a standard for permitting an insolvency proceeding presents a countervailing risk. For example, a system that permits a single creditor to force an insolvency proceeding (as in the United Kingdom) may give too much leverage to creditors and permit initiation of proceedings without sufficient information suggesting the existence of a general default that requires collective action. Thus an important aspect of every insolvency system is the extent to which it draws accurate and precise lines for sorting out cases where the filing of a petition is the result of a single creditor action and not an instance of real insolvency. Of course, an attempt to seize the debtor's property in an individual action may lead to a needed insolvency filing by the debtor, a filing that might not have been made but for the pressure of the individual action. The same is true of an enforcement action or repossession by a secured creditor.[22] These actions may serve as informal creditor triggers for the filing of an insolvency proceeding.

The power to initiate corporate rescue proceedings may be given to creditors. However, it should be noted that it is usually true in Commonwealth countries (and other jurisdictions adopting English insolvency law principles) that only the debtor is able to commence formal rescue procedures.[23] It is likely that involuntary rehabilitation proceedings, permitted in the United States and a few other countries, are not common and are perhaps not likely to be successful. With regard to the methods for attracting or forcing debtors into filing rehabilitation

---

[22] *See supra* 2.2.7.
[23] However, it would be rare in such jurisdictions for debtors to resort to corporate rescue without first consulting with its major secured creditors.

procedures while there is still time to save the business, see Section
3.6.1.2 below. Note also that in many jurisdictions (for example, France)
proceedings may be initiated by public authorities.

At the same time, it is important to remember that a number of systems
are unitary, in that they contemplate a proceeding being initiated without
an initial choice between liquidation and rehabilitation, with that choice
made following an observation period (e.g., France, Germany, Mexico).
Those systems have some important advantages,[24] but one cost of such a
system is the complication of the choice of initiation standards because
both liquidation and rehabilitation situations have to be envisioned.

In systems that are not unitary, so that the original application represents a choice of liquidation or rehabilitation, there may be a mechanism
for conversion from one to another. Such a system permits the debtor
or a stakeholder to ask that the proceeding be converted from the initial
type of proceeding to one thought to be more appropriate.

3.4.4. *Assets Administered in Insolvency*

At the outset, the administrator needs to identify all of the property
belonging to the debtor, including property obtained after the commencement of the case. All systems dispossess the corporate debtor of all
or most of its property. The administrator must determine what property
is "the property of the insolvency estate or mass" or in general under the
administrator's control regardless of the theory of dispossession used in a
particular legal system. Closely related is resolution of the problems that
can arise in relation to other rights in such assets. These problems increasingly arise in relation to intangible property rights, the retention of which
might well be crucial to the ability of an enterprise to be restructured or
purchased by a third party and begin with a fundamental question: what
rights are to be treated as property? For example, is a government license
property of the estate?

In general, any interest the debtor had at the moment of filing that
can be sold or exchanged may be considered part of the property to be
administered and sold by the administrator. There may also be interests
that cannot ordinarily be sold (for example, an unassignable contract)
that should nonetheless be part of the administrator's property.[25] How-

---

[24] *See infra* 8.1.1.
[25] *See infra* 3.9.7.

ever, some types of property raise conflicting policy issues. What about lists of customers and their shopping and personal preferences that (in some countries) conflict with the customers' rights to privacy? While their use by a rehabilitating debtor may be unobjectionable, should they be sold to an unrelated company with whom the customer did not intend to deal?[26]

3.5. *Moratorium and Suspension of Actions*

There is a consensus among experts that the moratorium on debtor and creditor actions, and the consequent control by the court, ought to be a broad as possible. The broad stay provided by article 20 of the Model Law on Cross-Border Insolvency promulgated by UNCITRAL illustrates that consensus.[27] It is clear, nonetheless, that some exceptions have to be made and it is there that policymakers must consider certain alternatives.

3.5.1. *Lawsuits*

All modern systems forbid enforcement of judgments, but some might allow pending actions by or against the debtor to continue as far as judgment without special court approval. Generally, that exception creates some risks for stakeholders because debtors in the midst of financial crisis may not be devoting the attention or the resources to defending or prosecuting actions as they would under other circumstances. Thus, for example, a default judgment for an inflated amount might be entered against a debtor and taken as conclusive in the insolvency proceeding whereas, on a proper adjudication, the action might have been dismissed or judgment entered for a smaller amount. Such a result prejudices all other creditors. One of the virtues of an insolvency proceeding is that it usually permits all claims to be resolved in one court.

The Model Law itself excepts pending litigation under some circumstances. One concern is the running of a statute of limitations if suit cannot be brought, thus barring a claim from being made. Suits can be

---

[26] United States Bankruptcy Code §§ 332, 363(b)(1) (consumer privacy ombudsman).
[27] U.N. Model Law on Cross-Border Insolvency (1997). *See also* UNCITRAL, LEG-ISLATIVE GUIDE ON INSOLVENCY LAW 84–88 (2005) (discussing the scope of application of stays).

exempted for that limited purpose or the statute of limitations on claims can be suspended for a certain time or until the insolvency proceeding has been resolved.[28]

3.5.2. State Regulatory Actions

Regulatory actions that are not designed to collect money for the state but to protect vital and urgent public interests may be exempted from the stay. For example, if a debtor's operations violate general health and safety regulations, creating a present danger to others, then the state must be permitted to take necessary enforcement actions.

3.5.3. Other Exceptions

Other common exceptions include setoffs (discussed at Section 3.9.9), closure of certain financial contracts (such as derivatives), and payment to critical vendors in reorganization cases.

3.5.4. Secured Creditors

Aside from timing, perhaps the most controversial aspect of the moratorium is its application to secured creditors. It is not uncommon for the moratorium in European business rescue jurisdictions to exclude secured creditors (e.g., Belgium, Denmark, Netherlands) who would thus be free to pursue enforcement actions against the debtor. Some Commonwealth jurisdictions exempt only major secured creditors, that is, creditors holding a charge over substantially all of the debtor's assets. The secured creditors are not exempt in rescue cases in France, Italy, Germany, and the United Kingdom, among other countries. Making secured creditors subject to the stay may be seen as more justifiable in rehabilitation proceedings than in liquidations because an argument can be made that, by subjecting the secured creditor to the stay, a reorganization is more likely to be achieved that will benefit creditors generally.

A paradigm case would be one in which a secured creditor has a security interest (or charge) in a piece of manufacturing equipment that is being used to produce widgets. This piece of machinery is central to any possible reorganization of the corporate debtor. If the secured cred-

---

[28] *E.g.*, in the United States Bankruptcy Code § 108.

itor were allowed to take this asset and sell it to reduce its own liability, the other creditors would be likely to receive nothing in the corporate insolvency. However, if the secured creditor were subject to a moratorium, this would perhaps increase the likelihood that the bank holding the security interest in the machinery could be protected at the same time that the unsecured creditors could benefit from the cash flow generated from the sale of widgets produced by the manufacturing equipment. Of course, to justify this intrusion into the secured creditor's rights, the insolvency law might ensure that the secured creditor is adequately protected for any diminution in value of the secured asset that occurs during the period that the creditor is prevented from asserting its pre-existing rights against the machinery. This simple example demonstrates the importance of understanding the place of the moratorium, or stay, in a reorganization structure as well as the policy justification for delaying the secured creditor's assertion of its rights.

3.5.4.1. *Protection*

The protection for secured creditors restrained by a moratorium can take a variety of forms. Clearly the adversarial process of discretionary access regimes provides the opportunity for those who are opposed to the debtor's entry into the protective regime to state their case and to provide evidence in support. Where the regime is automatic at the instance of the debtor, there will invariably be a right for those who believe that the regime is inappropriate to apply to court to have the protection set aside. For example, in Australia, where the regime is automatic, protection of other interests is provided by the requirement for the appointment of an administrator, who is almost always a qualified accountant.

In the United States, the creditor may apply early, and often, for "relief from the automatic stay" unless it is granted "adequate protection" of its security interest. That protection is typically given by periodic payments from the debtor or by an additional lien on other property of the debtor, along with insurance coverage and similar protections. In addition, under the United States system, if the protection given to the secured creditor turns out to have been inadequate, it becomes a "super-priority" creditor, ahead of almost all others, in the remaining assets of the debtor. In other systems, secured creditors may have additional protections.[29]

---

[29] *See infra* 3.6.1.2. *See also* UNCITRAL, LEGISLATIVE GUIDE ON INSOLVENCY LAW 207 (2005).

Germany is an example of a civil law jurisdiction that bars lawsuits while giving the administrator the right to dispose of assets subject to liens (with some exceptions), but with protections for creditors, including a right to suggest more favorable dispositions and a right to interest.[30]

3.5.4.2. *Receivership Regimes*

Inevitably, the moratorium will have limited effect in the more than 80 common law countries that have fixed and floating charges.[31] However, this is beginning to change. One of the driving forces for this change has been the promulgation of the London Approach and its adoption worldwide in an effort to increase the effectiveness of out-of-court restructuring. The London Approach[32] has been adopted by many Asian countries in the aftermath of the Asian financial crisis. For example, in Hong Kong the Hong Kong Monetary Authority (HKMA) and the Hong Kong Association of Banks (HKAB) jointly issued guidelines for multi-bank workouts that adopt as a central tenet the need for a standstill. Similar guidelines were adopted elsewhere in Asia, including the Jakarta Initiative in Indonesia, the Bangkok Approach in Thailand, the Corporate Debt Restructuring Committee ("CDRC") in Malaysia, the Hong Kong Approach, and the Workout Accord in Korea.

Once banks start adopting standstills in out-of-court restructurings, the notion of being bound by a moratorium in a formal insolvency proceeding is not as onerous as it might have seemed prior to the promulgation of the London Approach. Hong Kong is a case in point because the new proposed corporate rescue procedure provides for a moratorium. If enacted, this will be the first statutory ban on the actions of secured creditors in corporate insolvencies in Hong Kong. However, to gain the support of the banking community, it was necessary to ensure that the moratorium would be in place for as short a period of time as necessary to achieve its purpose. In Hong Kong it has been proposed that the moratorium should initially be in place for one month, with the possi-

---

[30] Eberhard Braun, Commentary on The German Insolvency Code §§ 165–169 (2006).

[31] Id, text at n. 37.

[32] *See infra* 5.5.2.

bility of extension by the court for up to six months. Beyond six months, the agreement of creditors will be necessary. Further protection has been incorporated into the proposed Hong Kong legislation through special treatment being provided for "major secured creditors," which are defined as creditors with a charge (fixed and/or floating) over substantially all of the assets of a company. Where a provisional supervision is commenced, within three days of commencement the provisional supervisor must notify in writing any major secured creditor. The major secured creditor has three days to respond to the provisional supervisor as to whether or not it will support the provisional supervisor's efforts to draft a proposal for voluntary arrangement. If the major secured creditor agrees, it too will be bound by the moratorium. If it does not agree, then the provisional supervision will immediately cease and the major secured creditor will be able to assert its pre-existing rights and appoint a receiver (or receiver and manager) to protect its interests. In contrast, all non-major secured creditors will be bound by the moratorium subject to a right to seek exemption where the facts so justify.

The other large element of change was noted earlier—the fact that the country of origin of the receivership system, the United Kingdom, has adopted new legislation that greatly restricts its use, opting in favor of a rehabilitation system governed by an administrator charged with observing the interests of all creditors. It is fair to say that in all such systems, the trend is strongly in favor of subjecting secured creditors to the moratorium, although with often elaborate provisions for protection of the value of its collateral as discussed herein.

3.5.5. "Gap" Moratorium

When a "gap" arises between an initial filing and the opening of an insolvency proceeding, either: (i) the general moratorium must be imposed immediately upon the filing of the application, voluntary or involuntary; or (ii) provisional measures must be made available immediately, on an emergency basis if necessary. In the first case, if there is an abuse of the process, procedures may (and should) provide for an emergency hearing, if necessary, to release the stay in whole or part. If there is instead a delay in imposing the moratorium, then creditors will often find that key assets have simply disappeared. It must be emphasized that these concerns are even greater in a world in which enormous amounts of money (and even property) can be moved very quickly around the world. Once control is achieved, then the debtor can be permitted to operate in the ordinary course of business, with or without a monitoring system, until the court decides to open or to decline to open a proceeding.[33]

3.6. *Governance: Management*

3.6.1. *Administrator/Debtor in Possession*

This section discusses the appointment and operating functions of an administrator, while Section 7.2 focuses on the qualification and regulation of that official. When addressing the issues involved in the management of a bankrupt enterprise, a distinction must be drawn between liquidation and corporate rescue.

3.6.1.1. *Liquidation*

In regard to the liquidation or winding up of an insolvent company, there is a broad consensus that the pre-commencement management should be replaced by qualified independent officials (administrators) with authority to administer the estate for the benefit of creditors. Such an official is generally entitled to take control of the property of the company upon his appointment, and the company and third parties should surrender property to him at that time. The official would have the authority to delegate certain powers back to the company directors and officials who would be required to report back to the administrator. Although there is general agreement as to this principle, there are several issues that are less likely to find such broad support.

The usual procedure would be for an independent official to be appointed by the court upon the commencement or declaration of the liquidation. In an involuntary case, to appoint an official before a winding-up order or order for relief is made, the court must balance certain factors. To enable an independent official to be appointed prior to the making of an order could create great hardship for a company if a winding-up order or an order for relief was not eventually made. On the other hand, if an official cannot be appointed as of the date of the filing of a petition, this might lead to the dissipation of the company's assets and thereby dis-

---

[33] *Cf.* UNCITRAL, LEGISLATIVE GUIDE ON INSOLVENCY LAW 90 (¶ 47) (2005) (discussing the use of provisional measures to protect the debtor's assets where a preliminary moratorium is unavailable).

advantage the company's unsecured creditors. In addition, where there is no doubt that the company is bankrupt and will have to be wound up, the company itself may be anxious for an interim appointment to be made so that preparations for the winding up can begin as early as possible.

Therefore, most jurisdictions ensure a reasonable resolution to this issue by providing that an administrator shall generally be appointed upon the making of the winding-up order or the order for relief; however, upon the filing of a creditor's petition, where cause is shown, the court may appoint an interim administrator (often with more limited duties) until the time arises for the appointment of a permanent administrator. In those jurisdictions where the legislation fails to set out the powers of the interim administrator, a court order may do so.

Most jurisdictions provide that the official should be appointed by a court. However, Commonwealth jurisdictions usually provide for an out-of-court insolvent liquidation procedure called a creditors' voluntary winding up. Such procedures are often more efficient and cheaper than the court supervised alternative and provide for the appointment of an administrator, initially by the company, with the creditors retaining a right to choose their own administrator (liquidator) if they so choose. Such procedures are only appropriate where the official chosen is suitably qualified and independent.[34] It should also be pointed out that in such cases, provision is also usually made for the conversion of a voluntary winding up into a compulsory winding up where, for example, the complexity of the winding up or the suspicion of bias warrants close, direct court involvement.

Many jurisdictions prefer the formality of a court-appointed official, often a government official (such as an Official Receiver or Official Assignee).[35] In some jurisdictions a government official may initially be appointed. He might be given the authority to determine whether or not to carry on in that capacity or he may be subject to later replacement by an official chosen by the creditors. Increasingly, the individuals so chosen must be registered insolvency practitioners who have qualified as such through the obtaining of relevant insolvency experience and/or the satisfactory completion of a formal course of instruction. One model is for a roster system in which once an insolvency practitioner becomes a

---

[34] *See infra* 7.2.

[35] Many of these officials belong to a worldwide association, the International Association of Insolvency Regulators. http://www.insolvencyreg.org/index_main.php (last visited April 2007).

member of the "administrators" panel, the practitioner is then appointed
in rotation with the other members (again, sometimes subject to replacement at the discretion of the creditors). In some jurisdictions (e.g., the
United States) the administrator is usually legally trained; elsewhere (e.g.,
Commonwealth jurisdictions) the official is usually an accountant. Overall, the worldwide trend is for more and more insolvency work to be del-
egated to the private sector, subject to court supervision. Thus, in the
United Kingdom, for example, even in the case of a compulsory winding up, which has the most direct court involvement and supervision,
the liquidator will frequently be a member of the insolvency practitioner
profession.[36]

It is important to mention again one of the important differences
between American and English liquidation law: the effect of insolvency
law on the rights of secured creditors. In the United States, secured creditors are bound by the stay and must go to court to seek adequate protection of their collateral but it is the administrator who has legal control
of the property throughout the reorganization. In contrast, in England
and Commonwealth jurisdictions that adopt the English approach, for
the most part the rights of secured creditors (whose security consists of
a fixed charge) operate independently of liquidation procedures. Where
the security is a floating charge, the matter is more complicated.[37]

3.6.1.2. Rehabilitation

In rehabilitation a number of jurisdictions appoint an administrator as in
liquidation but a number of others permit prior corporate management
to remain in control, an approach often called the "Debtor in Possession."
One reason for the difference might be to take into account the fact that in
a rehabilitation scenario a company may well have spent weeks or months
negotiating with its creditors before any court process has taken place as
to the terms of a possible rescue. Thus, when a petition is filed it may
well be in a pre-packaged form or well along the way to the resolution of
many of the issues. The presumed expertise of business people to run the
company, rather than an accountant or lawyer appointed by the court,
is another reason. Moreover, in some jurisdictions only the company is

---

[36] *See infra* 7.2.
[37] *See supra* 2.2.

able to petition for rescue, not the creditors, and retention of management control is therefore an incentive for timely filing.[38] Although the different approaches to control of rehabilitation are discussed more fully in Section 4.3, it should be noted here that there are commonly these options:

   i. exclusive control of the proceeding by an independent administrator or supervision of management by an independent administrator or supervisor; or

  ii. exclusive control of the proceeding shifting to an independent administrator only if existing management proves incompetent or negligent or has engaged in fraud or other misbehavior.

The first option has two alternatives:

   a. exclusive control of the proceeding by an independent administrator; or

   b. supervision of management by an independent administrator or supervisor.

The norm in Commonwealth jurisdictions and other jurisdictions following English company law is the (i)(a) approach in that once a company is ordered wound up the management's powers cease and an independent administrator, a member of the independent insolvency practitioner profession (usually initially trained as an accountant), is appointed. At the other extreme, adopting the second option, is the United States with a strong debtor-in-possession culture. Two countries adopting the middle ground—the (i)(b) approach—are Canada and Mexico.

The new Chinese insolvency law offers another permutation—it provides for the appointment of an administrator to manage the debtor's property and business affairs but also permits the debtor to apply to the court for permission to manage its property under the supervision of the administrator.

A DIP, or modified DIP approach, may prove particularly useful for closely held, family run companies whose management might be reluctant to petition for corporate rescue if it automatically leads to their replacement by an outside administrator.

---

[38] That limitation may be *de jure* or, as in the United States, *de facto* because of the risks and costs of involuntary proceedings.

3.6.1.3. *Administrator's Financial Responsibility*

A very important factor in any insolvency system is the extent to which an administrator, in either liquidation or rehabilitation, is personally liable for his or her activities as such. In virtually all systems, the administrator will be liable in a civil action for damages from the administrator's misfeasance or malfeasance, although the standards (for example, negligence versus gross negligence) may vary. It is common for that reason to require that the administrator (if not a government official) post a bond or other guarantee that an injured party can recover for the administrator's wrongdoing.

More difficult is the decision whether to make the administrator liable personally for obligations incurred in the ordinary course of the insolvency proceeding. The benefits from doing so include the fact that suppliers to the insolvency can feel more sure they will be paid even if the assets of the insolvency are inadequate to do so and therefore will be more willing to supply on credit. It is also true that the administrator will be more careful about incurring debts if any shortfall, after application of the debtor's assets, will come from the administrator's pocket. Yet, the risk is that the administrator will grow too cautious, unwilling even in liquidation to take steps that might maximize value (such as preparing goods for sale or advertising extensively) because of the risk of personal liability far in excess of the fees that might be earned in the proceeding. In rehabilitation, the risk is much greater because the substantial expenses of running the business could fall on the administrator and the administrator's family if the attempt is unsuccessful, and it is even more likely that the amounts at risk in that case would dwarf the amounts reasonably to be earned as fees. Thus a system that is serious about rehabilitation must probably decide to make only the assets of the debtor or the estate liable, not the personal assets of the administrator.

As has already been pointed out, in the United Kingdom the receiver, despite owing his or her appointment to the exclusive initiative of the secured creditor, can be held liable for negligence where this causes loss to others who have interests in the insolvency, for example a guarantor of the company's debt or, indeed, other creditors. In this respect, the role and liabilities of the receiver are not without their complications and originally were virtually free from liability except at the instance of the secured creditor by whom the appointment was made.[39]

---

[39] *See* Harry Rajak, *Can A Receiver Be Negligent?*, in The Corporate Dimension, 129 (Barry AK Rider ed., 1998).

In due course, however, as pointed out elsewhere,[40] English judges chipped away at the receiver's erstwhile invulnerability.

3.6.2. *Governance: Creditors and Creditors' Committees*

3.6.2.1. *Organization of Creditors*

A number of systems, including those in many common law countries, contemplate decisions being made by full meetings of creditors at crucial junctures in a proceeding. Other systems provide for creditor participation primarily through creditors' committees elected by mail or by proxy. In general, the former approach is most useful with smaller companies or where creditors are located in the same geographical region while the latter is more useful when there are many creditors or they are widely scattered. Many creditors will be unable or unwilling to "throw good money after bad" by devoting time and resources to participation in insolvency proceedings. Thus all systems try to encourage creditor participation or even control of proceedings, but it is also necessary to provide for guidance of the proceeding by professionals alone where creditors are not active.[41] Some systems, as in Germany, use a full assembly of creditors for ultimate decisions but may employ an interim representative creditor council prior to the convening of the assembly.[42]

In a number of systems there may be appointed a single person to represent creditors or a certain group of creditors.[43]

3.6.2.2. *Creditors' Committee Functions*

A creditors' committee or other creditor representatives can play a valuable role in insolvency cases and provide "double protection." They may be consulted on non-routine matters and have a right to be heard on key decisions. The creditors' committee may also play an important role in disseminating information to creditors and in organizing creditors.

The scope of a creditors' committee in a liquidation is much narrower than in a rehabilitation. In a liquidation, the committee's main functions

---

[40] *See supra* 2.1.4, 2.2.7.

[41] Some systems also provide for special procedural protections for employees as creditors. This subject is dealt with below. *See infra* Chapter 6.

[42] Braun, *supra* note 30 at §§ 67–73.

[43] One example is the new Mexican law. *See* ALI Mexican Statement at 49.

are to supervise the administrator and to provide the necessary approvals where required. In a rehabilitation, in addition to providing these functions, the committee also plays an integral role in approving (and perhaps negotiating) the reorganization plan or proposal.

In general, a committee can serve a useful function as a sounding board and in monitoring activities of the administrator, in processing and distributing information to its constituents and in organizing creditors for decisions on critical issues. Efficiency should be tempered with accountability and transparency. Greater transparency and creditor participation are generally required when regulations or institutions are weak.

The court should take into account the views of creditors' committees. They should be consulted by the administrator or the judge and should be given an opportunity to oppose major actions that will affect their interests. Having an ability to veto actions outright is less significant where secured creditors have already been given the right to take their collateral. In general, creditors tend to act rationally if they have full access to information to make decisions and have a financial stake involved. A creditors' committee may also serve as a restraint on unreasonable creditor expectations.

3.6.2.3. *Transparency and Approval Rights*

It is important to distinguish between issues of transparency and management. Transparency is designed to protect creditors by giving them notice of issues that affect their interests and affording them an opportunity to be heard. Notice does not in itself imply the right to approve or make management decisions, as discussed above. Nonetheless, creditors and a creditors' committee can serve as an effective check and balance on the activities of an administrator or liquidator with regard to major decisions. A system will permit creditors to monitor effectively where they are given an opportunity to obtain relevant, accurate, and current information on the debtor's enterprise, trading activities, and financial affairs so that administrators can be held accountable for their conduct. However, it often is true that, before the enterprise will agree to disclose confidential information, it will require the creditors' committee to sign a confidentiality agreement to not disclose the information to competitors or others without prior approval. While notice to the entire creditor body may not be required, notice for the committee, major creditors (including secured creditors), and fiscal creditors may be obligatory.

Significant events might be published in an appropriate public journal to provide additional notice to creditors at large. For some major decisions, the dissemination of notice often must go beyond the lists of known creditors. For a sale of property of the estate to realize as high a price as possible, parties outside the insolvency process must also be notified. It is often in regard to the sale of significant assets that problems arise and assertions are made that an insider or associate is benefiting from its inside information at the expense of other parties. It is here that judicial hearings can serve an important role in reassuring other creditors that their concerns are being considered and that fairness will be done. Notice is too often ignored in understanding and evaluating insolvency systems. It is not a routine formality but central to an effective process.

3.6.2.4. *Organization of Creditors' Committees*

The primary problem is that insolvency law in practice often creates disincentives for active involvement. For a creditors' committee to function properly and effectively, creditors must commit the time and energy to make the committee a success. However, this can often be a time-consuming, if not costly, endeavor. When creditors realize that they are unlikely to receive a substantial recovery in a liquidation or a reasonable payout in a restructuring, they frequently will make the rational decision that their time and energy could be better spent elsewhere. Thus, it is not unusual for the first few meetings of creditors to be well-attended but for participation to drop off as a case carries on. In smaller cases, there may be no committee at all.

Because of this natural tendency for creditors to lack interest in the process, one should not underestimate the relevance of other aspects of the insolvency process—such as the enactment of effective avoidance and investigatory powers—in increasing participation rates. However, rather than paying greater attention to this connection, law reform efforts sometimes focus on streamlining the existing procedures—such as by lowering the numbers necessary for quorums for creditors meetings (as occurred in personal bankruptcy law reform in Hong Kong in the 1990s).

Of course, different insolvency systems take on varying levels of creditor participation. The United States system is unusual both in the levels of participation and in the amount of time dedicated to the insolvency process by creditors. It is not unusual in large cases in the United States for there to be several unsecured creditors' committees including separate committees for unsecured debenture holder or for employee claimants.

Arguably, part of the explanation for these occurrences is the fact that all official committees can hire legal and other professional advisors (to be paid for by the estate) and once one committee is armed in this way others will follow. Another factor is the United States proclivity for debating matters in open court.

The traditions and practices in other jurisdictions are quite different. However, it is unfair to conclude (as have some United States courts)[44] that other systems are less fair than American procedures because they rely primarily on the skills of an experienced insolvency practitioner serving as administrator rather than on the active involvement of creditors in the process and the holding of more judicial hearings. A balance must be struck. Each approach has its merits and when evaluating each system one must balance the increases in time and costs that result from holding more frequent judicial hearings and involving more professionals in the committee process against the benefits resulting from the increased transparency of the process.

For example, in jurisdictions where there are fewer well-trained insolvency professionals, the civil law approach of the appointment of an interventor or inspector (or another creditor representative) has its merits. The reliance on such an individual is also tied to the overall insolvency culture and the level of participation sought by creditors. There is a tradeoff—there is no doubt that the use of an interventor or inspector is more efficient than a full-blown creditor committee approach; on the other hand, it is not as democratic and transparent.

Another difficult area is the composition of the committee. At one extreme is the committee of inspection (British in origin) in which a variety of parties with an interest in the proceedings, including both creditors and shareholders, may serve on the committee;[45] at the other extreme is the United States plethora of committees with not only separate committees of secured creditors but also the possibility of separate creditors' committees for trade creditors, bondholders, and employees.

Rules and procedures are required to deal with such things as the calling of meetings of creditors, the eligibility of persons to attend and par-

---

[44] *See, e.g.*, criticisms of Australian corporate insolvency procedures in *Interpool, Ltd v Certain Freights of M/V Venture Star*, 102 BR 373 (DNJ 1988), *appeal dismissed*, 878 F2d 111 (3d Cir. 1989).

[45] Only recently in 2001 did the Hong Kong courts rule that shareholders need not necessarily be represented on a committee of inspection in a compulsory winding up of an insolvent company. *See Re Hung Fung Holdings Ltd* [2001] HKCFI 1009 (9 October 2001).

ticipate in meetings (including voting rights and establishing a quorum), and the chairing and general conduct of meetings. The committee itself should operate according to by-laws, or another governing document, adopted by the committee to normalize and define the parameters of its operations and deliberations, but practices in this regard vary widely. One point often overlooked is the procedure for voting. Because it is often the case that creditors lose interest as the proceedings carry on, it may make a real difference whether voting is only extended to creditors who appear in person at meetings or by proxy or whether it should be extended to creditors generally and allow for voting by mail or fax. In this regard, the use of creditor representatives can prove of assistance.

Jurisdictions are beginning to take into account the potential benefits of the Internet in organizing creditors.[46] Internet websites and email mailing lists could be created to disseminate information or even for voting. Going forward, the web might well offer a cost-effective method for increasing the involvement of creditors in the process.

3.7. Administration: Collection, Preservation and Disposition of Property

Once the debtor's interests in property have been ascertained, the property must be collected. To assist the administrator in collecting the property of the debtor, the insolvency legislation and rules need to include a combination of sticks and carrots to ensure that company directors comply. One such stick is to make the failure to comply with the requirements a ground for the disqualification of the director.[47] In Hong Kong, although these sections are not used as frequently as they are in England, they do address common problems such as the non-submission of books of account and the submission of incomplete books. A recurring problem in Hong Kong is that a Hong Kong company goes into liquidation but most of its assets are in mainland China. When the directors either fail to submit proper books of account or submit incomplete books, it makes it difficult, if not impossible, for the liquidator to locate the assets. These problems also demonstrate the cross-border difficulties that can occur.

Attention must also be paid to the ability of administrators to force third parties to turn over property belonging to the estate. To what

---

[46] See, e.g., http://www.enron.com/corp/ (website last visited April 2007).
[47] See supra 3.3.1.2.3.

extent may the administrator exercise such powers, with or without court coercion, and to what extent may such third parties raise defenses such as professional liens?[48] More modern systems adopt the principle that all such property should come under the physical or legal control of the court or the administrator, with the court then in a position to adjudicate conflicting claims to the property. Strong legislation backed up by strong decisions in the United Kingdom and South Africa have served to favor the insolvency administrator as against claims by third parties, for example, to retain documents relevant to the insolvency, or to resist providing information as to events prior to the onset of the insolvent liquidation, for fear of self-incrimination.[49]

The administrator must also make a series of quick decisions, including whether to continue the business, with its salaries and other costs, in the hope of getting a going-concern price. If not, then employees need to be laid off, utilities shut down, and so on as soon as possible. It will also be important to ensure the preservation of estate assets, which may require insurance, for example, but may also require the fast sale of perishable assets or assets declining rapidly in market value. Notice provisions may be limited in this last instance.

Problems in the collecting of assets are exacerbated when the assets are located in foreign countries. Of course, when the directors themselves file an insolvency petition, they can take steps to minimize this occurrence—for example, when an airline files for an insolvency proceeding, it is sensible to do so when as many planes as possible are in the air heading back to the jurisdiction in which the insolvency is occurring. But in regard to those planes that are still on the ground when the petition is filed, it is likely that the administrator will have difficulty in convincing many foreign jurisdictions that his claims should take priority over the various local mechanics' liens against the planes.[50]

When an administrator tries to collect the debtor's property, conflicts might well arise with other parties asserting rights to those same assets. There are two areas that need to be addressed specially: secured creditors and retention of title creditors.

---

[48] Professional liens may include liens of accountants and lawyers securing payment for their services.

[49] Sections 234–237, United Kingdom Insolvency Act 1986; *British & Commonwealth Holding plc (Joint Administrators) v. Spicer & Oppenheim* (Re British & Commonwealth Holdings plc (No 2)) [1993] AC 426; *De Lange v Smuts NO and others*, South African Constitutional Court—1998 (3) SA 785 (CC); 1998 (7) BCLR 779 (CC).

[50] *See infra* 8.1.

3.7.1. *Rights of Secured Creditors*

The earlier discussions have noted the very different positions of secured parties in various jurisdictions, especially with respect to control of their collateral.[51] There are also differences in rights to the proceeds of the sale of collateral. In some jurisdictions like the United States, the secured party has first priority in those proceeds ahead of all claims except the costs of sale. In other jurisdictions, certain preferred creditors (especially employees)[52] or even the unsecured creditor body may sometimes come ahead of the secured party.[53] In Germany, the costs of administration and sale come first and are percentages fixed by statute.[54]

Potential conflicts in jurisdictions whose law is based on English company law precedents might arise between the administrator and creditors holding a charge over book debts. In such jurisdictions, it is not uncommon for a secured creditor to take a fixed charge over book debts and their proceeds, with a proviso that if the fixed charge is not effective, then the book debts will be subject to a floating charge. The distinction is an important one: first, because a floating charge is more easily avoided than a fixed charge and, second, because a floating charge has a lower priority of payment than a fixed charge.[55] The issues regarding the distinction between fixed charges and floating charges have been among the most contentious in English security law. Cases have debated whether it is sufficient for the categorization of a charge as a fixed charge that the parties had intended that proceeds from book debts be deposited into a blocked account. The alternative position was that a charge over book debts could only be regarded as a fixed charge if the debtor was unable to access the money paid into that blocked account, without the permission of the chargeholder. A recent House of Lords case adopted the latter view, that is to say the case was less concerned with what the

---

[51] *See supra* 2.2.

[52] *See, e.g.,* Sec. 132 of the recently enacted PRC Enterprise Insolvency Law (adopted at the 23rd Session of the Standing Committee of the 10th National People's Congress on August 27, 2006, and effective on June 1, 2007), which included a special priority for various types of worker claims (wages, medical fees, and more) provided that the labor claims occurred prior to the promulgation of the new bankruptcy law and existed until the date the law came into operation.

[53] The new law in the United Kingdom has such a provisions *vis à vis* the floating charge. *See* § 176A, UK Insolvency Act 1986.

[54] Braun, *supra* note 30, at §§ 170–171.

[55] *See supra* 2.2.

charge said than with what the parties' actual rights were.[56] This decision has been seen as concluding this debate—at least for the present.

3.7.2. Retention of Title Claimants

Another possible class of claimants involves retention of title holders (for example, sellers who retain title in goods sold until the purchaser pays for the goods in full).[57] In these disputes, as with conflicts over book debts as discussed above, the resolution of the issue involves reviewing the documentation that sets out the rights (in this case providing a seller of goods with a retention of title, requiring the separate storage of the goods, and giving the seller a right of re-entry upon default by the purchaser) and ensuring that the procedures followed by the purchaser complied with the requirements. One of the problems for holders of retention of title interests is that even if the documentation is properly drafted, the holder will lose if the company failed to store the goods in a way that makes them easily identifiable. Part of the difficulty in jurisdictions that follow this approach is that these interests may not be registrable.

3.7.3. Other Priorities

Nearly all systems give priority to administration costs, including the compensation of the administrator and various professionals and the obligations of contracts adopted or created by the administrator. Obviously, without such priority no one would provide goods or services during the proceeding.[58] It is commonplace for insolvency systems to provide priorities among unsecured creditors as well, although some recent reforms suggest a trend toward reducing or eliminating priorities (e.g., Austria, Germany, United Kingdom). The favored creditors will ordinarily be paid in full or up to some stated limit before the other unsecured creditors receive any payment. Although priority systems vary greatly in whom they favor, a big three dominate: secured creditors (including title claimants, as above), employees, and taxing authorities. In some jurisdictions certain priority (or "preferential") creditors will enjoy a measure of priority even over secured creditors. One instance is discussed above.

---

[56] *National Westminster Bank plc v Spectrum Plus Ltd* [2005] UNITED KINGDOM HL 41.
[57] *See supra* 2.2.3.
[58] Some systems put these charges ahead of secured creditors as well.

Recently, the issue of the competing priorities between employees and secured creditors has emerged as one of the most contentious issues in insolvency law reform.[59] This is the very issue that held up Chinese law reform efforts for several years and continues to delay an enactment in Hong Kong. Under the old mainland Chinese laws—both the 1986 Trial Insolvency Law for SOEs and the 1991 Civil Procedure Law for non-SOE legal person enterprises—in bankruptcies, workers enjoyed statutory priority for their claims over unsecured creditors but were paid after secured creditors. However, various State insolvency policy decrees provided for special treatment for workers of some insolvent SOEs, pursuant to which workers' resettlement rights (and certain medical and pension benefits) took priority over the rights of secured creditors. In drafting the new Chinese insolvency law, a key issue was determining which approach to follow. The 2002 draft adopted the approach in the 1986 and the 1991 laws in which workers were given a more traditional priority. However, the 2004 draft moved in the other direction and even exceeded the scope of the PRC insolvency policy decrees, first by giving *all* workers priority over secured creditors and, second, by extending this protection to a broader scope of employee claims. This issue continued to be debated until the summer of 2006 when a compromise was finally reached regarding the rights of employees *vis á vis* secured creditors: under the PRC Enterprise Insolvency Law, secured creditors will have priority over all workers' claims arising *after* August 27, 2006 (the traditional approach as contained in the earlier Chinese insolvency laws); however, certain wage, medical, and insurance claims of workers arising before August 27, 2006 (and continuing to existing as of June 1, 2007), shall have priority over the claims of secured creditors. (This was one of the few areas in the new law where a policy disagreement was settled by a compromise). In most jurisdictions the amount of such old claims would not be significant. However, given that some SOEs have not paid workers wages for significant periods of time (many months and, in some cases, years), in some instances these might well be substantial sums.[60]

Meanwhile, in Hong Kong the issue has not been able to be resolved. Over a decade ago, the Hong Kong government proposed the Provisional Supervision regime, whereby a company in financial distress would be

---

[59] *See infra* Chapter 6.

[60] Charles D. Booth, *The Race of Two Tortoises: Insolvency Law Reform in Hong Kong and China*, 2(2) ABA CHINA LAW REPORTER 3–6 (Nov. 2006); republished in INSOL ELECTRONIC NEWSLETTER (Jan. 2007).

permitted to appoint a qualified professional to take over the management of the company and develop a rescue plan. The Hong Kong Law Reform Commission proposed that workers for companies using this new procedure would be able to rely on the Protection of Wages on Insolvency Fund ("PWIF"), which provides financial assistance to workers of companies that enter compulsory liquidation. However, the Hong Kong government, fearful that the PWIF would become a corporate bailout fund, rejected the use of the PWIF and instead inserted an unusual requirement into the commencement criteria included in the Companies (Amendment) Bill 2000: to utilize the Provisional Supervision procedure, a company would first have to either pay, in full, all the wages and other entitlements owing to the company's workers or set up a trust account with sufficient funds to make such payments.

Of course, the obvious question raised by these proposals was how a company in financial distress was supposed to find sufficient funds to pay all workers their full entitlements. Rather than addressing this concern, the government inserted the same proposal in the Companies (Corporate Rescue) Bill 2001. A government consultation paper issued in September 2002 proposed a cap on such payments to bring the amounts payable to workers in a Provisional Supervision in line with the amounts that workers would receive in compulsory liquidations. However, this cap would still require the company to pay individual workers up to HK$278,500 (roughly US$36,000),[61] and little legislative progress has been made since the conclusion of the consultation process in November 2003.[62]

Beyond the big three beneficiaries, the variation is remarkable. For example, the United States for some reason favors grain farmers and fishermen over other worthy claimants. Canada is like other jurisdictions in favoring landlords, while the United States disfavors them.

One other major variation among systems relates to shareholder claims of fraud in the sale of securities. The issue is whether those claims should be treated as general unsecured claims (like most fraud claims) or should have the lower position associated with the securities to which the fraud related (for example, the purchase of common stock, with com-

---

[61] *See* Philip Smart & Charles D. Booth, *Provisional Supervision and Workers' Wages: An Alternative Proposal*, 31 HONG KONG L.J. 188–199 (2001).
[62] *Id.*

mon shareholders ranking below all creditors). In the United States, for example, such claims are "subordinated," while in Belgium they are not.[63]

The international trend is to cut back on the categories of protected creditors in an effort to increase the distribution to unsecured creditors generally. In the case of workers' claims, this is easier in those jurisdictions where the government is able to provide sufficient protection of workers' claims outside an insolvency proceeding.

Tax claims are another target. Australia has abolished the priority for tax claims; interestingly, tax collection has actually increased as it appears that the Australian tax authorities are more vigilant in policing their debtors now that they can no longer rely on a priority in an insolvency proceeding. On the other hand, critics argue that these changes merely shift the burdens of insolvency onto other shoulders, mostly the taxpayers'.

3.7.4. Procedure

Procedures for resolving disputes over claims made against the debtor's assets will reflect the procedures generally following in litigation in each country. Peculiar to an insolvency proceeding, however, is the role of the administrator, who generally has the job of objecting to claims that appear invalid or overblown, although creditors usually have the right to object as well. This centralization reduces costs and is more efficient than expecting each creditor to object for the common benefit.

Systems vary in their emphasis on thoroughness versus speed in the claims process. The United States, for example, makes a claim "allowable" in the amount claimed, unless an objection is made. Germany has a similar system. A variety of rules can be found concerning deadlines for filing claims and whether a debtor's listing of a creditor is sufficient to constitute a claim.

In looking at systems as a whole, the most important factor is whether the claims process delays the proceeding as a whole, whether liquidation or rehabilitation. A system that permits disposal of assets or approval of reorganization to go forward while resolving claims later is likely to produce larger dividends for creditors. However, that approach also creates some difficulties as to voting.[64]

---

[63] *Lernout & Hauspie Speech Products N.V. v. Stonington Partners, Inc.*, 310 F.3d 118 (3d Cir. 2002).

[64] *See infra* 4.4.2.

3.8. *Disposing of the Debtor's Assets*

The insolvency law should provide a mechanism by which sale of assets subject to conflicting claims—ownership, leasehold, or lien—can go forward without waiting for a final resolution of those claims. The assets can be sold "subject to" a later determination of the rights of the claimants. If absolutely necessary, they can be sold with those rights still attached, but the prices obtained will obviously be very low. Some jurisdictions offer a far better approach, which is to sell a debtor's assets "free and clear" of all other liens or interests, leaving the claimants to dispute over the proceeds obtained in the sale. Because the law strips all conflicting interests from the property being sold, it will bring the best possible price from buyers glad to have judicial confirmation of their clear ownership.

It is very important to ensure, in the case of liquidations or of liquidating reorganization plans, that the assets are sold for a reasonable sum. The sale of assets is a major source of potential corruption or insider dealing in an insolvency system. It is the norm, of course, that assets disposed of in a liquidation will fetch a lower sales price than similar assets sold under normal market conditions. Nevertheless, various procedural protections can be put in place to ensure that the process is fair and that it maximizes the purchase price. The sort of protections found in modern systems include the following:

- having valuations prepared by neutral, independent professionals (especially important when dealing with real estate and specialized industrial property);[65]
- providing proper notice to creditors and prospective purchasers and permitting disgruntled creditors to seek legal redress if they have concerns or objections in regards to the process;
- in some cases, requiring pre-bidder qualification and minimum prices; and
- preventing and punishing bid rigging (that is, collusion among bidders).

Of course, this is another area of the law where there often is a large gap between the theory and the practice. It is important that the mechanisms be both flexible and transparent. Even in jurisdictions where the laws are clear and there are procedures in place to prevent insiders or associates from buying back corporate assets at "sweetheart" rates, it is usually the

---

[65] *See supra* 3.2.

case that the proceeds from such procedures are on the low side. This result is further exacerbated in jurisdictions with poorly functioning market economies or in insolvencies of state-owned enterprises where the government wears many hats in the proceedings and might well serve (or have a close relationship with the party that is serving) as seller, buyer, and auctioneer, all in one.

One device increasingly used, especially in the sale of whole businesses as going concerns, is the "stalking horse" bidder. The administrator arranges a contingent sale to an interested party at a set price, but the contract states it may be cancelled (broken up) if a higher bid is received in a stated time. To give the first bidder an incentive to enter into such a contract, it will be paid a "breakup" fee of a substantial amount if its contract is displaced by a higher bid. This device is sophisticated and sometimes controversial but has become important in recent years.

Another problem is presented when a jurisdiction's non-insolvency laws prohibit or restrict foreign ownership in certain industries or sectors. In an insolvency, such national policies are likely to lead to a lower realization for assets and thus smaller distributions to creditors.

Overall, there are no factors more important in the disposal of assets than maximum transparency and maximum publicity. Publicity attracts buyers and transparency defeats fraud and collusion.

Finally, in keeping with the goal of maximizing the estate for the benefit of creditors, the administrator may be entitled to abandon assets with negative or insignificant value, providing the abandonment does not violate compelling public policies (for example, abandonment of an environmentally dangerous property). Notice to creditors of abandonment should be required, however, as a check against carelessness or abuse.

3.9. *Contracts*

3.9.1. *Introduction*[66]

Most insolvency laws allow the administrator to elect to continue or repudiate ("accept or reject")[67] contracts based on a cost-benefit analysis

---

[66] *See generally*, UNCITRAL Legislative Guide, 119; Roy Goode, PRINCIPLES OF CORPORATE INSOLVENCY LAW §§ 6–16–24, 154–162 (3d ed. 2005). (United Kingdom); Eur Prin. 45–47, § 6; Ian F. Fletcher, INSOLVENCY IN PRIVATE INTERNATIONAL LAW 78–79 (1999).

[67] Many different terms are used for the same actions. "Assume" is used here for

of what is in the best interest of the creditors, accepting good bargains the
debtor had made and rejecting bad ones.[68] In particular, rehabilitation
may depend on the ability to enforce contracts notwithstanding a right
of cancellation in the event of insolvency, to cancel contracts (including
labor contracts) to enable the enterprise to downsize its workforce to a
reasonable level, or to avoid burdensome contracts. The principle encourages policy makers to take account of other policies that may provide a
compelling case for altering the commercial expectations and bargains
of the parties.

The calculus of costs and benefit of performing a contract is somewhat
different in insolvency than in a normal business context. If the contract
is accepted, in most countries it must be performed or damages paid in
full as a cost of the case.[69] If the contract is rejected, the damage claim of
the counterparty is usually treated as a pre-insolvency unsecured claim,
which receives only a small percentage payment in most cases.[70] Thus
acceptance can only be justified where the benefit to creditors is greater
than the full cost of performance, while rejection is appropriate when the
cost of performance by the debtor would be greater than the sum of:

a. the benefit of reciprocal performance still due from the counterparty; and
b. the expense of paying a low-percentage damage claim for breach of
   contract.

The decision is made almost entirely on the basis of the creditors' interests, not those of the counterparty, but many insolvency systems provide
certain protections for the counterparty as well, especially in the case of
acceptance and continued performance.

Many contracts contain clauses forbidding assignment of the contract,
which would prevent the debtor's rights from passing to the administrator. Many contracts also contain "insolvency clauses" (also known as
"ipso facto" clauses) that cancel the contract or permit its cancellation in

---

"adopt," "accept," "perform," or "opt to perform." "Reject" is used for "disclaim," "disas-
sume," or "refuse to perform." "Assume" means to agree to perform a contract and "reject"
means to breach it.

[68] For example, see the Mexican law, LCM article 88.

[69] For example, in France such costs become "Article 40" expenses and debts of the
estate. Anker Sorenson and Paul J. Omar, CORPORATE RESCUE PROCEDURES IN FRANCE
(1996) at 87, 171–172. Germany, *see* Braun, *supra* note 30, at 225–226.

[70] Apparently, rejection damages are given a higher priority in Japan. *See* Council of
Europe (1996) at 67.

case of the insolvency of one of the parties (see below). If these clauses are enforced in an insolvency proceeding, they will lessen or eliminate the power of the administrator to maximize the value of the estate by accepting good bargains and rejecting or disclaiming bad ones.

Discussions of contracts in insolvency often refer to "executory" contracts. Obviously, nothing can or should be done about a contract that is fully performed on both sides. Thus an executory contract is one in which performance remains to some extent undone. Yet if the only performance left is payment by the debtor to the counterparty or payment by the counterparty to debtor, little thought is required about any contract issue, because there is nothing left but a debt. It is the mutual dependence of obligations that makes adoption or rejection of a contract an important and often difficult business decision. Unfortunately, this state of mutual dependence has sometimes been elevated from a business difficulty to a legal one with the claim that only a contract with performance due on both sides is executory enough (has a quality of "executoriness") such that *it is permitted to be* adopted or rejected.[71] This mistake—a supposed legal rule that only a contract with executoriness can be adopted or rejected—in turn can give rise to a great conceptual tangle. The key point is that mutuality is not a legal condition but an occasion for business judgment as to whether the performance to be received by the debtor by adoption is worth more than the cost of the debtor's performance.

There are detailed rules governing different types of contracts, including employee contracts[72] and leases of real estate.[73]

3.9.2. *Decision to Terminate the Contract*

Confusion can be avoided by a clear understanding of the fundamentals of the problem. If the administrator determines to reject (not perform and therefore breach) a contract, the estate is merely doing what any party to a contract might do. The counterparty will be entitled to a damage claim, as with breach by a solvent party, except that its claim will be paid in tiny insolvency currency (perhaps the infamous 10 cents on the dollar) rather than in full currency units. The counterparty's harm comes from breach of contract, a risk with any contract, greatly worsened by

---

[71] *See* Jay Lawrence Westbrook, *A Functional Analysis of Executory Contracts*, 74 MINN. L. REV. 227 (1989).
[72] *See infra* Chapter 6.
[73] *See, e.g.*, Braun, *supra* note 30, at 235.

insolvency. The harm is just the same, in most cases, as the harm suffered by other creditors whose contracts happened to have been finished by the time the insolvency proceeding began, so that the debts to them were already fixed. (Excluded from this section are rights *in rem* or other rights to obtain specific property, which are discussed elsewhere.) As such, the counterparty has no more entitlement to 100 percent payment or 100 percent performance than any other unfortunate general creditor. To give it full payment or performance is to violate the equality principle, unless creditors generally will benefit from doing so.

In many systems, the counterparty may not receive non-damage remedies even if it would have been entitled to such remedies outside of insolvency. The reason is that other remedies—for example, delivery of goods the debtor had manufactured but not shipped prior to the start of the insolvency proceeding—would represent the equivalent of 100 percent payment to the counterparty, while other creditors of the same class—almost always general, unsecured creditors without priority—would be receiving far less. Therefore other remedies would violate the equality principle. On the other hand, this view is not always followed. Some systems, for example, will permit a buyer of goods to demand shipment even though the effect is to prefer the buyer over other unsecured contract creditors. The policy reason for this result is not clear but it is consistent with the rule in many civil law countries outside of insolvency that buyers may demand delivery of goods from defaulting sellers.[74] Similarly, in common law countries, performance in kind may be required where the contract is for the sale of real estate (immovable).[75]

3.9.3. *Decision to Continue the Contract*

Where an administrator decides a contract should be accepted, the counterparty is merely being held to its bargain with the debtor. Outside of an insolvency proceeding, if it made a bad bargain, it would nonetheless be required to perform. In principle, continuation of the contract in insolvency asks no more. Thus if the contract provides for the counterparty to sell the debtor goods for 1,000 currency units and those goods are now worth 2,000 units in the market place, the administrator will adopt the contract, pay 1,000 units for the goods, and sell them for 2,000 units, thus benefiting all the creditors by increasing the distribution to them. The

---

[74] For the situation of sellers, *see supra*, 2.2.3.

[75] For example, this is true in the United Kingdom. Roy Goode, PRINCIPLES OF CORPORATE INSOLVENCY LAW (2d ed. 1997) at 126.

good bargain has been preserved for their benefit and the counterparty, having been paid as provided by the contract, has no legitimate complaint. Any insolvency system should permit such results and most do.

The counterparty might have what amounts to an option to get out of the contract if the contract contains an "insolvency termination" clause, permitting termination of the contract if either party enters an insolvency proceeding. Because on the facts of the example just discussed there is no risk to the counterparty, its reason for termination might be merely that it wants to get out of a bad bargain and make the 1,000 units profit for itself. To avoid that result, some countries override such clauses, making them unenforceable in insolvency while others permit them to be effective.[76] This policy decision is an important one, especially in the context of rehabilitation, where the power to accept good bargains may be essential to rescue.[77] It represents another instance of the balancing of the interests of other creditors and other stakeholders generally against the interests of a creditor counterparty to an incompletely performed contract. Much the same situation may arise from an "anti-assignment" clause that forbids the debtor from transferring its rights under the contract to a third party. As discussed below, if such a clause is enforced in an insolvency proceeding, it might prevent the estate or administrator from acquiring the debtor's rights in the contract.[78] Again, some systems render such a clause ineffective against an administrator so as to preserve the value of the debtor's bargain for the benefit of creditors. If such clauses are permitted, the counterparty may get a windfall by virtue of escaping from its bad bargain.

Nonetheless, some policymakers favor limiting an administrator's power by full or partial enforcement of an insolvency-termination clause. Reasons supporting the right of a counterparty to cancel contracts under such clauses are in reality arguments against the administrator's power to accept or breach contracts. These arguments include the following:

---

[76] For example, see the LCM, art. 87; Braun, *supra* note 30, at 250, § 119; Eur. Prin. 45–57, § 6.

[77] *See generally* Goode, *supra* note 75, at 128, 149–150, 323 (criticism of rule enforcing such clauses, especially in rehabilitation proceedings).

[78] Conceptually, such a clause has that effect in systems that conceive of the debtor's property being "conveyed" by operation of law to a legal entity, the insolvency estate, at the moment the proceeding is opened. In those systems, an anti-assignment clause might be claimed to prevent the property from passing into insolvency at all. Those insolvency systems that conceive of the debtor's property as remaining in the debtor, but taken from his possession and control by the administrator, may not have the same difficulty with an anti-assignment clause.

- Where the parties have made several contracts between them, the insolvent can "cherry pick"—that is, claim selective performance of contracts profitable to the insolvent but cancel others. It is unreasonable for a defaulter to have an advantage denied to the innocent counterparty. One response would be a rule permitting a court to aggregate apparently separate contracts where the parties intended mutual dependence. For example, the debtor may have entered into a franchise contract with a franchisor while also getting from the franchisor a lease of the real estate where the debtor would operate the franchise. The parties may have intended that the two apparently separate contracts depend upon each other but may not have used specific language to make this clear. In that case, the administrator might be required to accept both or reject both, as if they were one contract.[79] On the other hand, if the debtor has two separate contracts to buy two different types of goods from the same counterparty and there is no contract language linking them together, the law may conclude that they are truly separate and the debtor may accept or reject either of them in the interests of creditors.
- If the administrator accepts some contracts and rejects others, the result may be to prevent netting.[80] One response is to permit netting of some contracts and not others, leaving to the courts the sometimes difficult task of isolating contracts that should be eligible for netting from those that are not. Alternatively, a finance ministry could maintain a list of contracts exempted for netting purposes. If a selective approach is not adopted, then all netting must be permitted or none at all, and either of those choices will produce inefficiencies.
- The insolvent estate is often unable to perform so there is no point in forcing the other party to await a largely theoretical choice by the administrator. If, however, the law permits a counterparty to terminate unilaterally under an insolvency or non-assignment clause, two serious problems are created. The first is that rehabilitation will often become impossible because the business cannot maintain crucial contracts in the early stages of recovery. The second problem, which arises even in liquidation, is that the possible benefit of assigning a profitable contract to an eligible transferee is lost. A response to this difficulty is to adopt a procedure that forces an

---

[79] See *infra* 3.9.4 regarding the "cum onere" rule.
[80] Netting is discussed below under setoff and netting. See *infra* 3.9.9.

early decision on continuance of a contract and to deem the contract ended if the decision is not made within the prescribed period.[81]

- It is inappropriate to compel a transfer of contracts to a different unknown transferee. This point is clearly correct. As discussed below, countries may provide that no approval of an assignment of the contract by the administrator unless the assignee is identified and determined to be ready and able to perform the contract.

3.9.4. *Risks to Counterparties*

The most common risk to a counterparty is through continuation of a contract. Although the counterparty is being held to its agreed bargain, continuation of a contract with a party in an insolvency proceeding presents risks not ordinarily present. The most important risk to the counterparty is the risk of non-payment. For example, if the terms of a contract provided for an extension of credit, in which the debtor was not required to pay until 60 days after delivery of the goods, then enforcement of the contract by its terms would require the counterparty to assume the risk of non-payment by the administrator for a period of 60 days. Even if the contract provided for payment on delivery and the administrator promised to make such payment, the counterparty who had to expend substantial sums to prepare the goods for delivery would run a risk of harm if by the time of delivery the administrator was no longer able to pay for the goods.

Some systems react to these risks by requiring the administrator to provide some sort of guarantee of payment or performance to the other party, perhaps by a bank guarantee or a letter of credit, even though the original contract made no such provision.[82] In other systems, the administrator assumes personal liability for such contracts, so the counterparty has a solvent defendant in case of breach.[83] In still other systems,

---

[81] For example, in a liquidation case in the United States a contract is deemed rejected (breached) unless the administrator adopts it within 60 days of the opening of the proceeding. 11 U.S.C. § 365(d)(1). In Mexico, the LCM sets a 20-day period in article 92, third paragraph. *See* ALI Mexican Statement 2002, sec. I, 2. Germany, Braun, *supra* note 30, at 227.

[82] For example, the Mexican law provides that the contract continues unless the conciliator (administrator) objects. If it continues, the debtor must perform or secure performance by a guarantee of some kind. ALI Mexican Statement 2002, sec. I, 2.

[83] For example, see Ian F. Fletcher, THE LAW OF INSOLVENCY (2d ed. 1996) at 373–379, and Goode, *supra* note 75, (1997) at 245, 317 (in United Kingdom system, an administrative receiver is personally liable for adopted contracts but an administrator is not, although a new contract takes priority over administrator's fees).

however, the counterparty is forced to bear the non-payment risk on the theory that it assumed the risk of the debtor's insolvency by entering into a contract with the debtor. That result is supported by the argument that the risk is no greater by accident of timing. If, for example, there were two creditors, A and B, with contracts allowing for payment 60 days after delivery, and A delivered the day before the proceeding began while B's contract was still unperformed on that date, a defender of the assumed-risk theory would say there is no obvious reason B should be better treated than A just because of the difference in timing of performance. This policy decision—the allocation of the risk between perhaps blocking rehabilitation by requiring assurance of payment or, on the other hand, forcing the counterparty to take the risk of non-payment—is a highly important one as a practical matter.

The most common increase in contractual power granted to the administrator is the power to cure a default that may not have been curable under the ordinary law of contracts. Thus a debtor might have fallen several months behind on its land-lease rental payments before the insolvency proceeding began. If the administrator wishes to continue the lease, the law may permit cure of the default by payment of the arrears even if such cure would not ordinarily be permitted without the consent of the landlord. In a rehabilitation case, for example, such a result may be justified by a desire to ensure that a landlord who will be paid in full is not permitted to frustrate a rehabilitation favored by the great majority of creditors. The landlord, on the other hand, may feel that renewed defaults are likely and it would strongly prefer in light of the earlier defaults to re-lease the property to another party.

One rule protecting counterparties that may be universal is that the administrator must elect to breach or continue a contract as a whole (*cum onere*). It would be obviously unjust and productive of much mischief if the administrator could elect some parts of a contract to continue while breaching others.

Other rules designed to protect counterparties, in addition to the procedural rules discussed below, include flat prohibition of continuation of certain kinds of contracts without the agreement of the counterparty. For example, some jurisdictions impose such a rule with regard to contracts with the government. Some of these are discussed below.[84]

---

[84] *See infra* 3.9.7.

Of great practical importance is the rule with respect to the existence or absence of personal liability of the administrator for performance of assumed contracts.[85] In some systems—for example the United Kingdom administration procedure—the administrator becomes personally liable for the performance of "adopted" (continued) contracts, while a liquidator is not so liable. Especially with regard to employees, that personal liability might operate as a significant disincentive to continuing the business of the debtor because there will always be a risk of failure and consequent liability for the professional who serves as administrator. More commonly, as noted above, the counterparty is protected either by a third-party guarantee (for example, a bond from an insurance company) or to a more limited extent by a right to priority payment from the debtor's assets.

3.9.5. *Assignment of Contracts*

In more sophisticated systems, there is also the possibility of assignment of a contract by the administrator to a third party for performance. Obviously, this second stage may involve an even more complex set of benefits and risks for both the estate and the counterparty. A common example would be a debtor lessee who has a below-market lease for retail space. The landlord would like to terminate the lease and re-lease to another party at the higher market rate. The administrator would like to continue the lease and sell its rights under the lease (often called a "sublease") to a third party, thus realizing the debtor's good bargain for the benefit of creditors. If the lease is freely transferable, then the only legal question is the one just discussed: under what, if any, circumstances may the administrator continue the contract and thus exercise the debtor's rights, including the right to transfer?

However, it is often the case that the contract has an "anti-assignment" clause. As noted above, that clause may prevent the administrator from acquiring any rights in the contract. In those systems where the administrator has the right to continue the contract despite such a clause,[86] there remains a further question as to the administrator's right to take the second step of transferring the contract to a third party.

One obvious point is that the counterparty never agreed to contract with the third party and may not wish to do so. In some systems, the

---

[85] *Cf.* 3.6.1.2.
[86] *E.g.*, the United States. 11 U.S.C. § 365.

contract will not be transferable. In the systems that override the anti-assignment clause so the administrator may transfer the contract to a third party, the counterparty is generally entitled to some protection. For example, the court may be required to determine that the third party is a solvent and capable party to such a contract. Or the administrator may be required to make some guarantee of the performance of the third party (such as a bond) in a way that insulates the counterparty from unreasonable additional risk. On the other hand, once assignment is approved, the law may provide immunity from further liability under the contract for the estate or administrator.

3.9.6. Procedure

While avoiding the details of procedure, which necessarily vary from one system to another, it is important to focus on some procedural points of special importance in the area of contracts. The first is timing. Most systems have some time limit within which the administrator must decide to continue or not continue each pre-insolvency contract of the debtor.[87] Some have specific limits in the statute while others require the counterparty to make a demand for a decision, after which the administrator has a certain time to decide.[88] Most systems anchor this procedure with a default rule: if the administrator does not declare continuance or non-continuance within the specified time, then the contract continues or does not continue. Systems that adopt non-continuance as the default rule[89] sometimes have a different rule or no rule in a rehabilitation proceeding as opposed to a liquidation.

Two other procedural points often arise in the contract field. One is that some systems require judicial approval of the administrator's deci-

---

[87] For example, in the United Kingdom the counterparty can demand a decision within 28 days. Fletcher, *supra* note 83, at 193–194. In France, the time is one month. Sorenson-Omar, *supra* note 69, at 85. In Indonesia, the period is set by the court if the parties cannot agree on a time. Benny S. Tabalujan, INDONESIAN INSOLVENCY LAW (1998) at 74–75.

[88] It is sometimes provided that certain types of contracts are subject to special timing rules. For example, in France a lessor can demand surrender of the lease if rent is not paid for two months. Sorenson-Omar, *supra* note 69, at 86. In the United States, a commercial lease of an immovable or a movable must be adopted or rejected within 60 days. 11 U.S.C. § 365(d)(3), (10).

[89] For example, this rule prevails in Indonesia. Tabalujan, *supra* note 87, at 76. The Mexican system is one that adopts continuance as the default rule. See LCM art. XX. The same is true in Belgium and, for the most part, in Italy. Harry Rajak, Peter Horrocks & Joe Bannister, EUROPEAN INSOLVENCY: A PRACTICAL GUIDE (1993).

sion while others leave it entirely to that official (for example, the United States and the United Kingdom, respectively). The second is the question of continuation of a contract by conduct. That is, if the administrator acts in a way consistent with continuation of a contract (as by encouraging employees to continue to work), even though no formal continuation is declared, will the administrator and the insolvency estate be bound? This question is quite sophisticated and often not addressed in the insolvency statute. For example, the law in the United States on this point is quite unclear. On the other hand, in the United Kingdom the possibility of adoption by conduct is so clear that the statute expressly protects the administrator from adoption of employment contracts by conduct during the first 14 days of an administration (rescue) procedure.[90]

There is a third question even less often addressed: what are the obligations between the administrator and the counterparty during the period within that the administrator is allowed to consider whether to continue the contract or not? Must the counterparty perform as required by the contract during that time? Must it prepare to perform where such preparation cannot await the administrator's decision? In either case, if the contract is not continued, the counterparty may have incurred damages after the opening of the insolvency proceeding while waiting for the administrator's decision. The law may have to determine to what extent the resulting claim should be paid pro-rata as a pre-proceeding claim or in full as a claim incurred by the administrator for the benefit of creditors.

3.9.7. *Special Contracts*

Because contracts are of so many different sorts in so many different parts of a society, the general rules dealing with a debtor's contracts are often subject to exceptions for special contracts. To some extent, these exceptions are inevitable because of the unusual social and economic

---

[90] Section 99(5), sch. B1, United Kingdom Insolvency Act 1986. In relation to employment contracts, an administrator will be liable (subject to the protection that any such liability will be charged on and payable out of property of that the administrator had custody) where he or she has "adopted" the contract of employment, and subject to the provision that "action taken within the period of 14 days after an administrator's appointment shall not be taken to amount or contribute to the adoption of a contract." *See also* Goode, *supra* note 66, at 9–49, 286; 9–53–58, 290–294.

problems inherent in certain contracts. On the other hand, that fact makes a perfect disguise for the desire of various creditor groups to evade the collective rules of insolvency proceedings so they may benefit disproportionately from special treatment. The policymaker will be constantly presented with pleas for special treatment in this area. The key question will be whether the pleader is genuinely in a position importantly different from many other contractual parties.

To take the classic example of a contract that may not be adopted: if the debtor was a portrait painter, the counterparty is not required to permit the administrator to adopt the contract and paint the counterparty's portrait. Indeed, the administrator probably cannot assign the contract to another good portrait painter because the nature of the contract is so personal. This principle is much expanded in some systems to forbid continuance of contracts that specifically contemplated performance by the debtor uniquely, even though the debtor is a corporation and might change its management and employees at will. An example is a court decision in the United States making a patent license such a "personal" contract where the licensee goes into an insolvency proceeding, so that the administrator cannot accept and assign the license.[91] While the result is controversial in the United States, it illustrates how far the principle is sometimes taken. Another common exemption is for contracts with the government.[92]

Most systems will not permit the administrator to force the extension of credit by continuance of a contract to make a loan. This rule, however intuitively appealing, actually requires some difficult distinctions in those systems that do not have a general rule requiring complete protection for a counterparty. For example, if a contract for the purchase of goods by the debtor can be continued without cash payment before delivery or a third-party guarantee, as it can be in some systems, then how can that forced extension of credit by the seller be distinguished from a loan?

---

[91] Some cases in the United States have gone so far as to deny acceptance even in rehabilitation cases, where the debtor is in fact the same person with whom the counterparty original contracted. *See, e.g., In re Catapult Entertainment, Inc.*, 165 F.3d 747 (9th Cir. 1999). Norway is another country where licensing agreements may not be adoptable. Rajak, Horrocks & Bannister, *supra* note 89, at 507.

[92] Yet another example: Under the recent Mexican law, no contract for services may be rescinded, on whatever side the debtor may be—provider or purchaser. ALI Mexican Statement 2002, Sec. I,2.

Insurance contracts are also in a special category in many systems, with a great variety of results,[93] as are contracts with utilities, which are often required to continue services.[94]

Employment contracts are given unique treatment in most insolvency systems. Employment contracts are of two main types: the collective rights won through a union and individual contracts with employees. Both types of contracts are heavily protected in most systems, but only in systems with extensive experience with rehabilitation has it been necessary to go much beyond the priority of employee claims. In a rehabilitation, questions include the possibility of changing wage rates and work rules to permit the business to continue. In this area, the insolvency rules intertwine with labor laws in ways that make it very hard to generalize. On the other hand, it must be candidly stated that rehabilitation is very often not workable unless employees are prepared to sacrifice wage rates and traditional work rules in the interest of preserving the business and therefore their jobs. Ultimately, these questions are less matters of contract than of labor policy versus rehabilitation policy.[95]

Contracts for the sale of goods are not "special contracts;" indeed, they are almost the central example of treatment of contracts in most systems. Nonetheless, it should be noted that these contracts are often subject to special rules that have evolved over centuries of trading.[96]

3.9.8. *Leases*

Leases in many legal systems may be regarded as a hybrid form, lying between contract law and property law. Thus it is not surprising that many systems have special rules for leases,[97] although most treat them under the general conceptual and legal structure associated with contracts. Real property (immovable) leases may have different rules than personal property (movable) leases. Within the category of immovables, there are often distinctions between residential leases and commercial

---

[93] For example, in Mexico see ALI Mexican Statement 2002, sec. I,2; in the United Kingdom, *see* Fletcher, *supra* note 83, at 194; Goode, *supra* note 75, at 131–132.

[94] For example, the United States provision (United States Code § 366) and the United Kingdom provision (IA § 233).

[95] *See infra* Chapter 6.

[96] *See supra* 2.2.3.

[97] *E.g.*, Germany. 108 ff. IO; UNCITRAL, LEGISLATIVE GUIDE ON INSOLVENCY LAW 129 (§§ 137–138) (2005).

leases. The special social questions associated with a habitation may protect the residential lessee more thoroughly than a commercial lessee. Commercial leases are often of very great importance in rehabilitation cases. On the one hand, below-market leases represent an asset that can be sold, for example, where the debtor wants to close a certain retail store but has a good price on the lease. On the other hand, the ability to escape leases for money-losing locations by payment of only a part of the remaining rent may be an important advantage of an insolvency proceeding for a retailer whose survival depends on contraction of its business.

A common problem with leases, especially of immovable property, is a sub-lease, where the original lessee has assigned a lease granting all or part of the leased premises to another party and later the original lessee files in insolvency. The question is whether or not the sub-lessee's rights are dependent upon performance of the original lease by the original lessee, now in an insolvency proceeding. Generally, the answer depends upon non-insolvency law: what is the effect on the sub-lessee of a breach of the original lease by the original lessee? Ordinarily, the parties will have negotiated a clause in the sub-lease dealing with this very question. Much the same problem arises where there is no sub-lease but the original lessee has granted a security interest in its lease to secure repayment of a loan. Much the same answer should apply.

Increasingly, the form of a lease transaction is being used to provide finance, creating an economic relationship very similar to a secured loan. The treatment of this sort of "financial" or "financing" lease is discussed in Section 2.2.

3.9.9. Setoff, Netting, and Derivatives

In some common law countries setoff is permitted between solvent parties but becomes compulsory on insolvency. In others, setoff is not required but is almost always in the interest of the counterparty. Generally, setoff is permitted only between two pre-petition debts or two post-petition debts, but not between a pre-petition and a post-petition debt, because the difference in value between the two types of debts (that is, their different rights to priority in distribution) is usually so substantial that setoff would lead to injustice.

Where setoff is compulsory—that is, where it takes place as a matter of law without an election by either the debtor or the counterparty—it is not subject to court control and may be governed by different choice-of-law rules.[98] On the other hand, in some countries, including the United States, setoff is an election by the counterparty and is restrained by the automatic stay, so it may not be exercised without court approval once a proceeding has begun.[99]

However, many countries provide an exception for certain financial contracts.[100] Policymakers have been persuaded that a number of these financial contracts should enjoy virtually complete exemption from the insolvency process (including the moratorium, the contract rules, and the distribution rules), giving the counterparties to these sorts of contracts far more favorable treatment than most creditors.

Netting is a more controversial subject.[101] Nonetheless, some jurisdictions (e.g., Belgium, France, Luxembourg) have granted exceptions to the general insolvency rules for certain types of netting, again primarily in the area of financial contracts, but its acceptance is significantly less widespread than for setoff. The policymaker has similar policy considerations to weigh in considering exemptions for netting.

The United Kingdom has a heady mix of principles. Netting is provided for by legislation in the financial services sector in domestic cases.[102] Yet, the netting arrangements of an international agreement were specifically rejected by the House of Lords as incompatible with United Kingdom insolvency principles. Finally, it might be mentioned that the United Kingdom falls into the category of jurisdictions in which insolvency setoff is compulsory.[103]

3.10. *Avoiding Pre-Proceeding Transfers*

Typically, insolvency systems permit recapture actions for as many as four common types of pre-proceeding transactions. These transactions may be subject to being treated as legally void, so that property the debtor

---

[98] Goode, *supra* note 66, §§ 8–16 – 8–49; pp. 224–246. Some countries prohibit setoff post-proceeding.

[99] *See* 11 U.S.C. § 553. *See also* UNCITRAL, LEGISLATIVE GUIDE ON INSOLVENCY LAW 155 (2005).

[100] In general, these are contracts that include "repurchase agreements" or "repos," "swaps," and, more generally, "derivatives."

[101] "Netting" for present purposes means offsetting all amounts due under various contracts between the two parties.

[102] Sections 159–165, United Kingdom Companies Act 1989.

[103] *National Westminster Bank Ltd. v. Halesowen Presswork and Assemblies Ltd.* [1972] AC 785.

has transferred, or its value, may be recovered by an insolvency representative from the person receiving the transfer. (Some systems also permit avoidance or cancellation of an obligation arising from a disfavored transaction; references herein to "recapture" are meant to include such actions unless the context suggests otherwise.) The four types are: transfers in intentional fraud of creditors; transfers at an undervalue; preferential payments to certain creditors; and invalid security interests.[104] As to each of these, legal systems vary as to whether the transferee—the person who received the property—can be required to return it if the person receiving the transfer acted in good faith, gave value, or had no knowledge of the crucial facts. Some systems permit such defenses by the transferee, while others require a return of the property regardless, although with some protection for any value actually given by the transferee. In addition, many systems exempt certain types of transactions from recapture. A common example is the exemption of certain financial transactions, such as borrowing against stock or closing a derivative contract. Financial contracts are frequently exempted from insolvency rules because of arguments from the financial community that their contracts require preferred treatment if the financial system is to function properly.[105]

3.10.1. *Generally*

Three of the four types of avoidable pre-proceeding transactions are avoidable because they are generally regarded as unfair or financially harmful to the interests of all of the debtor's stakeholders, especially if they are executed in contemplation of a likely insolvency. These are transfers in intentional fraud of creditors, transfers at an undervalue, and preferential transfers to certain creditors.[106] A transaction may fall into these categories retrospectively—that is, it may be a transaction that would not be regarded as morally or legally wrongful ordinarily but is

---

[104] However, Germany has much broader provisions that may permit avoidance of almost any action that disadvantages creditors. Christoph G. Paulus, *Lessons to Learn from the Implementation of a New Insolvency Code*, 17 CONN. J. INT'L L. 89 (2001).

[105] See, for example, § 165, United Kingdom Companies Act 1989. *See also* 3.9.7.

[106] These general types of avoiding actions also appear in many systems in forms directed at specific sorts of conduct. An example is the Canadian "settlement," which voids gratuitous transfers within one year of proceeding. *See* American Law Institute, Transnational Insolvency Project, International Statement of Canadian Bankruptcy Law (2003) [hereinafter "Canadian Statement"] at 25.

seen as harmful in light of insolvency. As discussed below, this area is one in which a delicate balancing of competing social benefits is struck by each jurisdiction. When the balance suggests that a particular transaction is harmful, it may become legally avoidable. One tool that insolvency systems often use to strike the necessary balance is an allocation of the burden of proof in different ways for different transactions. For example, a particular sort of transfer may be avoidable only if the person receiving the transfer knew certain facts, but there may be a presumption that person did know those facts unless that person proves otherwise.[107]

These avoidable transactions are different from other issues arising in an insolvency proceeding, including various other types of fraud or improper conduct, because the insolvency representative seeks to void a specific transfer of the debtor's property (or cancel a specific obligation) that arises from a specific category of transaction often seen in the context of insolvency.

These three types of avoidable pre-proceeding transactions are made avoidable for the following reasons, *inter alia*:

  i. To prevent fraud (for example, transfer of assets to hide them for the later benefit of the debtor);
 ii. To ensure distribution among creditors *pari passu* or by whatever priority system the law establishes for distribution;
iii. To prevent favoritism, where the debtor wishes to advantage certain pre-proceeding creditors at the expense of the rest;
 iv. To prevent a sudden loss of value in a company that may force the debtor into an insolvency proceeding that may have been unnecessary or that may impoverish the debtor just before court supervision is imposed; and
  v. To create a framework for out-of-court settlement so creditors will know that last-minute seizures of assets by other creditors can be set aside, an assurance that makes it more likely that creditors will be willing to work with debtors to arrive at workable settlements without court intervention.

These five policies, in turn, have evolved from three general principles in insolvency cases: equal treatment of creditors with similar legal rights,

---

[107] The German system of changing burdens for different types of transactions is illustrative. Braun, *supra* note 30, at §§ 130–131, 270–273. Another example is from the United States system: a provision that presumes insolvency for the 90 days before bankruptcy, for the purpose of preference avoidance. United States Bankruptcy Code § 547(b)(3). *See infra* 3.10.8.

maximization of value to be shared, and encouragement of out-of-court settlements. They in turn are balanced against policies concerned with free and predictable commercial transactions, as discussed below.

The right to recapture transfers arising from these types of pre-proceeding transactions is generally limited to transactions that took place within a certain period before the opening of an insolvency proceeding, often called the "suspect period." In some systems the period is a fixed number of days, weeks, or months while in others it is measured from the time the debtor became insolvent in one sense or another. Some systems have one suspect period for all types of transactions while others have different periods for different categories. The suspect period may also vary for transfers to "insiders," such as officers, directors, and their relatives. There also may be changes in the burden of proof with respect to insiders.

The fourth type of avoidable transaction, cancellation of a security interest, rests on a different footing. The cancellation of a security interest improperly created or perfected under security law is simply an instance of enforcement of the rules concerning such interests in the context of insolvency. The laws governing security interests have certain requirements, and creditors who fail to meet those requirements cannot expect to see their security interests enforced. The policies served are those established in the laws permitting the grant of security to creditors.[108] On the other hand, as noted above, even a security interest valid under those non-insolvency laws may be avoidable in insolvency under one of the first three headings listed above. For example, the grant of a security interest shortly before the opening of an insolvency proceeding, although otherwise valid, may be found to have been preferential because it favored unfairly a certain creditor at the expense of the rest.

Although some or all of these four types of pre-proceeding transactions may be subject to avoidance or a Paulian action by a creditor outside of an insolvency proceeding, the insolvency representative generally has more opportunity and more incentive to bring such actions than any one creditor. As a result, these actions are perhaps the most unique and characteristic consequence of commencement of an insolvency proceeding.

---

[108] *See supra* 2.2.

3.10.2. *Intentional Fraud*

Virtually all legal systems give creditors the right to avoid or cancel transactions executed by the debtor with the intent to defraud creditors. A typical example would be a transfer to a trusted confederate, often a relative, with the agreement that the property would be held for the debtor's benefit and re-transferred when the debtor's creditors had ceased their efforts to collect (a "*fiduciacum amico*"). Typically, the greatest difficulty in these cases is proof of the intent to defraud. Some systems have presumptions or other legal methods for making it easier for a court to find intentional fraud under certain circumstances. For example, in Germany a transfer within the proceeding 10 years can be avoided if the debtor intended to disadvantage its creditors and the person receiving the transfer knew of that intention. If the person receiving the transfer knew of the debtor's illiquidity and the disadvantage to the creditors that would result, that person is presumed to have known of the debtor's intent.[109] In many systems, these doctrines have evolved into rules that eliminate any requirement of bad intent on the part of the debtor, as explained below concerning transactions at an undervalue. Where a debtor's fraudulent intent is found, systems vary as to the existence or absence of a requirement that the person receiving the transfer also have a bad motive or guilty knowledge, a point discussed under the heading "Defenses" below.

3.10.3. *Transactions at an Undervalue*

A debtor who has no intent to defraud may nonetheless be in great need of cash and may therefore sell property at a price substantially below its real worth in order to obtain a quick sale. The result may be to reduce the amount of property available to creditors when an insolvency proceeding is commenced. In a number of jurisdictions, it is possible to recapture such transfers, although frequently the person receiving the transfer is assured of getting the return of the actual amounts paid to the debtor for the property. Generally, the debtor must have been insolvent in one sense or another at the time of the transfer or the transfer must have been within the suspect period.

For example, in Germany such a transaction done during a three-month suspect period may be recaptured if the person receiving the

---

[109] *See, e.g.*, Braun, *supra* note 30, at 269 (German law).

transfer knew the debtor was illiquid. The same transaction might be set aside in the Netherlands if done within one year of insolvency, if the debtor knew of damage to creditors from the transaction (presumed) and it is shown that the person receiving the transfer knew of the prejudice to creditors. In the United States, a transfer can be avoidable, and the property recovered, regardless of the intent of the debtor or the knowledge of the transferee, if the debtor was insolvent at the time of the transfer, the value given the debtor by the other party was "less than reasonably equivalent value," and the transfer was made within one year of the filing of the insolvency proceeding.

The changes in knowledge required or, just as important, in the burden of proof concerning knowledge are well illustrated by a German example. If the debtor transferred property to another during the suspect period, the transfer might be characterized in three ways: as a congruent delivery, an incongruent delivery, or an immediately detrimental contract. If a transfer is a congruent delivery—that is, a transfer performed by the debtor within the suspect period—and was in perfect accordance with the underlying contractual or legal obligation, it would not be avoidable unless the receiving person had knowledge that the debtor had ceased to fulfill its obligations as they became due or knew about the filing of the petition. If, however, such delivery did not take place in accordance with the underlying obligation—i.e., if such delivery was performed before the due time, if what was delivered was different than what was owed, or if there had been no obligation at all for such delivery—then such delivery was incongruent and recoverable if the receiving person could not prove its ignorance about the debtor's ceasing of payments or the filing of a petition. The third category—the immediate detrimental contracts such as an undervalue sale—covers more broadly what is already dealt with by the section on transactions for inadequate consideration, except as to remedy. If the contractual obligations were performed within the suspect period, the section on immediate detrimental contracts allows for a full recovery of the delivered goods—and not just that part for which no consideration was given.[110]

The ultimate example of a transaction at an undervalue is a gift. Because the debtor receives no exchange for a gift, if it is given at a time when the debtor is in financial distress and unable to pay creditors, it is often avoidable. In a number of systems (for example, Canada) the gift

---

[110] To be sure, in detail these rules are a bit more complicated than described here. *See* Braun, *supra* note 30, at 269–273.

may be avoidable regardless of insolvency or financial difficulty or of the parties' intent or knowledge if it is given within a stated period before an insolvency proceeding.

It is noteworthy that these transactions may not involve any moral or legal failing by the debtor or the person receiving the transfer. Often they would be valid and unavoidable under normal circumstances. A transaction for a below-market price is simply a bargain ordinarily. A gift to charity might even be admirable in the usual case. It is the debtor's inability to pay creditors that makes these transfers subject to challenge and possible avoidance. An old legal proverb explaining the difference is "A man must be just before he is generous." Another factor is the difficulty of proving intent to defraud. A rule that looks at results, not intent, will be easier to enforce, while an innocent transferee can be protected by defenses, discussed below.

A central question in this category is how great the undervaluation must be to make the transaction avoidable. This determination is generally left to the courts by the use of standards like "reasonable value" or "market value."[111]

3.10.4. *Preferential Transfers*

Most insolvency systems provide for voiding a payment or other transfer of debtor property to a creditor when the transfer gives that creditor an unfair advantage in recovery over the other creditors with the same legal rights. The common example is a payment to one unsecured creditor shortly before the filing of an insolvency proceeding, enabling that creditor to obtain a larger percentage of what it is owed than the other unsecured creditors. There are various requirements and limitations imposed on avoidance of such transactions but the most common are that the debtor must have been insolvent in some sense at the time of the transaction and that it took place within the suspect period.

Some systems, including the English, require that the debtor be "influenced" by a desire to prefer the creditor.[112] This requirement means that the law in those jurisdictions is focused on the avoidance of debtor favoritism for certain creditors rather than maximization of value or encouragement of settlement. The great importance of this requirement

---

[111] *See supra* 3.2.

[112] Historically, the test was a tougher one that the debtor "had a dominant intention to prefer."

is illustrated by the United States case of *In Re Maxwell Communication Corporation plc*,[113] in which the application of United States law, which has no intent requirement, or English law, which has such a requirement, determined whether US $100 million of payments to three banks would be recoverable as preferential.

The leading English authority, *Re MC Bacon Ltd*, holds that the word "desire" is subjective—and therefore that the debtor must have wished to improve the creditor's position. Thus, where the creditor puts genuine pressure on a debtor to pay or threatens legal action against the debtor, the debtor's payment will not be found to have been influenced by a desire to prefer the creditor.[114] Given this rule, a creditor in such jurisdictions can thus take certain steps to minimize the likelihood that the debtor's payment will later be characterized as a preference.

Unlike the subjective English approach, the American approach is to look more to preferential effect than to intention or desire. Such an approach may, at times, be under- or over-broad, but it has the advantage of ease of administration.

Although the concept of avoidance of payments that give a preferred position to a certain creditor is connected with the concept of fraudulent or undervalued transfers, it represents a distinct concept with its own justification. A fraudulent transfer is not necessarily made to a creditor, but a preferential transfer is always made to a creditor. For that reason, a preferential transfer is nearly always made for equivalent value because the transfer discharges all or part of the debt that is being paid, while a fraudulent or undervalued transfer may be attackable precisely because too little was given to the debtor in exchange. The problem with a preferential payment is that it gives one member of a class of creditors (for example, the class of general unsecured creditors) a greater percentage of the debtor's assets than is that creditor's legal entitlement.

Other types of transactions during the suspect period that may be avoidable are: (a) pre-payment of debts not then due to be paid; and (b) payments by commercially unusual methods.

Preferential payments are like undervalued transfers or gifts in that they are often perfectly proper transactions under normal circumstances but are viewed differently when the debtor is insolvent and an insolvency proceeding is filed shortly afterward. In some systems a preferential

---

[113] 93 F.3d 1036 (2d Cir. 1996). English law applied: no preference
[114] Philip Smart, Charles D. Booth & Stephen Briscoe, HONG KONG CORPORATE INSOLVENCY MANUAL, p. 82 (2002).

payment must involve a blameworthy intent or knowledge of the debtor and the creditor who received the payment, although often providing that certain circumstances create presumptions that such an intent or knowledge was present. In other systems, however, no such intent or knowledge is required.

3.10.5. Defenses

Although the avoidance of harmful transactions serves important policies, it also creates some serious risks in the marketplace. The assurance that legal and customary transactions are final and legally protected is very important. The possibility of avoidance of an otherwise proper transaction risks introducing uncertainty into the market, with a consequent reduction in efficiency and an increase in costs. For that reason, the gains from avoidance actions in an insolvency context must be carefully balanced against the costs imposed on ordinary market transactions. Different insolvency systems have drawn the line at different points. The principal method for protecting the market has been to give defenses to the person receiving the transfer. The defenses may include a claim that this person lacked a certain knowledge or state of mind, gave full value, or was engaged in a protected sort of transaction. Where such a defense exists, a person in the market who fits one of these categories need not be concerned about the risk of having to return the property obtained in a transaction.

Sometimes these protections are stated as defenses, while in other jurisdictions they may instead be one of the elements that constitute the avoidance action. In either situation, presumptions are often employed, depending on the circumstances of the transfer.

3.10.5.1. Defenses to Avoidance Other Than Preferential

Excluding defenses to preferential transfers, discussed below, the most common defenses by a transferee to an avoidance action are based on the transferee's innocence or lack of knowledge. Yet in some countries, including the United States, the bankruptcy law does not recognize this defense for the initial transferee but grants it to subsequent transferees from the initial transferee.

There may also be a partial defense for a transferee who gave value for a transfer. The transferee may be entitled to return of the value actually given, although it may also have to show its good faith or lack of knowledge. Thus, for example, in Canada an avoidable transfer to a related party at an undervalue is avoided only to the extent of the undervalue, permitting the person receiving the transfer to retain the value actually given.[115]

3.10.5.2. *Defenses to Preferential Transfer Avoidance*

The concern to protect the marketplace may be especially strong as to preferential transfers, so there are often more defenses to such an action. Lack of knowledge of the debtor's insolvency is a commonly recognized defense, although not universally recognized. Another defense often found is that the payment was made in the regular course of business. As noted above, several countries require that the debtor have an intent to prefer the creditor. There are also a number of defenses that protect particular types of transactions.

3.10.6. *Suspect Periods*

There are two approaches to calculating the "suspect period" in which transactions are subject to review under the foregoing rules. One is to state a fixed period in the statute. The period may be a certain time before a request for an insolvency proceeding is made or before such a proceeding is actually opened. The other is to measure the period from the time that the debtor first ceased to make payments as they became due, an event known as "cessation of payments." Fixed periods often vary depending on the type of transaction involved and upon circumstances, such as the relationship between the debtor and the person receiving the transfer. For example, the recent Estonian statute provides for a two-year period for a preferential transfer to a creditor who is related to the debtor, unless it can be shown that the debtor was not insolvent at the time. The two may be combined, so that some "cessation" systems also have an outer limit on the length of the suspect period, while a fixed-period system may require insolvency or illiquidity as a further condition to avoidability. In some systems, the relevance of the suspect period is only to create a presumption of necessary intent or knowledge in the debtor or the person receiving the transfer or both.

---

[115] *See* ALI Canadian Statement at 25.

The time periods vary greatly from jurisdiction to jurisdiction. For example, the time period for avoiding a gift is four years before a request for insolvency proceedings in Germany but only one year in Switzerland. For deliberate fraud with knowledge by both debtor and the person receiving the transfer, the period stretches backwards 10 years in Germany but only five in Switzerland.

Many jurisdictions—including both the United Kingdom and the United States—dramatically increase the suspect periods for transactions involving payments to "associates" or "insiders." Associates normally include the spouse or relatives of corporate directors, partners, employees, and employers. It normally also extends to corporate groups both upstream and downstream. In addition, in the United Kingdom and many jurisdictions adopting its approach, where it is found that a suspect transaction involves certain associates, the relevant desire to prefer will be presumed (unless the contrary is shown).[116]

3.10.7. Security Interests

Among the transfers that can sometimes be avoided are those involving security interests. It is significant in this section to discuss only a key difference between two different grounds for avoidance of such interests.

One reason for avoiding a security interest is that it is invalid under the law governing security, regardless of insolvency. Thus, for example, those systems that require the public registration of certain sorts of security may provide that the security will be unenforceable or void in an insolvency proceeding if the registration was not made. Although this result is consistent with insolvency policy, the insolvency proceeding is merely an appropriate occasion for enforcing the requirements of the law of security interests.

On the other hand, a security interest may be valid under security law (for example, it may be properly registered in systems requiring registration) but may be avoidable on one of the grounds set forth above.[117]

---

[116] However, due to one of a series of drafting errors in Hong Kong, this is not the case for corporate directors who receive preferences. Smart et al., *supra* note 114, at pp. 83–84. These drafting errors exist in Hong Kong because the changes to the corporate preference provisions were made by incorporating the definition of "associate" from personal bankruptcy law rather than through the promulgation of a definition better suited to corporate transactions.

[117] *See supra* 3.10.1.

3.10.8. *Procedure*

Generally, it is the administrator of the insolvency who is authorized by law to bring Paulian actions. Such actions in many systems require a full lawsuit just as in the case of a commercial lawsuit of the usual kind. As indicated above, such litigation may require of either party proof of state of mind or knowledge, which is very difficult. The difficulty of proof may mean that the party with the burden of proof will most often lose. Perhaps even more difficult are questions of valuation, especially if the relevant time for valuation is some time in the past. For an appraiser to testify as to the value of a property claimed to have been transferred at an undervalue two years before is very difficult, especially if property values have been volatile since that time. As with other elements of an insolvency system, the shape of the avoiding powers may depend on the resources available to the system. If accountants and appraisers are hard to find and expensive to employ, then a system may focus on intentional or reckless transfers rather than merely unwise ones.

3.11. *Avoiding Post-Insolvency Transfers*[118]

Obviously, the debtor should not be allowed to transfer property to others after an insolvency proceeding has been opened. Some systems, as in the United States, treat this problem as a question of avoidable transactions. Others, for example in Germany, consider that the dispossession of the debtor of its property makes it conceptually impossible for the debtor to have transferred any interest to another after the proceeding has commenced.[119] Regardless of the theory, the effect is the same: a general rule that post-opening transfers by a debtor are ineffective and any property so transferred should be returned to the administrator and any obligation so created should be unenforceable against the property subject to the insolvency.

On the other hand, many systems reflect a concern about persons receiving such transfers who may have been unaware of the insolvency proceeding at the time of the transfer, especially if such a person gave value in good faith in the transaction. Some systems therefore make such transactions valid as to such innocent persons until notice of the

---

[118] UNCITRAL Legislative Guide, §§ 70–73, pp. 98–99.
[119] Braun, *supra* note 30 at § 81, at pp. 191–193.

insolvency proceeding has been published. Other systems make most such transfers void or voidable, but provide some exceptions. For example, in the United States such transfers are avoidable, except: (i) those made to innocent purchasers of immovables until the insolvency has been recorded in the land records;[120] and (ii) those made by third parties holding certain assets of the debtor who transfer them to others in good faith and without knowledge of the insolvency proceeding.[121] On the other hand, any exception creates a risk that creditors will be deprived of property to which they should be entitled. In some systems the risk continues over a substantial period of time (typically until some formal method of notice is satisfied by publication or otherwise), increasing the risk greatly as the "notice" period is expanded.

Similar issues are presented by transfers made *to* debtors after an insolvency has commenced. For example, is payment to a debtor of a pre-existing debt a valid satisfaction of that debt if made after insolvency proceedings have commenced? Once again, some systems make the answer dependent upon publication of the insolvency while others have a general rule of non-satisfaction of such debts, with stated exceptions because of lack of notice or other factors.

Finally, questions arise about the validity of transfers made and obligations incurred by debtors after the filing of an insolvency proceeding but prior to the court's ruling thereupon (that is, prior to the opening of a proceeding). In some systems, this "gap period" only arises in involuntary cases because the filing of a voluntary application leads automatically to opening of a proceeding. In other systems, where even a voluntary filing leads to the opening of a proceeding only after a court determination that an opening is appropriate, transfers during a gap period may arise in any case.[122] As with the notice problem, the longer the gap period provides an exception to the no-transfer rule, the greater the risk to creditors.

3.12. *Special Treatment of Partnerships*

The insolvency of general partnerships creates its own set of problems. Without exploring the details, we note here the key issues each insolvency system must address. Unlike the insolvency of legal entities such

---

[120] United States Bankruptcy Code § 549 (c).
[121] United States Bankruptcy Code § 542.
[122] *See supra* 3.4.3.

as corporations where the legal separateness and individuality provide a kind of anchor for the doctrinal treatment of that entity, the case is different with partnerships because they are somewhat hybrid institutions lying between the poles of personal liability of the partners and that of the economic unit. Three questions reflect the central points. All three relate to the treatment of the partnership as a single entity or as a collection of individuals:

> Is the partnership eligible to file an insolvency proceeding as an entity distinct from the individual partners?
>
> If the partnership files an insolvency proceeding, is the power to enforce the individual partner's liability reserved to the insolvency administrator?
>
> Are the assets of the partnership and the individual partner segregated for purposes of access and priority by their respective creditors?

The questions arising from the dual nature of partnerships are clearly reflected in the German legislation: even though partnerships (in particular the so called Offene Handelsgesellschaft [OHG] and the Kommanditgesellschaft [KG]) generally are not entrusted with their own legal individuality, they do have some legal capacities that reflect the economic need of treating them as more than just an aggregation of several (natural and/or legal) entities. One of these capacities is that a partnership as such is potentially subject to an insolvency proceeding; i.e., a partnership can be the debtor in an insolvency proceeding. One has, thus, to distinguish precisely between the insolvency of that partnership and those of its partners—they do not necessarily go hand in hand. To the degree, however, that the partners are personally liable for all debts owed by the partnership, the partnership's creditors have next to their regular insolvency claim against the insolvent partnership an accessory claim against the partners who might not yet be in an insolvency proceeding. To avoid in such an instance the risk that those creditors will act against the partners directly, Section 93 of the German Insolvency Ordinance entrusts the administrator during the course of the partnership's insolvency proceeding with the exclusive right to enforce such claims against the partners; they are to be realized to the benefit of the estate as a whole. The United States has a similar approach.

How complicated this issue might become in practice is amply demonstrated by the law of the United Kingdom; it provides more than 10 different ways of dealing with a partnership's insolvency. The main (but not exclusive) legislative guidance is the Insolvent Partnerships Order 1994. As a general paraphrase, however, it is fair to summarize that the law's main task is to balance the various interests at stake. Thus, it is up to the creditors to decide to pursue their claims against the partnership or against a single partner (or several of them). While it is self-evident that the partnership's estate is to be used for the benefit of its creditors, things are seen to be different with respect to the estate of the individual partners. There, by contrast with the United States and German examples, a common law rule states that the partners' individual creditors should take priority over the partnership's creditors unless the partnership's liquidation estate has absolutely no funds (i.e., the presence of just one British pound in the partnership insolvency estate would allow application of this rule).

A somewhat comparable approach is to be found in the Austrian Bankruptcy Ordinance, Section 57. According to this law, the partnership creditors are admitted to each partner's insolvency proceeding only with a claim reduced by the dividend they have received (or are to receive) in the partnership's proceeding. That is to say that these creditors are forced to seek satisfaction first from the partnership's estate; as such, the partnership creditors are subordinate to the partner's personal creditors. In the partner's insolvency proceeding, however, those same creditors of the partnership are of equal rank with the individual creditors of the respective partner.

In contrast to the English example, legislation gets much simpler once a partnership is excluded from the insolvency regime; then one has to deal only with the insolvency of the single partners. France is an example of this legislative approach. The partner's personal debts add to the debts resulting from the partnership's activities and the respective personal liability of that partner.[123]

These key issues demonstrate the difficulty of discussing partnerships in a book devoted to the insolvency of business corporations because every issue is ultimately tied to the rules governing individual bankruptcies, a subject beyond our scope. However, the key issues discussed do represent the conceptual link between the two types of proceedings.

---

[123] Code civil, art. §§ 1872–1, al. 2 and 1873.

CHAPTER FOUR

CORPORATE REHABILITATION PROCEEDINGS

4.0. *Introduction*

In almost all developed countries, as well as in a number of developing countries, insolvency systems have two distinct formal pathways for handling the problem of debtors unable to pay their debts as they fall due. First, there is the traditional approach, which can be said to have dominated insolvency systems up until a generation or so ago and that is often called liquidation. This refers to the process by which the unpaid or underpaid creditors seize control of the assets belonging to the debtor (most often through a representative, not surprisingly often called a "liquidator") and arrange for the piecemeal sale of these assets and distribution of the proceeds amongst themselves. This process generally entails the dismantling of the business belonging to the debtor and, with that destruction, the loss of employment for the employees, the termination of transactions and assignments before completion, and other wasteful or disruptive consequences.

Second—perhaps in reaction to what was seen as unnecessary wastefulness—the approach of debtor rehabilitation has been developed.

A number of general points should be made in connection with this bifurcated approach to bankrupt debtors. In the first place, the idea of rehabilitation is also rooted in legal tradition but not the same tradition as that from which liquidation originates. The latter may be described as a formal process, most commonly arising from a court order initiating a process that takes place under the supervision of the court.[1] The traditional rehabilitation process, by contrast, may be more informal; it springs from the collective concerns of creditors and is subsequently translated into an agreement with the debtor as to the future conduct

---

[1] However, it should be noted that many Commonwealth jurisdictions supplement the compulsory, court-centered procedure with a streamlined creditors' voluntary liquidation procedure.

of the business. The importance of the process in this context lies in its independence of any assistance from, or approval by, any court or other public institution. Yet its inability to bind creditors who refuse to be party to the agreement made a formal rehabilitation pathway inevitable.

4.1. *History and Key Issues*

The concept of a formal business rescue regime in modern times can be traced back at least to 1926 when, under the description of Judicial Management, it was introduced into South Africa by the South African Company Law Amendment Act of that year.[2] This regime was adopted almost in its entirety by Australia in 1961, where it was called "Official Management."[3] Both these regimes have been widely recognized as failures.[4] Following the recommendations of the wide-ranging Australian Law Reform Commission Report, Official Management was abolished in 1993 and replaced by the regime of Voluntary Administration. South Africa's Judicial Management remains on the statute book,[5] and although much work has been done on radical reform in this area,[6] a new implementing statute (a Companies Act) with a wholly new business rescue regime is still in bill form and its enactment is not expected before 2010.

Insolvency "rehabilitation," or "reorganization" or "rescue" is everywhere devoted to maintaining all or a major part of a business as a going concern. It may be devoted to saving the company (which remains in the hands of the original owners) or merely to saving the business (which is sold to the highest bidder as a complete unit). The former was often the goal with rehabilitation laws and the original Chapter 11 in the United States, while the latter is the common result under some more recent enactments and in many contemporary Chapter 11 cases.

---

[2] For another view of this history, see Philip Wood, PRINCIPLES OF INTERNATIONAL INSOLVENCY 21–27 (2007).

[3] *See* Part IX, Australian Companies Act 1961.

[4] On Judicial Management, see Harry Rajak & Johan Henning, *Business Rescue for South Africa* 116 S. AFR. L. J., 262, 264–272 (1999). On Official Management, see Australian Law Reform Commission (the Harmer Report, 1992) 45. For a plea in defense of Official Management, see McCabe, *Official Management v. Reorganisation Under Chapter 11 of the United States Bankruptcy Code: In Defense of Official Management* [1992] 20 AUSTRALIAN BUSINESS LAW REVIEW 320.

[5] Now at §§ 427–440, South African Companies Act 1973.

[6] See, for example, Rajak & Henning, *op. cit.*

The Common Law of the United Kingdom, on the other hand, has its own provision for business rescue—the institution of receivership that, for one reason or another, was rejected by the South African legal system.[7] Flexible and responsive principles of equity in the legal system were skillfully fashioned to create this institution, which is discussed more fully below[8] and which may be regarded as the mainstay of the United Kingdom's business rescue provision for the last hundred years or more.

Nor is the United Kingdom unique in the creation of a Common Law system to provide for the possibility of a rescue rather than a liquidation of a bankrupt business. The United States, which shares the same Common Law system as the United Kingdom, developed what was described as the "equity receivership" as an instrument for the reorganization of bankrupt corporations, both independently of and alongside Federal Bankruptcy Acts, for the period of at least 100 years prior to the enactment of the US Bankruptcy Code in 1978.[9] Unlike the United Kingdom's institution of receivership, the equity receivership in the United States has passed into history, eclipsed by statute, although its debt to the common law is clear. "When [the U.S.] Congress finally added a meaningful corporate reorganization option to the Bankruptcy Act in the 1930s," Professor Skeel tells us, "it took all of its cues from the railroad receivership techniques that had long been used in the courts."[10]

The modern era in statutory rehabilitation regimes was initiated by the United States, with Chapter 11 of its Bankruptcy Act of 1978. Some countries like the United Kingdom followed this lead by creating statutory regimes for the first time; in other cases, like Australia and Germany, the newly created regimes in 1993 and 1999, respectively, replaced outdated ones. In Central and Eastern Europe, after the fall of the Soviet Union, new bankruptcy codes were enacted in some countries and, in

---

[7] This is a vastly interesting topic but not one we can pursue here. A starting point for those interested in this kind of divergence between legal systems may be the South African Appellate Division decision of *Conradie* v. *Roussouw* [1919] AD 279 (South African Law Reports), in which South Africa rejected the Common Law doctrine of Consideration in contract.

[8] *See infra* 5.5.1.

[9] *See* DAVID SKEEL, JR., DEBT'S DOMINION (2001) 17, 48, 57–69; Clifford Billig, *Corporate Reorganization: Equity vs. Bankruptcy*, 17 MINN. L R 237 (1933).

[10] SKEEL, *supra* note 9, at 48.

other countries, long dormant codes from the pre-Soviet-era were resuscitated and updated. The German reform has been especially important and influential.[11]

This new-style rehabilitation regime can now be found in a substantial number of legal systems throughout the world, and the process of rescue and rehabilitation of a bankrupt business (as opposed to its liquidation) is recognized by all recent international treaties and other instruments dealing with insolvency proceedings.[12] It is important to observe that all such regimes are created by statute and that such statutes usually lay down a comprehensive procedure to be followed by whoever seeks protection under the regime. One might describe such regimes as "formal rehabilitation" regimes, although terms such as "rescue," "reorganization," "restructuring," "arrangement," "administration," "composition" or "reconciliation" are all used.

There is little significance, if any, in the differing terminology thus employed, but it may be of interest to note that in the United Kingdom, for example, discussion has centered on the desirability of avoiding reference to words such as insolvent, insolvency, and bankruptcy when describing business rehabilitation regimes. It is thought by some that avoiding the use of such words helps to remove a stigma that might otherwise attach to those associated with the insolvent business that is likely to benefit from the regime. If it is indeed the case that a business rehabilitation regime might be shunned, despite its potential for beneficial use, on account of the terminology used, then clearly it would be desirable to avoid the off-putting terms.

4.1.1. Formal and Informal Rescue and Rehabilitation Regimes

Under the old-style business rehabilitation regimes, where the entry threshold was often intolerably high, the realistic choice for debtor and creditors alike usually lay between a private workout and a formal liqui-

---

[11] *See* Harry Rajak, *Rescue Versus Liquidation in Central and Eastern Europe*, 33 Tex. Int'l L. J. (1998) 157, 165 ff.

[12] See the European Union's, Council Regulation (EC) on Insolvency Proceedings, No 1346/2000, arts. 1(1), 2(a) read with Annex I, UNCITRAL, Model Law on Cross Border Insolvency (1997), preamble (e), art. 2(a), OHADA Uniform Act Organising Collective Proceedings for Wiping off Debts arts 1, 2 (http://www.jurisint.org/ohada/text/text.06.en.html); World Bank Principles & Guidelines for Effective Insolvency and Creditor Rights Systems, Introduction and Executive Summary, ¶¶ 12–15; Principles 17–26.

dation.[13] Even where the entry threshold to the formal regime is substantially lower, a private workout in the form of a creditors' composition—which could be seen as an example of an informal business rehabilitation regime—retains its attractiveness. By taking an informal route, the rehabilitation can be conducted without the necessity of oversight or approval by the court, which can be costly, complicated, and time-consuming.

This lack of court oversight may, however, also be a disadvantage where, for example, the debtor takes advantage of it to defraud the creditors. There is a further disadvantage with informal rehabilitation in that there is nothing equivalent to the automatic stay or moratorium provided by legislation to prevent a creditor from initiating or continuing legal proceedings, or, where appropriate, self-help remedies[14] against the debtor for payment of a particular debt. And if a substantial number of creditors favor an informal rehabilitation but one creditor demurs and threatens legal proceedings against the debtor, there will be a temptation to remove the threat to the business life of the debtor posed by the rogue creditor by assisting or encouraging the payment of that creditor in preference to the others.

This difficulty is often described as the "hold out" problem, because it is in the interest of one creditor to threaten to "hold out" in order to receive better treatment than other creditors with similar legal rights. Naturally, the other creditors will be unwilling to agree under those circumstances. A type of commercial blackmail might thus be seen to be encouraged. Furthermore, and of particular relevance to an insolvent debtor with assets in a different jurisdiction, the contract enshrining the informal workout is unlikely to give sufficient authority to anyone seeking the repatriation of assets belonging to the debtor from a foreign court.

One of the developments in large corporate bankruptcies in the United Kingdom in the past two decades has been a mechanism to secure

---

[13] For example, under the ancient German company rehabilitation regime (vergleichsverfahren) for a composition to be accepted, a minimum of 35 % of the claims of the unsecured creditors had to be guaranteed. This regime did not provide an automatic stay and did not apply to preferential or secured creditors. *See* Oscar Couwenberg, *Survival Rates in Bankruptcy Systems: Overlooking the Evidence*, 12 EUR. J. L. & ECON. 253 (2001) (this article is of much value and can also be found at http://www.som.eldoc.ub.rug.nl/FILES/reports/themeE/2001/01E15/01E15.pdf).

[14] For example, a creditor who has supplied goods to the debtor may be able to assert rights of ownership against those goods in the possession of the debtor (by reference to a provision in the contract of supply in terms of which the supplier retained ownership until the goods had been paid for in full) and simply remove those goods from the debtor. For a discussion a creditor's right of retention, see *supra* 2.2, 2.2.7.

agreements among the banker creditors of the debtor. This mechanism is known as the "London Approach" and is masterminded by the Bank of England. It is specifically designed to secure agreement among the debtor's bank creditors. Here, of course, we are concerned with a huge indebtedness owed to several, sometimes dozens, or even hundreds of banks and where the economic and possibly political consequences of the outright failure of the debtor are unthinkable. This particular approach to rescue and rehabilitation is discussed elsewhere.[15]

4.1.2. *Survival of the Business and Liquidation*

It is an oversimplification to see the survival of the business and liquidation as mutually exclusive. Liquidation can entail either liquidation of the debtor itself (where the latter is an incorporated organization) or merely liquidation of the business. The former is a technical term describing the process, invariably laid down by statute, as a result of which the debtor's assets are realized, the creditors' claims are met as far as possible, and the debtor's personality extinguished. The latter is a non-technical term that describes the process by which the business is brought to an end by dismantling its constituent parts: dismissing the employees, selling the assets piecemeal to different purchasers, and so on. A liquidation of the debtor itself, therefore, may involve the sale of the debtor's business as a going concern and its continuation in the hands of the purchaser.

While liquidation may result in the continuation of the business—and thus be seen as a rehabilitation procedure—it suffers from one serious disadvantage for this purpose. In many jurisdictions, the liquidator (or other official charged with the responsibilities of liquidation) is required to dispose of the assets as quickly as possible and is permitted to carry on the business of the debtor only insofar as this is necessary for the liquidation process.[16] This may further depress the value of the debtor's assets. To overcome this disadvantage of liquidation, the United Kingdom Insolvency Act included in the part of the statute that created the statutory business rehabilitation regime—Administration—a power that

---

[15] See *infra* 5.5.2.

[16] This principle is deeply established in U.K. insolvency law. It rests on a 19th century decision, *Re Wreck Recovery and Salvage Co.* (1885) 15 Ch D 353, and might be even more firmly applied today in view of the added jurisdiction now available to insolvency practice of Administration.

enables the administrator to effect "a more advantageous realization of the company's assets than would be effected on a winding up."[17]

The extra flexibility that Administration brought to United Kingdom insolvency in this respect has all but eliminated the difficulty that a liquidator might face in not being able to continue the business, except strictly for the purposes of the winding up. Of course, petitioners must be sure, where an extended period is desirable in the liquidation of the business, that Administration, and not Liquidation, is the chosen course. In jurisdictions where there is a single insolvency gateway rather than—as in the United Kingdom—a separate gateway for rescue and liquidation, this problem should not arise. And in the United States, technically a dual gateway jurisdiction, the problem hardly arises on account of the ease and popularity of electing the rescue route. It would appear that no rule similar to that of the United Kingdom exists in the United States, requiring any continuation of the debtor's business in a liquidation process to be used solely for the purposes of the liquidation.[18]

Alternatively, the liquidation regime may be destructive of the business for the opposite reason. Given that liquidation is more than likely to require court oversight and approval, it may be too cumbersome to enable the liquidator to act with the speed that may be necessary—given the nature of the business—to ensure survival of the business as a going concern. Businesses that rely on commission agents (who may have built up substantial goodwill) may only be able to survive if there is as little hiatus as possible between the onset of liquidation and the transfer of the business to a purchaser wishing to continue it. To overcome this disadvantage, a liquidator in the United Kingdom has the power, exercisable without requiring court involvement or sanction, "to sell any of the company's property by public auction or private contract, with power to transfer the whole of it to any person or to sell the same in parcels."[19]

4.1.3. *A Single or a Dual Gateway?*

Some jurisdictions, for example France and Germany, provide a single entry point for insolvent debtors moving into a formal regime. The

---

[17] *See* § 8(3)(d), UK Insolvency Act 1986.

[18] *See* Douglas G. Baird, THE ELEMENTS OF BANKRUPTCY, 1992, p. 14.

[19] Sch. 4, Part III, para. 6, read with secs. 165 and 167, Insolvency Act 1986. *Cf.*, UNCITRAL, LEGISLATIVE GUIDE ON INSOLVENCY LAW 26–27 (2005) (advocating the value of flexibility in this regard).

rationale for this is to maximize the possibility of a rehabilitation. Under the French law that created this type of regime, the *redressement judiciaire*, a statutory observation period enables the court to decide whether a long-term rehabilitation is possible or the debtor must be put into liquidation. Other jurisdictions, for example the United States, have separate entry points for a prospective rehabilitation of an insolvent debtor and for the liquidation of the debtor. Research in France shows that the overwhelming number of debtors ended up in liquidation; and more recent legislation in 1994 provides for a drastic reduction in the observation period, leading in certain instances to the almost immediate consignment of the debtor to the liquidation regime.[20]

The fact that liquidation can act as a framework for rehabilitating the debtor's business reduces the significance of whether the system has a single or dual gateway into an insolvency proceeding. The important point is not to lose an opportunity of rescuing a salvageable business. As long as the liquidation regime is sufficiently flexible, the business can—where appropriate—be transferred as a going concern. The entity in which the business was housed will, of course, be lost and with that the potential for any return for the original investors. Interestingly, the United Kingdom has both separate gateways for the rescue and liquidation of insolvent companies, as well as a single gateway. As we shall see, one of the purposes for which administration is permitted is the better realization of the company's assets than would be achieved in liquidation—a rescue of sorts but essentially a liquidation within the rescue regime. And, as we have seen, there is a certain amount of flexibility within liquidation such that sometimes a rescue might be fashioned and put into effect within liquidation.

Although a sale of the debtor's business in liquidation is rightly seen as a rehabilitation of that business, there is good reason for encouraging rehabilitation through the rescue regime, rather than through liquidation, wherever possible. Apart from the loss (in liquidation) of the debtor's equity, rehabilitation carries with it a potentially higher return for unsecured creditors than in liquidation. While accepting without

---

[20] Régis Blazy, Bertrand Chopard, Agnès Fimayer, Jean-Daniel Guigou, *Financial Versus Social Efficiency of Corporate Bankruptcy Law: the French Dilemma?*, 3d Annual Conference on Empirical Legal Studies Papers (2007). Although the United States technically has a multiple-entry system, recent empirical work suggests that Chapter 11 of the Bankruptcy Code functions like a single entry system for most corporate debtors that are larger than tiny. Elizabeth Warren and Jay L. Westbrook, *The Success Of Chapter 11: A Challenge To The Critics*, 107 MICH. L. REV. 603 (2009) (Most significant corporate debtors file in Chapter 11 and the courts then promptly separate winners and losers).

reservation the proposition that seeking to keep alive a business that has no likelihood of survival is a serious waste of resources, the dynamic effects of rehabilitation should not be ignored or underestimated. Rehabilitation may carry with it the endeavor and commitment of equity holders and unsecured creditors, and this may be crucial in effecting the business's rescue. In assessing the likelihood of rehabilitation, therefore, the opportunity must be provided for evaluating the degree of active and beneficial support that the rehabilitation will be likely to receive from the debtor's equity holders and unsecured creditors.

4.2. Structural Features of Rehabilitation Statutes

Many of the conditions considered to be indispensable to a commercially and economically effective rehabilitation procedure raise issues of cultural and economic significance. Their consideration should begin with an overview.

4.2.1. Access

Some jurisdictions permit the debtor to take steps of its own accord leading directly to the establishment of the rehabilitation regime and the protective moratorium against the creditors' claims ("automatic access").[21] In contrast, other regimes require initiation of a process—almost always a court process—during which the court will investigate the claim that the debtor should be placed in the rehabilitation regime and decide one way or the other. The extent to which it is likely that the debtor will regain financial independence is invariably of central concern to the decision-maker in this process and it is therefore appropriate to describe such regimes as having "discretionary access."

Two variations in jurisdictions with automatic access should be observed. In the United States, the debtor can obtain automatic access to protection under Chapter 11 of the United States Bankruptcy Code 1978 by filing a notice in the Bankruptcy Court, which *ipso facto* triggers the rehabilitation regime and its protective moratorium. In Australia, on the other hand, the rehabilitation regime (called "voluntary administration")

---

[21] The United States and Australian business rescue regimes have been longstanding examples of automatic access at the instance of the debtor. Recent legislative changes have now brought automatic access to the UK, *see infra*.

is initiated by the mere resolution to this effect by the debtor's board of directors. It is put into effect by a written appointment by the debtor company of an administrator once the board has resolved that in its opinion the company is insolvent or is likely to be become insolvent and should be placed in voluntary administration.[22]

The Australian system is not restricted to this form of entry into the business rescue regime. The Administrator can also be appointed by a liquidator[23] or by a chargee,[24] although not by the court.[25] The United Kingdom, on the other hand, having begun with purely discretionary access, has recently extended its statutory business rescue provision so as to include automatic access at the instance of the debtor, although this is subject to certain conditions. This approach deserves some detailed attention.

By its Insolvency Act 1986, the United Kingdom established two regimes, the Corporate Voluntary Arrangement ("CVA") and Administration. Only the latter provided a moratorium against the claims and enforcement processes of creditors. The CVA was designed partly as a regime to facilitate the establishing of the plan to mark the final stage of a successful Administration but also as a stand-alone regime to effect a business rescue in circumstances where there was no substantial threat of a creditor taking potentially fatal enforcement proceedings against the debtor. The original Administration, unlike the CVA, called for substantial court involvement and discretion.

When first enacted in the Insolvency Act of 1986, the legislation laid down, first, that the debtor or a creditor seeking the protection of an Administration had to present a petition to the court and, second, that the protective regime would only come into existence if the court accepted that it was likely that:

a. the debtor and all or part of its business would be likely to survive; or
b. an Administration would enable a more advantageous realization of the debtor's assets than would have been possible on a winding up and made an order to that effect.

---

[22] § 436A, Australian Corporations Act 2001.
[23] *Id.* at § 436B.
[24] *Id.* at § 436C.
[25] *Id.* at § 435C (1)(a). The court may, however bring the administration to an end, *Id.* at §§ 435(3)(a), 447.

This original Administration regime has now been restricted to large corporate entities operating within sectors of the economy designed to finance large infrastructural initiatives, such as the transport and water industries, building societies, and the public/private partnership initiative.[26] The new Administration regime—which applies to all company debtors, other than those referred to in the previous sentence—was created by the Enterprise Act 2002 and came into force in September 2003.[27] It completed a package of reform of business rescue provisions in the United Kingdom that had been begun with the Insolvency Act 2000 and that created a radically revised CVA regime.

The new United Kingdom provision provides something of a third way between the automatic and discretionary entry business rescue regimes. Essentially, the new Administration and CVA regimes provide for automatic entry, which quickly activate the moratorium against creditors' claims and enforcement processes. At the same time, because access is subject to certain conditions, the legislation has preserved entry into Administration by petition to the court.

Given the now singular nature of the United Kingdom's "automatic entry subject to conditions," these "conditions" are worthy of note. In addition to the application of the condition, applied under the ancien regime, that the company debtor must be insolvent or nearly insolvent, automatic Administration is barred to a company debtor:

- if within the last 12 months, the company has been in Administration on an out of court appointment by the company or the directors or by application to the court by the company or its directors;[28]
- if within the last 12 months, a moratorium was obtained with a view to a [company] voluntary arrangement but the arrangement was not achieved;[29]
- if within the last 12 months, a moratorium was obtained with a view to a [company] voluntary arrangement and the arrangement was achieved but ended prematurely;[30]

---

[26] § 249, UK Enterprise Act 2002.
[27] It was contained in § 248 and schedule 16 of the Enterprise Act 2002, which were to be inserted as § 8 and schedule B1 of the UK Insolvency Act 1986.
[28] ¶ 23(1), Sch. B1, UK Insolvency Act 1986.
[29] Id. at ¶ 24(1).
[30] Id.

- a winding up petition or an Administration application has been presented and not yet been disposed of; or
- an administrative receiver is in office.[31]

In addition, certain companies are excluded from the new CVA on account of their involvement in major financial and international financial transactions.[32] In fact this regime is only open to any company which qualifies as being a "small company" within the meaning of the UK's Companies Act 1985,[33] and the following conditions must be satisfied:

- the company must not be subject to any of the following: Administration, winding up, administrative receivership, voluntary arrangement, or provisional liquidation;[34]
- if, during the 12-month period ending with the filing for a moratorium, there had been a moratorium in force for the company, that moratorium must have been followed by a fully completed (i.e., not prematurely ended) voluntary arrangement;[35]
- during the 12-month period ending with the filing for a moratorium, there must not have been in office an Administrator appointed to the company either by the company itself or by its directors;[36]
- there must not have occurred both (a) a voluntary arrangement on a proposal by either an Administrator or a Liquidator which was terminated prematurely and, (b) during the 12-month period ending with the filing for a moratorium, an order by the court under Section 5(3) either, (i) if the company was being wound up, staying all proceedings in the winding up of the company or, (ii) if the company was in Administration, stating that the Administration cease to have any effect.[37]

A discretionary access regime presents the problem of the interim period between initiation of the procedure and the decision by the court. This is

---

[31] ¶ 25(1), Sch. B1, UK Insolvency Act 1986.
[32] *Id.* at Para 2(2), Sch. A1.
[33] § 247(3).
[34] ¶ 4(1)(a)–(e) Sch. A1, UK Insolvency Act 1986, the retrospective effect of § 129(2), which backdates the commencement of the winding up to the date of the presentation of the winding up petition, does not apply, so a company whose winding up has commenced by the date on which the notice is filed for the moratorium solely by reason of § 129(2) is not regarded as being wound up for the purposes of Sch. 4(1)(b)—see Sch. 4(2).
[35] ¶ 4(1)(f) Sch. A1, UK Insolvency Act 1986.
[36] ¶ 4(1)(fa), Sch. A1, as amplified by ¶ 22, Sch. B1, UK Insolvency Act 1986.
[37] ¶ 4(1)(g) Sch. A1, UK Insolvency Act 1986.

likely to be the debtor's most vulnerable period, given that in almost all instances, it will be making a public statement of its insolvency and that anything between a few hours and a few weeks might elapse between the presentation of the petition and the court's decision granting the order of Administration. This problem was solved in the UK—in relation to its old-style Administration—by a provision to the effect that the initiation of the Administration proceedings itself, automatically brought into immediate effect a preliminary protective moratorium prohibiting any enforcement procedures against the debtor, except the appointment by a secured creditor of an administrative receiver under the provisions of a floating charge.[38] This preliminary moratorium remained in force at least until the court reached its decision and was continued if the court decided to grant an administration order.[39]

Without a provision automatically triggering the moratorium on presentation of the petition, a debtor might be seriously compromised in searching for the protection of the business rescue regime. The petition might be challenged on the ground that the debtor did not meet the insolvency or near insolvency standard and the delay caused by this might make the difference between the survival or death of the debtor. In these circumstances, it is imperative that procedures are available for ensuring that, if there is such a requirement, it can be established one way or the other, simply and quickly.[40]

An insolvency or near-insolvency requirement will clearly have some effect on when a debtor seeks the protection of the rescue regime. Such a requirement will prevent too early a move for such a protection. Creditors would rightly object to a moratorium at a time when the debtor was able to meet their claims. On the other hand, it is important for any effective business-rescue regime that debtors be encouraged to initiate rescue proceedings earlier rather than later. The opening of a proceeding while the debtor still has assets and operations of value, before all has been lost, is of special importance in rehabilitation. The hospital is of no use if the patient is already in a terminal condition.

The two Japanese rehabilitation procedures provide an illustration of different approaches. In a civil rehabilitation proceeding, a secured

---

[38] § 10, UK Insolvency Act 1986; *see* (c) "Sufficient Protection for all Interests", below. *Infra* 4.2.3.

[39] § 11, UK Insolvency Act 1986.

[40] *See supra* 3.4.3; *see also* UNCITRAL, Legislative Guide on Insolvency Law 45 (2005).

creditor can enforce its security interest but a debtor can apply for a temporary stay that prohibits enforcement of a security interest for a certain period. On the other hand, commencement of a corporate reorganization proceeding automatically operates as a stay on the enforcement of security interests.

Where there is an automatic moratorium, there is a risk of debtor abuse. Because most creditors operate in the dark, at least to some extent, they often have too little information to be able to accurately assess whether the debtor, who has sought the protection of the rescue provision, has truly reached a stage of financial distress so close to insolvency that the creditor will not be able to succeed in opposing the maintenance of the proceeding. Policymakers must make a difficult choice. Systems that place too heavy a burden on a debtor both as to seriousness of financial condition, and proof as to that condition, discourage filing until it is too late for effective rescues to be undertaken. On the other hand, a system that permits abuse of the moratorium will lose the confidence and support of creditors.

More often, perhaps, the risk is that debtors will fail to initiate insolvency proceedings soon enough. It is possible—indeed desirable—to tackle this issue from both creditor and debtor standpoints. As noted in the section on enforcement of security,[41] an effective system of enforcement of both unsecured and secured debts is one answer to this problem. If a debtor has not paid, but can pay, then threatening to seize its assets is likely to produce payment. On the other hand, if the debtor cannot pay, that same threat is likely to precipitate an appropriate insolvency filing by the debtor.

From the debtor's standpoint, two common approaches may encourage appropriate early initiation by debtors. The first is to provide sanctions against officers and directors who unduly delay initiation. These sanctions have been discussed above.[42] The second is to provide incentives for filing (or to curtail disincentives). The debtor-in-possession rule, which permits the company management to run its own rehabilitation effort, greatly reduces the disincentive that loss of control of the company presents to management. Management is likely to be much more willing to seek insolvency protection if it has a prospect of continuing its employment and its direction of the enterprise. This advantage, although

---

[41] *See supra* 2.2.7.
[42] *See supra* 3.3.1.2.

considerable, has to be weighed against the concerns that naturally arise from leaving possibly inefficient management in control, a problem that some systems seek to meet by entrusting the management of the debtor both to the board, and to an outside, neutrally appointed monitor.[43]

Another incentive operates at the level of the debtor's shareholders, rather than its management. If the rehabilitation regime permits equity to retain some interest in the business, subject to creditor approval, then it is much more likely that shareholders will encourage management to initiate any necessary rehabilitation proceeding. Otherwise, shareholders have little incentive but to encourage the company to continue trading and hope for the best. Experience suggests that even a small hope of equity participation in a rehabilitation plan may have an important effect in obtaining its cooperation. Note that this incentive can operate even if management is to be replaced in the proceeding by an administrator, as long as the equity holders have some possibility of a stake in the rescue. Thus there are two distinct issues that are often confused: will the owners or managers of the debtor be allowed to manage the insolvency and will the owners be permitted some hope of salvaging some value from the company?

4.2.2. Timely and Efficient Administration of the Proceedings

As noted earlier, at least three different formal approaches can be identified in answer to the question of how to administer the rehabilitation regime proceedings. Once again, the United States and the United Kingdom provide the extremes. In the United States, the debtor continues to manage the business in the rescue regime, as it had done before; whereas in the United Kingdom the management of the business passes to an "Administrator," namely a person who has the professional status of an insolvency practitioner. The third approach, which can be found, *inter alia*, in the Netherlands and France, is a combination of the previous management and a third person appointed by the court.[44] The latter (called the *administrateur judiciaire* in France, and the *bewindvoerder* in the Netherlands) has both powers and obligations in relation to the assets and the business of the debtor. In the absence of cooperation between the

---

[43] *See infra* 4.2.2, *see supra* 3.6.1.

[44] For descriptions of this management model, see Harry Rajak, EUROPEAN CORPORATE INSOLVENCY LAW (H. Rajak et al. eds., 2nd ed., 1995) (chapters on France and Holland), pp. 132–155 and 460–464, respectively.

original management of the debtor and the third person, the latter may ask the court to bring to an end the protective rehabilitation regime.

In addition to these formal approaches, it is worth noting that in practice it is not uncommon for an Administrator in the United Kingdom to seek—and often to find—cooperation with the existing management. Much will depend on the circumstances of each case, especially the reasons for the insolvency and the anticipated reliability and responsibility of the original management. In the new-style Administration regime, which retains the feature of an outside, professionally qualified insolvency practitioner being appointed to act as Administrator with all the powers of the board of directors, this appointment will now frequently be made either by the board of directors itself or by the creditor (almost invariably the debtor's bank) that holds a floating charge.[45] It seems highly likely that, at least in the cases where the appointment is made by the board, there will be an increase in fruitful cooperation between the Administrator and the board in the management of the debtor.

In enacting this new-style Administration, the United Kingdom had to deal with the problem of the competition between the debtor and its bank creditor. Until 2003, the latter was often entitled to appoint an Administrative Receiver—as opposed to an Administrator—to manage the debtor in the regime of Administrative Receivership, rather than Administration.[46] The big difference between these regimes was that the Administrative Receiver was under a primary obligation to the bank creditor, whereas the Administrator's primary responsibility is to the creditors as a whole. It was in recognition of this huge role played by the bank creditor in the management of its bankrupt debtor that the bank retained a share of the right to appoint the Administrator in the new-style Administration.

Now that both debtor and bank creditor are committed to Administration, the issue may well come down to "whose Administrator?" Under the new legislation, before a company or its directors can make an appointment out of court, they must give five business days' notice to a floating charge holder who is empowered to appoint an Administrator.[47] In giving the requisite notice, the company or its directors must reveal to the floating charge holder the identity of the proposed Administrator.

---

[45] See infra 4.3.1.

[46] The regime of Administrative Receivership and the changes effected in 2003 are described below. See infra 4.2.3.

[47] ¶ 26, Sch. B1, UK Insolvency Act 1986.

This could open up depressing possibilities as the company and the float-ing charge holder cultivate their particular pet Administrators. One may hope that the professionalism of the insolvency practitioners will elimi-nate this kind of competition. It is unrealistic to expect the same degree of cooperation between the board and the Administrator where the latter is appointed by the bank creditor, as existed when the appointment was made by the board; but it is realistic to expect the same degree of coop-eration as existed between board and Administrative Receiver under the prior regime.

In the United States, there may also be something similar by way of informal cooperation between dominant creditors and a board of direc-tors, despite the stark picture to the contrary that the concept of the debtor in possession often conjures. It is clearly sometimes the case that, prior to the debtor's filing for protection under Chapter 11, an arrange-ment will have been arrived at whereby the funding of the debtor in an insolvency proceeding will have been arranged and some members of the board of directors selected in accordance with the wishes of the dominant creditors.[48] It is also worth remembering that the U.S. Bankruptcy Code also enables the court to appoint an examiner or a trustee to assist or replace the existing management of the debtor.

It is invariably the case that whoever manages the debtor while the latter is in the rehabilitation regime is under an obligation to prepare a plan for the payment of the debts of the business and the future regulation of the debtor.

4.2.3. Protection of Secured Parties

Apart from the protection afforded by supervision of the process, almost all systems have a particular provision for each of the different interests. Thus, the Netherlands is one of those countries in which the morato-rium does not apply to secured and preferential creditors. In Australia, receivership provides special protection for a creditor whose claim is secured by a floating charge that permits the appointment of a receiver

---

[48] This statement hardly needs authority, it being implicit in much that is now written about Chapter 11; *but see e.g.* David A. Skeel, Jr., *Creditors' Ball: The "New" New Corporate Governance in Chapter 11* 152 U. PA L. R. 917 (2003); Lubben *The "New and Improved" Chapter 11* 93 KY. L. J. 839 (2004); Henry Hu & Jay Lawrence Westbrook, *Abolition of the Corporate Duty to Creditors*, 107 COLUM. L. REV. 1321 (2007). *See also, infra*, 4.5.4.

where the charge has become enforceable.[49] The Australian institution of receivership is modeled closely on the office of Administrative Receiver in the United Kingdom (formerly known as the office of Receiver and Manager). The appointment of an Administrative Receiver is a contractual right frequently conferred on the debtor's major creditor (invariably its bank lender) as part of the security known as the floating charge. Under this charge, the bank has security over all the debtor's assets and in appointing an Administrative Receiver, thereby enables the latter to exercise full control, akin to that of the board of directors over the debtor.

The business rescue systems of the United States and the United Kingdom permit the debtor or administrator to deal with assets belonging to the debtor and that constitute security for certain creditors' claims, provided those creditors are given alternative protection of a similar or improved nature. Furthermore, most systems provide for any creditor to apply to court for permission to enforce his or her claim during the moratorium. In deciding whether to accede to such an application, the court will probably adopt a balancing test, weighing the hardship to the creditor if he or she is not able to enforce the security, as against the effect on the success or failure of the rehabilitation and the commensurate benefit to the interests of all the other creditors. Although general in nature, this right of application to court to enforce a claim against the debtor is almost invariably restricted in practice to secured creditors.

Finding the correct balance between the interests of the secured creditor who often will wish to enforce his claim irrespective of the effect on the debtor and the interests of the creditors in general, who are likely to want to see the continuation of the debtor as the only realistic chance of any recovery, may be said to be at the heart of the business rescue provision. It is here that the court has to decide whether the moratorium should be maintained.

This balance has been considered with considerable sensitivity and sophistication by the English courts in a manner that is likely to be of value to all jurisdictions. It was the subject of two Court of Appeal decisions, in the first of which, *Re Paramount Airways Ltd, Bristol Airport plc v. Powdrill*,[50] the court held that the assertion of a statutory lien by the airport against the airline debtor in an attempt to enforce a claim for unpaid airport charges was prohibited by the moratorium and that the airplanes held under the lien had to be released. This was applied

[49] § 436C, Australian Corporations Act 2001.
[50] [1990] BCC 130.

in *Re Sabre International Products Ltd.*,[51] where the lien was asserted by a haulage contractor. This was forbidden by the moratorium, although, given that the creditor was being made to give up a form of security, it was incumbent on the Administrator to make reasonable alternative proposals to the creditor. This did not, however, save the creditor from having to pay the costs of the proceedings for having held on to the goods in the face of the demand by an officer of the court and thus having been in contempt of court.[52]

In the second of the court of appeal cases,[53] the court laid down the principles in accordance with which the Administrator should make his decision as to whether or not to grant leave to the creditor to begin, or continue, proceedings to enforce his claim. The court emphasized the fact that it has to conduct a balancing exercise, bearing in mind that the continuation of the Administration without granting leave to secured creditors to enforce their claims or repossess their goods would in effect be running the company at the expense of the secured creditors. On the other hand, if there was a genuine chance of a recovery and this would be impeded were the secured creditor's claim to be enforced, this was the purpose of Administration and permission should be refused.[54]

4.2.4. *Providing a Structure to Facilitate Fair Negotiation of a Plan*

Almost all systems recognize the enhanced status of secured creditors, although few follow the Dutch system under which the moratorium does not apply to secured creditors. This does not always prevent productive negotiations among all interests, especially where the debtor seeks the protection of the rehabilitation regime in good time and is able to take advantage of the moratorium to carry out effective restructuring of its assets and commercial undertakings.

---

[51] [1991] BCC 694.

[52] See also *London Flight Centre (Stansted) Ltd.* v. *Osprey Aviation Ltd.* [2002] BPIR 1115, where the creditor only acquired the lien after the commencement of the administration, made no application for leave to maintain it, and was obliged to surrender it.

[53] *Re Atlantic Computer Systems plc* [1990] BCC 859.

[54] See also *David Meek Access Ltd* [1993] BCC 175, *Polly Peck International plc (in administration) (No 4)* [1997] 2 BCLC 630, *Re Carter Commercial Developments Ltd.* [2002] BCC 803. In the United States, the value of the secured creditor's collateral must be "adequately protected." The protection is generally provided by periodic payments compensating for a decline in value, by an additional lien on unenbumered property, or by an "equity cushion," which is found to be adequate where the creditor is substantially oversecured. United States Bankruptcy Code §§ 361–362.

An ideal system—to which any actual system might be compared— might include in the period between the entry of the debtor into the business rescue regime and the approval of the plan in accordance with which the debtor will return to the (unprotected) market place, the following operations:

- investigating the causes of the debtor's failure;
- securing the debtor's assets so as to ensure that they are brought wholly under the control of the insolvency regime;
- taking whatever action is necessary to ensure that any causes of commercial failure are eliminated; and
- making a realistic assessment as to which parts of the debtor can survive unprotected in the marketplace, separating those, and then disposing of any parts that would continue to act as a drain on the resources of the debtor.

This is clearly a time when the debtor's future is best served by independent and realistic action. Needless to say, whoever is charged with executive responsibility may have to take action that will be unpopular with some people or interests associated with the debtor. This is likely to be easier where the debtor during this period is under the control of an outside, professionally qualified person. However, in systems where the debtor remains solely in charge of itself, the court can and should act to ensure that appropriate actions are taken. The question then arises: how can information be drawn to the attention of the court so as to ensure that such action is ordered? A related question arises where the process is under the control of the independent outsider: namely, how does this person acquire the necessary information so as to enable him or her to take appropriate action?

Clearly the creditors must be expected to play an important role in this process. It is common to many systems to facilitate and even require the establishment of a creditors' committee and to ensure a proper channel of communication between the creditors (through the committee if there is one) and either the person or institution in charge of the rescue process.[55]

Many systems insist on the provision of adequate information to all interests, without which there clearly cannot be fair negotiations leading

---

[55] The UNCITRAL, LEGISLATIVE GUIDE ON INSOLVENCY LAW recommends creditors' committees where a case includes a large number of creditors. *Id.* at 197–202 (¶ 99–115).

to a plan that both is realistic and takes account of as many of the interests in the debtor as possible. Other common features of structures facilitating the negotiation of a plan are meetings (where proposals by the management can be discussed) and voting procedures. Most systems require that a plan be approved by a certain percentage of the total creditor claims, an idea not without its complications when it is borne in mind that the notion of "creditors" may well need to be unpacked to take account of different interests such as secured and preferential creditors and creditors who are neither secured nor preferential. The amount of the percentage of approving creditors varies from system to system.

The goal of an acceptable plan calls for consultation, transparency, methods of securing appropriate information, and an effective system for the calling and holding of meetings, the establishment of appropriate majorities for the carrying of proposals, the qualifications for voting, and the taking and recording of votes. The issues of information gathering and voting are discussed further below.[56]

4.2.5. *Judicial or Other Supervision*

There are various levels of protection afforded by the many different regimes at various stages of the business rehabilitation process. In the United States, where the procedure is automatic and it is often the case that the original management will be in control of the debtor in an insolvency proceeding, the overall protection of other interests relies partly on the general principles of law outlawing fraudulent and reckless conduct and partly on the fact that the court plays a leading role in supervising the process. The general level of supervision in the United States may seem too minimal for many jurisdictions, although there is no empirical evidence to suggest that the process in the United States is more prone to fraudulent and reckless conduct on the part of the management than elsewhere.

Almost all, if not all, business rehabilitation systems are supervised by the court to one extent or another. It is also common for creditors or other interested parties to be allowed access to the court to seek redress in the event of any alleged unfair, prejudicial, or corrupt practice on the part of the management of the debtor, either under a specifically enacted

---

[56] See *infra* 4.4, 4.5.

statutory provision[57] or under general principles of law that grant remedies for loss caused by fraud and other unacceptable conduct.[58] The
widespread requirement for full information as to the management of
the debtor to be disseminated among all creditors[59] provides the basis on
which any malpractice may be detected and appropriate redress sought.
Some jurisdictions provide additional safeguards; for example, the United Kingdom requires that all administrators be members of the insolvency practitioners' profession, a body that maintains comprehensive
rules for disciplining members who fail to observe high standards in the
conduct of their work.[60]

4.2.6. Shareholders' Interests

The common picture is one of the primacy of creditors' interests over
equity interests. Thus, it is, in the main, the creditors who will have the
final say as to whether or not the plan for the future of the debtor is
approved. This follows naturally from the fact that in a world of limited
liability companies, insolvency is, by definition, a loss suffered by the
creditors of the business run by the bankrupt company. Of course, the
investors (or owners or shareholders—all synonyms) will lose as well, but
their plight attracts less sympathy because it was their business and they
ran it.

Thus, creditors are paid their debts before any distribution is made to
shareholders on the liquidation or partial liquidation of a solvent company. And, correspondingly, in the rehabilitation of a bankrupt company,
it is natural to ensure that creditors' interests are protected as far as possible before any thought is given to the interests of the owners of the business. This result could be seen most clearly in the United Kingdom's traditional Administrative Receivership regime, where often the outcome was
the sale of the business out of the bankrupt company with proceeds then
distributed among the creditors to the complete exclusion of the shareholders. In fact, a further hierarchy was very much in evidence there,

---

[57] *See*, for example, § 6 and ¶¶ 74–75, Sch. B1, UK Insolvency Act 1986.
[58] *See* Andrew Keay, MCPHERSON'S LAW OF COMPANY LIQUIDATION (2001) 820–830.
[59] *See, e.g.*, § 438D, Australian Corporations Act 2001, para. 57(3)(b), Sch. B1, UK
Insolvency Act 1986.
[60] Part XIII, at §§ 388–398, UK Insolvency Act 1986, and the subordinate legislation
referred to therein.

with the proceeds of the sale of the business being generally applied in discharging the claims of preferential and secured creditors, often to the virtual exclusion of the ordinary creditors.

Yet, some systems—notably Chapter 11 in the United States—permit the possibility of equity retaining some value. That approach may be of special value where a business that has fallen on hard times may depend for its recovery and survival on its owners. A famous chef, for example, may be the key to the survival of a restaurant. Rigid rules about eliminating equity may make it impossible for creditors to negotiate a satisfactory resolution with such essential equity owners, even where most creditors might wish to do so. In such circumstances, the route to a successful rescue may well be a preparedness on the part of the creditors to grant a continuing (although perhaps smaller) stake for all or some of the shareholders of the bankrupt company in the rescued company. This may be seen as little different from the necessity of granting priority to those prepared to finance the bankrupt company so as to ensure its survival over all those creditors whose debts were incurred prior to the insolvency.

4.3. Stabilizing and Sustaining Business Operations

4.3.1. Financing

Priority given to post-insolvency commencement lenders to induce the financing of a rescue process is effectively a surcharge against the entire estate and its assets. One form of priority for those advancing money or goods is an administrative priority that gives precedence in repayment over the general unsecured creditors, but not over a secured creditor, with respect to its collateral. An intermediate approach allows lenders and those advancing goods to take a security interest in the debtor's secured and unsecured assets. In some jurisdictions, a senior or priming security interest or lien can be granted in exceptional circumstances. Some countries make all options available to accommodate the unique needs and circumstances of particular cases, either by their bankruptcy code or by general principles of law, especially the law of contract.

Thus, if a court concludes that priority financing involving collateral is in the best interests of the creditors and is not prejudicial to the existing secured creditors, the court should be able to approve the financing. Such financing alternatives are likely to present a threat to unsecured creditors who may see the remaining assets of the debtor consumed by the financing party, leaving nothing for them if the rehabilitation effort fails.[61] This calls for a carefully balanced approach.

It is no exaggeration to describe the issues of post-commencement financing and priority as presenting some of the most difficult issues of the rescue process. It is undeniable that singling out a business for a rehabilitation attempt—however achieved—may deal a double blow to the existing unsecured creditors. In the first place, the latter are temporarily denied the normal commercial remedies for attempting to recover the property or money that they are owed. Second, the selected business will commonly require not only the negative help of a creditors' moratorium but also the positive assistance of a further cash injection. Without this, it is likely that most rehabilitation attempts will fail and thus bring into disrepute the rehabilitation process. And it is obvious that the further cash injection will only materialize if this new credit is prioritized sufficiently to make repayment probable. Thus, existing unsecured creditors both are denied their commercial remedies and suffer new creditors (or, at least, new credit) leapfrogging ahead of them. Added to this, they may have to stomach the grant to the erstwhile investors in the failed company a stake in the rescued company. Secured creditors, on the other hand, are generally protected against this possible watering down of their interest.

The issue of post-insolvency funding exposes not only the often opposing interests of secured and unsecured creditors[62] but also the tension between pre-existing creditors and those whose ongoing supplies are critical to the continuation of the business. The obvious necessity of giving priority to the providers of new cash or liens or to creditors who supply essential goods appears in the earliest and most restrictive of business rehabilitation regimes.[63] Yet even in the more modern systems, this priority must be carefully delineated so as to ensure the least possible interference with the claims of the pre-existing creditors. In France, for example, the law is drafted so as to ensure post-insolvency priority only where the new debts are incurred for the purpose of continuing the enterprise and only so long as the appointed administrator or the debtor have not exceeded the power conferred on them by the judgment establishing the rehabilitation regime.[64] On the other hand, these limitations must not be

---

[61] The UNCITRAL Legislative Guide recommends giving post-commencement finance providers a priority over, at least, unsecured creditors. *Id.* at 119 (¶¶ 101–102).

[62] *See supra* 2.2.

[63] *See* § 435, Companies Act 1973 (South Africa). A fine example in the modern rescue regime is § 233, UK Insolvency Act 1986.

[64] Article 40, Law of 25 January 1985.

constructed in a way that leaves those who supply essential goods to the bankrupt debtor unsure about whether they will be paid. Needless to say, the monopoly or near monopoly capacity to supply vital products for the continuation of a business provides fertile opportunities for commercial exploitation and potential havoc with traditional hierarchies in claims in insolvency.[65]

The position of secured credit is central to the question of what priority may be conferred on creditors who extend credit or deliver goods to the debtor after the onset of the insolvency. The traditional and still widely held position is to permit no interference with the control by a secured creditor over the property that constitutes the security. This substantial championing of the position of secured credit, however, must now be seen as under threat by imaginative provisions that go so far as to enable the uncoupling of the secured creditor from the debtor's assets that constitute the security (the collateral). Some jurisdictions even provide a priority for post-insolvency creditors ahead even of pre-existing secured creditors, although this must be seen as somewhat unusual.

The point is that the dynamic use of the debtor's assets, perhaps by new management, may have a marked effect in increasing the debtor's resources to the obvious benefit of all the unsecured creditors and that a secured creditor should not be permitted to hinder this. There is scope for allowing the debtor to dispose of property that constitutes security or collateral but this should not be prejudicial to the creditor with an interest in the collateral.[66]

At first blush it may seem surprising that the United Kingdom's Insolvency Act of 1986 has taken a lead in this regard. The United Kingdom, with its floating charge, has often been seen as a jurisdiction that elevates the protection of secured credit high above the claims of unsecured creditors and investors seeking a continuation of the business in the hope of its trading out of insolvency. Yet it is perhaps because of the extensive nature of the floating charge, very often drafted to ensure security for a single creditor (almost invariably the bank) over all the debtor's assets, that the legislature felt it was necessary to give other interests priority over this form of security,[67] including granting to an Administrator

---

[65] *See Leyland DAF Ltd v. Automotive Products plc* [1993] BCC 389.

[66] *See ¶¶ 70–71, Sch. B1, UK Insolvency Act 1986.

[67] See §§ 40 (2), 175 (2), UK Insolvency Act 1986, which enable preferential creditors in administrative receivership and liquidation, respectively, to look to the floating charge assets inasmuch as there are insufficient funds to meet their preferential claims. The

during a business rehabilitation attempt the right to deal with assets that constitute collateral.[68] This right extends to fixed as well as floating security, although careful safeguards for the secured creditor are built into this provision.

4.4. *Disclosure of Information*

4.4.1. *Who Gathers the Information?*

A crucial structural question is where ultimate authority lies in conducting the process of eliciting the information necessary for an informed assessment of the prospects of the debtor's business. This question is, of course, closely bound up with—and indeed, complicated by—the question as to who controls the management of the business during the protective rehabilitation regime.[69] The process of obtaining the information necessary to make an informed assessment of the prospects of the business will include examination of people who will have been members of the company management before the onset of the insolvency. If such people continue to manage the business while it is in the protective rehabilitation regime, can they be expected to disclose information that may well be painful, or even self-incriminating, to reveal?

In the United States, this problem is resolved by assigning the bankruptcy court an active supervisory role and by giving the creditors' committee a right to demand and receive a great deal of information. Thus the U.S. Bankruptcy Code authorizes a creditors' committee to "investigate the acts, conduct, assets, liabilities, and financial condition of the debtor, the operation of the debtor's business and the desirability of the continuance of such business, and any other matter relevant to the case or to the formulation of a plan."[70]

In the United States, the appointment by the court of an independent "examiner" is an alternative solution. The problem is also somewhat

---

expenses incurred by Administrators and Administrative Receivers may also be paid out of floating charge assets, see § 44 (1)(c), 99(3), Sch. B1, UK Insolvency Act 1986.

[68] *See* ¶¶ 70–71, Sch. B1, UK Insolvency Act 1986.

[69] *See supra* 3.6.

[70] United States Bankruptcy Code 1978, ¶¶ 1103(c)(2), 1106(a)(3); *see also* ¶¶ 47–48 Sch. B1, UK Insolvency Act 1986 on the power to seek information and ¶¶ 50–58 on the establishment and operation of the creditors' meeting.

mitigated by management changes. Empirical evidence suggests that it is not uncommon for the composition of the management to change when the business goes into the rehabilitation process, especially in the case of large debtors.[71] This is, however, insufficient as a general safeguard. Hence the importance of the court's active surveillance of the rehabilitation process.

In the United Kingdom, the role of the court is much less pronounced. From the beginning of the process, the court accepts a substantial dependency on the reliability and insight of the professional cast involved: lawyers (in the United Kingdom, this involves two separate lots, barristers and solicitors) and insolvency practitioners. The latter are in the main qualified accountants but now members of a separate and separately regulated profession.[72] As an example of a country that provides discretionary access to its rehabilitation regime, the judgment exercised by the court relies heavily on the report prepared by an insolvency practitioner on the likelihood of the debtor achieving the objects for which the administration order is being petitioned.[73] An insolvency practitioner is appointed as the administrator and has overall control of the rehabilitation process subject to the (much lighter) surveillance of the court.

There is much to be said for the idea that the preparation of an appropriate questionnaire, and gathering any additional information that may be forthcoming, is a vital operation that needs to be undertaken by someone who is highly skilled and close to, but independent of, the management of the debtor. A strong structure for ensuring maximum disclosure of useful and relevant information can be found in the rehabilitation processes of the United Kingdom and other countries where an independent administrator is appointed with authority over the rehabilitation process (e.g., France and the Netherlands).[74]

While the independence and professional qualification of an independent administrator who is an insolvency practitioner makes that person ideal for the process of eliciting information, it is less clear whether this person should also play a central role in managing the business. There is much to be said for managers, especially managers immersed in the

---

[71] Stuart C. Gilson & Mike Vetsuypens, *CEO Compensation in Financially Distressed Firm: An Empirical Analysis*, 48 J. Fin. 425 (1993); Lynn M. LoPucki & William C. Whitford *Corporate Governance in the Bankruptcy Reorganization of Large Publicly Held Corporations* 141 U. Pa. L. Rev. 669, 723 ff. (1993).

[72] *See supra* 3.6.

[73] *Id.*

[74] *See infra* 4.4.2.

very business of rehabilitation, taking up that role, provided there are safeguards against the obvious potential for corruption to which such a system can give rise. The United Kingdom's system permits such cooperation, while the systems in Canada and Mexico institutionalize it.

Following on the heels of eliciting information is the assessment of the prospects of the business. The stark choice here would seem to be between the adversarial process as it operates in the United States and reliance on the professional judgment of the insolvency practitioner as in the United Kingdom and elsewhere.[75] Again, a combination of a professional and the existing management may be a good compromise, remembering that professional judgment may also suffer from certain limitations, including over-cautiousness.

4.4.2. What Information and How Obtained?

Disclosure of basic data, including financial statements, operating statistics, and detailed cash flows, is a pre-requisite for sound risk assessment. Fundamental factors underpin the determination of which option—reorganization or liquidation—provides the best and quickest return for creditors. The administrator and creditors need to assess: (1) the company's immediate liquidity needs and whether new financing is prudent; (2) the company's business prospects and whether the business is viable on a long-term basis; and (3) if management is qualified to continue to lead the company. Assessment of long-term viability will often involve development of a business plan based on comparable historical data.

Time is of the essence and speed is vital in business rehabilitations, requiring fast decisions and actions before the value of the assets dissipates. Although incentives for gathering and providing information are somewhat intangible, all parties—be they lenders, potential lenders, directors, shareholders, courts, receivers, or administrators—require information that is complete, accurate and reliable, provided on a timely and frequent basis, and sufficiently comprehensible. The law generally prescribes, broadly, the substance of the information to be provided and how and when that information is to be provided, usually by officers and other relevant third parties. Safeguards may be needed to protect confi-

---

[75] The UNCITRAL Legislative Guide would impose on the debtor a duty to disclose relevant information but would ultimately charge the "insolvency representative" with gathering such information. *Id.* at 168, 179.

dential information (such as trade secrets). In addition to providing the type of information mentioned above, one or more officers of the debtor may be represented and required to attend a main (possibly initial) meeting of creditors and answer questions. In cases where information is withheld, a form of "public examination" of officers and directors or other persons may be required to compel the provision of relevant information.[76]

Some jurisdictions have developed disclosure requirements to the point of standardized information schedules that must be completed by the debtor or its management (with sanctions for false or misleading information) or by an independent person or administrator. Where the business of the debtor is to continue, important information will go beyond merely indicating possibilities to include projections of profits and losses, cash flow, marketing, industry trends, and other information relevant to the feasibility of a successful rehabilitation. Revenue and growth assumptions should be carefully scrutinized. Although it may not be considered necessary for the law to intrude and exhaustively recite such matters, it can be beneficial in countries that have little experience with formal (or informal) rehabilitation techniques to spell these out.

Other relevant information includes the causes of the debtor's financial difficulty and a review of past transactions that may be avoided under the avoidance provisions of the insolvency law.[77] The provision and analysis of information should not be left to the debtor alone but should be available to the administrator and the creditors' committee. Thus, it is important to provide for the appointment of an independent person to review or comment on the information.

There is a serious dilemma in relation to the search for information in cases where an outside independent Administrator or other officer is appointed to manage the debtor. Often this information is to be sought from people who have been responsible for the debtor's failure and who could be placed in a position in which they are asked to provide information as to their own negligent or even fraudulent conduct. The Anglo-American systems are extensive in their provision of the means for the acquisition of information in this context, and are also very insistent in wishing to protect a person questioned against self-incrimination.

In the United Kingdom this dilemma has been resolved decisively in favor of the Administrator's right to use the wide statutory powers to

---

[76] See *infra* and § 133, UK Insolvency Act 1986.
[77] See *supra* 3.10.

acquire information as to the operation of the debtor leading up to its entry into the business rescue regime. Thus, the Administrator in an Administration in the United Kingdom has power to ask the court to summon an appropriate person:

- to submit an affidavit containing an account of his dealings with the company;[78]
- to produce any books, papers, or other records in his possession or under his control that relate to the company.[79]
- to pay any amount that he owes to the company;[80] and
- to be examined on oath either orally or by interrogatories concerning the company or its promotion, formation, business, dealings, affairs, or property.[81]

This issue came before the Constitutional Court of South Africa in relation to a provision of that country's Insolvency Act[82] that purported to authorize the imprisonment of a person summoned to appear before a meeting of creditors and who refused to be sworn in by the presiding officer at the meeting, failed to produce any book or document that he was required to produce, and refused to answer a question lawfully asked.[83] The provision was challenged as unconstitutional, in particular as it allegedly infringed the right to freedom and security of the person guaranteed under the Constitution. The majority of the Constitutional Court upheld the exercise of the power conferred by the Insolvency Act, provided that the committal to prison, if required, was the act of a judicial officer.

In his judgment, Judge Ackermann, speaking for the majority, noted that in several foreign countries surveyed, government personnel other than judicial officers were not permitted to commit to prison a reluctant witness in an insolvency proceeding. He concluded that this was because non-judicial government officers lacked the independence of the judiciary. Judicial officers, on the other hand, including magistrates (in this case a magistrate had presided at the insolvency meeting in question) could commit to prison an uncooperative witness in aid of an insolvency inquiry.

---

[78] § 236(3), UK Insolvency Act 1986.
[79] *Id.*
[80] *Id.* at § 237(2).
[81] *Id.* at § 237(4).
[82] § 66(3), South African Insolvency Act 1936.
[83] *De Lange* v. *Smuts N.O. and others* 1998(3) SA (CC) 785.

An Administrator appointed under the Australian Corporations Act 2001 is under a similar obligation to "investigate the company's business, property, affairs and financial circumstances" of the debtor and is given equally wide investigatory powers to enable him to do so.[84]

4.5. *Plan: Formulation, Consideration, and Voting*

This section discusses the limitations that might be imposed on the process of formulating a plan and on the contents of a plan, the process of stakeholder consideration, and voting procedures.

4.5.1. *Formulation*

The decision of how much external public supervision should be given to possible rehabilitation plans is a delicate one that should be tailored to each jurisdiction's political, cultural, and economic circumstances. Flexibility is crucial, given the enormous variations in businesses and industries and the varying challenges faced by particular debtors. On the other hand, where expertise is limited, more structure and public supervision may ensure more realistic and sustainable plans. It is rare, now, for legislation to be over-prescriptive in this regard, given the major breakthrough achieved by the new wave of rehabilitation regimes in departing from the earlier generation's insistence on entitlement to the benefit of the regime being dependent on establishing the likelihood that the creditors would all be paid in full.[85]

Although restrictions on the plan are undesirable, a jurisdiction just beginning the development of a rehabilitation culture may wish to adopt rules that describe the key elements of a plan that must be addressed. Examples would include a clear and complete description of the rights of each creditor (or class of creditors) under the plan and default provisions that would go into effect if the debtor defaults in performing under the plan. There should also be a detailed explanation of the likely results for

---

[84] § 438B–438C, Australian Corporations Act 2001.
[85] *See supra* 4.1. Norwegian legislation lays down requirements for different majorities depending on the amount of the debt that a proposal would offer. If the proposal offers a minimum of 50 %, it requires approval by a majority of 60 % and, if less than 50 %, the required majority goes up to 75 %.

creditors if the plan is defeated and the debtor is put into liquidation. Plans or schemes in use in various countries can be consulted for the key points to be included.[86]

4.5.2. *Sponsorship and Negotiation*

Equally important is the question of who will negotiate and present a plan. As noted, the law should designate a party responsible for producing a plan within a set time. Typically, that party would be the debtor's management, the administrator, or the creditors' committee. Others should be permitted to present plans as well, but there should be a preference for the designated party to focus the negotiations in one place. In the United States, for example, the debtor's management, or an administrator if one is appointed, has the exclusive right to propose a plan for 120 days (and to confirm it within a total of 180 days) and that time can be extended by the court.[87] After that period expires, any creditor may present a plan. In the United Kingdom, the responsibility rests with the Administrator, who starts by setting out proposals for achieving the purposes of the Administration.[88] These proposals are then considered by the creditors,[89] followed by revisions, if necessary.[90] The court has a wide variety of powers if the proposals—as amended, if it is the case—are not approved.[91]

Major creditors are generally closely involved in negotiating details relevant to the treatment of their claims, as well as other significant details regarding the restructuring (e.g., asset sales, changes in management). Likewise, the creditors' committee, along with other important stakeholders, should have an important role in plan negotiations.

---

[86] *See, e.g.*, American Law Institute, International Statement of United States Bankruptcy Law at Appendix G, at 131 (sample plans in large cases in various countries). For further illustrations of typical U.S. plan provisions see any one of hundreds of reported cases, e.g. *In Re Kreider* 2006 Bankr. LEXIS 2948; 47 Bankr. Ct. Dec. 41. A Corporate Voluntary Arrangement ("CVA") often constitutes the plan that concludes a U.K. Administration, *see* Roy Goode, PRINCIPLES OF CORPORATE INSOLVENCY LAW (3rd ed., 2005) 396–405. *See also* UNCITRAL, LEGISLATIVE GUIDE ON INSOLVENCY LAW 214–215 (2005).

[87] United States Bankruptcy Code § 1121.

[88] ¶ 49, Sch. B1, UK Insolvency Act 1986.

[89] *Id.*, at ¶¶ 51–53.

[90] *Id.*, at ¶ 54.

[91] *Id.*, at ¶ 55.

4.5.3. *Voting and Classes*

In the UK, when the regime of Administration was first created in 1986, it was anticipated that a successful Administration would be concluded by a transfer of the process to either a CVA, which was also created by the Insolvency Act 1986,[92] or a Scheme of Arrangement,[93] a much older institution that had been created by and that is still set out in the Companies Act.[94] It was anticipated that the CVA would provide a simpler and quicker route for the majority of successful Administrations, and the Scheme of Arrangement—which provides for separate meetings and separate voting of each different class of creditors and each different class of shareholders—would deal with complex Administrations.

In the case of a CVA, the plan is not permitted to affect the rights of secured or preferential creditors without their consent, and such creditors do not have the right to vote on the plan. The requisite majority for the plan to be binding on all creditors is 75 percent of the value of the claims, at least half of which must be held by creditors unaffiliated to the debtor. There is also a requirement for a vote in favor of the plan by the shareholders of the debtor company, in which case the required majority is anything over half.

In the case of a Scheme of Arrangement, voting is conducted at separate meetings of each class of creditors and shareholders. For the scheme to be approved, each meeting must vote in favor by a majority of at least 75 percent in value. Unlike the position in the United States, there is no provision enabling the approval of the plan to be forced upon an unwilling class that did not support the plan by the requisite majority.

More often, however, the power to bind secured creditors and preferential creditors is critical to a feasible plan. In the jurisdictions where that power exists, those creditors are, naturally, allowed to vote, usually by classes. They must approve the plan if it is to be adopted, except as noted below.

Even more important than the question of the precise majority required is the issue of classes. Some systems lump together all unsecured creditors and demand a certain majority in that unified class. Others divide the creditors into classes according to the treatment each will

---

[92] Part 1, §§ 1–7.

[93] *See* § 8 (3)(b) & (c) (the old § 8), UK Insolvency Act 1986.

[94] The current one being that of 1985; *see* §§ 425–428 for the provisions relating to the Scheme of Arrangement.

receive, so that all the creditors in a class are given the same treatment (or the same choices). The advantage of the second system is that it permits different treatment of different creditors while avoiding potential conflicts of interest among creditors in a particular class. Different treatment of creditors with the same legal rights is often desirable. For example, banks and public bondholders may prefer very different treatment, even though both are secured or both are unsecured. More often, lenders and suppliers will have different interests even if they have the same types of claims from a legal perspective. Suppliers, for example, may more often be willing to receive less payment in exchange for quick cash, while banks would prefer a larger percentage of what they are owed, even if paid over a longer period.

This, indeed, is the French system. The creditors are divided into two separate classes, apparently not on the basis of preferential and non-preferential or secured and non-secured but on the basis of suppliers of goods and services on the one hand and credit establishments on the other. Two committees are formed and any creditor with five percent or more of the total debt of his class is entitled to be a member of the committee. The committees vote separately and the decision is taken by each committee by a majority of its members, representing at least two-thirds of the total amount of the debts owed to all the members of the committee.

In jurisdictions that support classification of claims, rules governing classification should be clearly stated and designed to avoid abuse. The primary purpose for classifying claims is to satisfy the requirement to provide fair and equal treatment of creditors, treating similarly situated claims in the same manner. Classification also makes it easier to ensure that special claims such as those of secured and preferential creditors are treated in accordance with the priority established under the law.

In some cases, classification makes it easier to treat the claims of major creditors, who may be persuaded to opt to receive a different treatment from the general class of unsecured creditors, where such treatment is necessary to render the plan feasible. In such cases, the treatment for these major creditors is generally on less favorable terms than other, similarly situated creditors. Finally, classification may be a useful means of overriding the vote of a class of creditors that votes against the plan where the class is otherwise treated in a fair and equitable manner.[95]

---

[95] This override, which has come to be known as a "cramdown" based on its effect,

Most laws require a qualified majority of creditors to vote in favor of the plan, with voting conducted en masse or by classes. In cases where classes vote separately, the requisite majority is usually required of each class. In some countries a hybrid test is used that requires class approval by a requisite majority of the total number of creditors in the class and by a qualified majority of the total debt of the class. Failure of one or other requirement would be fatal to class acceptance.

The two types of Japanese proceedings have different rules in this regard. In a civil rehabilitation proceeding, a plan is accepted if a simple majority of creditors who attend the creditor meeting and hold more than half of the total amount of unsecured claims to the debtor accept the plan. On the other hand, in a corporate reorganization proceeding, a plan is accepted by unsecured creditors if creditors holding more than half in amount accept the plan.[96]

In the new Mexican law, the voting process is more complex. First, tax and labor claims, which must be paid in full unless there is agreement to the contrary, are not included in the voting computation at all. Secured creditors are divided into those that subscribe to the plan of reorganization and those that do not. The majority required for approval of the plan is only 50 percent of the sum of "recognized" unsecured creditors plus the subscribing secured creditors, but the dissenting secured creditors must be paid at least the value of their collateral, and the dissenting unsecured creditors must receive no less than the entitlement of similar claims of creditors who do accept the plan.[97]

It would follow from this that unless secured creditors are fully protected by being able to exercise their enforcement rights at any time or by being able to veto any attempted use by the debtor of the assets that

---

allows the court to conclude that a rejecting class should be compelled to accept the plan where the class is to be paid in strict accordance with the relative priority of creditor claims and will receive under the plan a distribution in an amount equal to or greater than such creditors would receive in a liquidation proceeding. The rationale is that these creditors cannot claim "foul" if their recovery is at least as good as they would have received if they had prevailed in having the enterprise liquidated.

[96] We are indebted for these insights into Japanese business rescue provision to assistance from Professor Junichi Matsushita of Tokyo University and to the paper filed by Dr. Shinjiro Takagi at the World Bank's Global Forum on Insolvency Risk Management Standards and Strategies for the Next Decade, January 28–29, 2003, Washington D.C. Shinjiro Takagi, *Restructuring in Japan* 12 INT'L INSOLV. REV. 1 (2003).

[97] ALI Mexican Statement 2001 at 85–87.

constitute the security, they should not only be entitled to vote on any proposal but that voting on a plan should be by separate classes with a "cramdown" to prevent obstruction of a feasible plan. An insolvency system must address the electoral structure of forced acceptance of a plan. One is majority rule by a vote of creditors overall while the other is acceptance by the majority in each class. Dissenting minorities overall or by class are required to accept the results of the vote. Nearly all modern systems have this feature, which solves the "hold out" problem.[98] Fairness can be ensured, as in the United States and Mexican examples, by providing that dissenters must receive equal treatment with approvers.

As indicated above, "cramdown" usually refers to a rule that imposes a rehabilitation plan on a whole class, a majority of which has voted against the plan.[99] It constitutes an exception to the rule that a plan fails in a "by class" system unless every class accepts. The United States' system is one example with such a rule. Naturally, a cramdown rule requires strict control over the circumstances in which it can be used. In the United States, for example, cramdown against a secured creditor requires payment of the secured creditor's collateral value plus a market rate of interest (thereby giving that creditor the equivalent of the "present value" of its collateral), while cramdown against unsecured creditors requires that any junior interests, including the equity owners, receive nothing, so that the creditors effectively own the company.

Voting in separate classes also protects bona fide creditors from the oppressive behavior of certain creditors who may, for example, wish to undermine the debtor so as to further other, unrelated interests.[100] A related problem is presented by insider creditors. The concept of the "inside creditor" is well established in insolvency law. Essentially it connotes a creditor who can be expected to cast his vote as a creditor contrary to the interests of the creditors as a class, on account of wanting to favor the interest of a director or shareholder or other insider of the company. The creditor in question is likely to have a close relationship with the insider, as a spouse or other relative. The United Kingdom

---

[98] For information on "hold outs", see *supra* 4.1.1.

[99] For a discussion of the cramdown see Charles D. Booth, *The Cramdown on Secured Creditors: An Impetus Toward Settlement*, 60 Am. Bankr. L.J. 69 (1986).

[100] Consider the circumstances in the English cases (both of companies as going concerns) of *Re Holders Investment Trust Ltd.* [1971] 1 W.L.R. 583 and *Re Hellenic & General Trust Co Ltd.* [1976] 1 W.L.R. 123.

legislation describes a person in this position as being "connected with a company"[101] and disallows this creditor's vote in appropriate circumstances.[102]

Given that all creditors would be expected to cast their vote according to their own interests, it may not always be a simple matter to exclude certain votes as illegitimate, but the courts must be given the ability to exercise this power where, for example, corrupt or wholly unrealistic expectations of insiders influence the vote. It is conceivable that outside creditors, too, may have wholly unrealistic expectations, but this is unlikely to be decisive. If unsecured creditors vote to continue an evidently failing business in circumstances where this would jeopardize the interests of secured creditors, the latter would almost certainly vote decisively against continuation.

There may be a need for an independent assessment of the proposed plan, especially to assist small, unsecured creditors in deciding where their interests lie and in determining whether the plan is "feasible."[103] Sometimes, however, testimony by so-called experts engaged by opposing interests leads to an escalation of the court process with, quite possibly, a reduced chance of an independent assessment of the proposal. Some jurisdictions may consider permitting the court to engage an independent expert (e.g., an unconnected accountant or appraiser) whose report would be available to all creditors. France or the Netherlands might be said to fall into this category. Each arranges for the appointment of a neutral independent judge or other official to run (or assist in the running of) a debtor placed in the rehabilitation regime. The United Kingdom has, on the whole, a very reputable insolvency practitioner profession, but its close association with bank creditors might rule out its being able to act as independent experts.

4.5.4. Pre-packaged Plans

In recent years there has been considerable interest in what the United States calls "pre-packaged plans" or "pre-packs." The idea here is to try to combine out-of-court workouts with formal rehabilitation to get the

---

[101] See §§ 249, 251, UK Insolvency Act 1986.

[102] See e.g. art. 1.19(4)(c), UK Insolvency Rules 1985.

[103] Under the United States statute, the court must find that the plan is feasible in that its approval is "not likely to be followed by liquidation, or by the need for further financial reorganization," except as provided in the plan itself. 11 U.S.C. § 1129(a)(11). Opposing experts routinely testify on this point in the larger cases.

best features of each. Most of the restructuring of the company and the negotiation of a new capital structure is done outside of court, but then a rehabilitation plan is presented to an insolvency court for approval, often already endorsed by creditors. The main benefit of the formal proceeding is, once again, to force dissenters to acquiesce and thus resolve the hold-out problem.[104]

4.5.5. *Plan Approval*

There are some difficult questions as to the role of the court in plan approval and the answers will vary, depending on the legal culture of the jurisdiction and the level of commercial expertise expected of its judges. In all systems, the decision on whether to accept a rehabilitation plan is principally one for the creditors, although the court must be empowered to act against fraud, corruption, duress, or other malpractice in the voting process. Different interests may have very dissimilar information as to the state of the debtor and, consequently, the likelihood of effective survival. Some jurisdictions that have less of a laissez-faire tradition than, say, the United Kingdom and the United States, may wish to provide for an independent expert to assist the judge. In the Netherlands, for example, it is emphasized that even where the requisite majorities in favor of the proposal are attained, the court is not obliged to give its consent to the proposal. This is, of course, also true of the United Kingdom and the United States, but its emphasis in the Netherlands seems to suggest a more obtrusive role by the latter's courts in this process. Perhaps it would help if the independent report made available to the creditors prior to the vote is the report that is also available to the court. This might increase the reluctance of the court to interfere with the creditors' decision.

This is just one of a number of circumstances in the insolvency process where jurisdictions will differ, as much as a consequence of cultural factors as any other. Some societies are more likely to have judges (or other officials designated to decide questions such as the feasibility of a rehabilitation plan) who have a grasp of commercial practice. As a result, they are more likely to make accurate practical determinations about feasibility but are also highly unlikely to challenge the decisions of creditors in the absence of fraud, corruption, duress, or other similar vitiating factors. Where appropriate officials and judges are less likely to

---

[104] *See* Vanessa Finch, *Pre-Packaged Administrations: Bargains In The Shadow Of Insolvency or Shadowy Bargains*, 2006, J.B.L. 568–588; *see also infra* 5.5.3.

have been immersed in commercial practice, it is helpful if the court can be advised by an expert with an independent commercial judgment.

4.5.6. *Plan: Implementation and Amendment*

It is common in the rehabilitation regimes of the European Union for there to be some external monitoring of the agreed plan. Thus, in the United Kingdom, when a CVA has been reached, the insolvency practitioner—who will have performed certain functions in facilitating the CVA—becomes the supervisor of the plan. As such, he has power to seek the guidance of the court and is susceptible to complaints by creditors or anyone else dissatisfied by any act or omission on the part of the supervisor. In Denmark, the court may require the appointment of an administrator (*tilsynsførende*) to monitor the plan. The supervisor plays a similar role in the Netherlands, where he is called the *bewindvoerder*. When a plan has been agreed upon in Italy, the debtor manages the enterprise under the surveillance of a judicial commissioner. In the United States, there is no statutory provision for a plan monitor but it is increasingly common for a plan to provide for a "plan trustee" to monitor or carry out the plan's provisions.

A further variation lies in the extent of the court's involvement. This is extremely difficult to establish since, here again, the commercial culture will play a vital role. Thus, while in the United Kingdom, the court's approval is required and the court seems to play an active part, the reputation of the insolvency practitioner profession is sufficiently high to enable the court's oversight to consist, often, of a light touch. In the United States, the role of the court in the monitoring of the plan is minimal, but the court is perhaps more readily available to resolve disputes under the plan than in other jurisdictions.

Along with these law reforms, practices to deal with insolvency cases (liquidation cases and rehabilitation cases) are changing dramatically. Almost all courts in Japan are opening their gates wider to insolvency cases, and the cases are being handled more expeditiously. Before these reforms, the Japanese courts were reluctant to admit insolvent debtors to the older composition process for fear of debtors defaulting on any plan approved by the court.

Most jurisdictions require court approval to amend a plan once that plan has received court approval, inevitably introducing some formality into any subsequent alteration of the plan. In certain instances, with skillful drafting, it may be possible to create a less formal mode for altering the plan. In the main, however, this is likely to be satisfactory only where minor changes to the agreed plan are sought. Major changes will inevitably reignite the clash of various interests, which are unlikely to be resolved within the terms of a contractual provision. It would be unfortunate if the consequence of trying to make the plan self-sufficient added litigation as to the interpretation of the plan to the substantive business issues underlying the need for alteration. As elsewhere in this field, the critical consideration is reaching a balance that enables as much as possible to be accomplished informally while still retaining a seriousness that inspires confidence in those interested in a successful outcome.[105]

4.5.7. *Plan: Discharge and Binding Effects*

There are two important concepts in this area. The first is the need for commercial certainty by giving binding effect to the forgiveness, cancellation, or alteration of debts in accordance with the approved plan. This principle is particularly important for ensuring compliance with the plan provisions by the creditors who rejected the plan or who did not participate in the approval process. A plan must be seen to be final and binding or the necessary commitment from investors, lenders, employees, suppliers, and other key actors will not be forthcoming. In some countries (such as Canada), the approved plan is regarded more as a contract than as a court order, but it is better to put the past behind by replacing the old obligations in their entirety with those set forth in the plan. The requirement of notice to all creditors is emphasized in this regard[106] because the plan must bind all possible creditors to the maximum extent possible and because binding a creditor who did not have notice of the proposed plan may be a denial of natural justice (due process). Every creditor who was sent notice in a proper way and every creditor who had actual knowledge of the proceeding should be bound. Tied to notice is the extent to which systems take advantage of evolving technology to try to reach more creditors with actual notice through the use of emails, for example, rather than newspaper ads and traditional mail.

---

[105] The UNCITRAL LEGISLATIVE GUIDE recognizes the possibility of amendments to a plan but stresses the importance of notifying potentially affected creditors. UNCITRAL LEGISLATIVE GUIDE, 230–231 (¶¶ 66–68).

[106] *See infra* Chapter 6.

A successful plan will very often require the creditors to accept a reduction in their original entitlements; the quid pro quo consists of the continuation and recovery of the debtor. Loyalty shown by creditors at the recovery stage is likely to be repaid by continued business if and when the debtor regains its independence. With trust as an essential ingredient in this process, it is vital to eliminate, insofar as possible, fraud and corruption by debtors (perhaps in collusion with some creditors) that, for example, might conceal assets or otherwise misrepresent the state of the business to the mass of creditors.

On the other hand, there may be a doctrine that requires claims of fraud or concealment to be raised, if known or reasonably knowable, before the plan is approved, or else be barred. There may also be a short period given for revoking a plan for fraud so as to avoid prejudicing the expectations and reliance of innocent persons. Of course, civil and criminal penalties for persons who engaged in fraud will remain available.

There is a connection between the requirements for a final discharge and those of full disclosure to enable fully informed decisions to be made by all those interested in the rehabilitation. Some businesses will inevitably be impervious to rehabilitation, and the sooner this is established, the better for all concerned. Governments may provide appropriate incentives in the form of tax relief for bad debts and—for debtors—exemption from investigation where the debtor has acted openly and honestly. In the United Kingdom, for example, there is a regime under which those who were directors of a company that goes into insolvent liquidation may be put through the process leading to their disqualification from acting as company directors for a specified period. Where directors have assisted the rehabilitation process and acted candidly and truthfully, however, they can expect to avoid this process. In jurisdictions where a quick decision can be made in clear cases of honest and open conduct that the disqualification process will not be invoked, the potential for such sanctions will serve as a useful incentive for management to act appropriately.

4.6. *Conclusion*

One cannot overemphasize the importance of providing a system under which debtors are encouraged to seek the help of the protective rehabilitation regime early enough to ensure that the maximum benefit can be achieved, with the caveat that too great an incentive (negative or positive) to seek this help early might have the effect of pushing some debtors into rehabilitation regimes too soon, with possible adverse consequences for existing creditors.

The issue here is linked with that of ease of access. In general, the more complicated and expensive the procedure for access, the more reluctant a debtor is to seek the help of the rehabilitation regime, especially at a time when, to the debtor, recovery would seem probable. This would argue for the United States' system of automatic entry, but European countries and countries that were formerly British colonies have a long history of resistance to automatic entry to a regime that bars creditors—however temporarily—from their enforcement rights. There are, it must be recognized, certain cultural sensitivities that have to be considered. Throughout Europe, even where practice suggests that protection under a rehabilitation regime is readily granted, court involvement is still, generally, insisted upon. Only in the United Kingdom have recent proposals been made for providing automatic access into a protective rehabilitation regime without court sanction, although even there this reform has been hedged in with certain significant qualifications.[107]

The rehabilitation culture in Europe is less well-developed than it is in the United States. In general, the structure of rehabilitation regimes in Europe is comprehensive, but it would be fair to add that there is little participation by unsecured creditors and stockholders in the process. The general assumption is that such interests do not have much to gain from the rehabilitation process and that to attempt to do so is a waste of time and money.[108]

In the United Kingdom, it has been argued that the ubiquity of the floating charge and administrative receivership, with its propensity for overall control of the insolvent debtor, has been a major disincentive to the active participation of unsecured creditors and stockholders. Some contend that this is a major cause of the lack of confidence that prevails in the business rehabilitation process. They say that the receivership system negates the many enterprising features in the rehabilitation processes of the United Kingdom and other western European countries, including such features as the establishment of creditors' committees, the requirement of sharing full information as to the conduct of the rehabilitation process, and so on. The predominant legal and commercial culture is of considerable significance in the operation of the rehabilitation regime.

---

[107] *See supra* 4.2.1.
[108] *See supra* 4.2.6.

It is certainly true that the recent United Kingdom reforms introducing automatic entry to the rescue regime and drastically limiting the role of administrative receivership explicitly acknowledged the need to stimulate business rescue.

It would be no exaggeration to say that the United States' Chapter 11 regime is viewed with considerable skepticism by financing institutions in Western Europe. It is highly likely that this procedure is inadequately understood and the actual practice not appreciated. Given this widespread skepticism, coupled with the reluctance of governments to antagonize the financial sector, an effort to stimulate a rehabilitation culture in Western Europe by introducing the Chapter 11 approach is unlikely to be successful unless it is a carefully monitored and controlled form of Chapter 11. A system not unlike Chapter 11 was introduced in Germany in 1999 but there are, as yet, insufficient reports as to how it is working. Despite a number of apparent "success stories," it cannot be said with any confidence that this new rescue regime has been fully accepted by insolvency practitioners.

Key differences from Chapter 11 are that the German system, as a rule, replaces management with an Administrator from the start[109] and that it is a "unitary" system—that is to say, it could lead either to rescue or liquidation—with an observation period of up to three months. In principle, the survival of equity investors in a rescue will depend on the agreed plan, which, of course, is in the hands of the creditors.

Central to the success of assessing the prospects of the business are two issues: who will undertake the assessment and what information will be available to this body or person in the performance of this task. But arriving at legislative solutions to resolve these tensions and conflicts among creditors is just part of the process. It is not an easy task to replace in one fell swoop a liquidation regime with a well-functioning corporate rehabilitation procedure. Rehabilitation cultures do not take hold overnight. Law reformers and practitioners alike should appreciate that this is a slow process that can only take hold if other necessary institutions—cooperative creditors, qualified judges, and effective lawyers and insolvency professionals—are also in place. The recent law-reform experience in Asia in the aftermath of the 1997 financial crisis—perhaps "experiments" is the better word—demonstrates this point. Having a well-crafted corporate rehabilitation law on the statute books in

---

[109] Although it should be noted that the appointment of a rescue officer to the existing board of the firm under rescue has some precedent in Germany.

a growing number of jurisdictions in Asia has not led to a significant increase in the number of insolvency cases; and where cases have been commenced, such law has not led to a dramatic increase in successful restructurings. However, the experience in Asia demonstrates another point—which is the subject of the next chapter—that perhaps the most important piece of the process in developing an effective corporate rescue system is the establishment of an informal, out-of-court rescue procedure.

CHAPTER FIVE

INFORMAL WORKOUTS AND RESTRUCTURING[1]

5.0. *Introduction*

There seems to be a consensus in most commercial cultures that informal procedures that solve problems are preferable to litigation with its much added expense and time. By definition, such procedures are not enshrined in law, although background legal rules may shape them in important ways. Thus in this chapter we seek to provide a discussion that enables the reader to evaluate informal approaches in various legal situations and as to debtors in various circumstances.

An informally agreed solution may enhance the trust and goodwill that are often vital to the future commercial relationships among the parties. This is particularly true where the issues concern the attempt to rescue an insolvent debtor with potential for survival and where continuing support for the debtor from existing customers or clients will be an important factor in the survival. Furthermore, an informal procedure can enjoy secrecy, something that might be of special value in circumstances where adverse publicity might have a further detrimental effect on the weakening debtor.

An informal procedure would in appropriate circumstances provide something more flexible and less rigid than the process available under formal rescue regimes. Many cases of corporate financial difficulty require an earlier and more active response from key bank and financial institution creditors, which is normally not possible under formal rescue regimes. It is less confrontational and so provides a better environment for market negotiations, both between creditors and the debtor and among creditors themselves. It is perceived to carry a lesser stigma than the formal process.

---

[1] For instructive and entertaining descriptions of the workout process, see Michael Mortitz & Barrett Seaman, GOING FOR BROKE: THE CHRYSLER STORY (1981); Tom Wolfe, A MAN IN FULL, Chapter 2 (1998).

Some countervailing considerations are heard. It may be thought that informal arrangements are not sufficiently transparent and may advantage large and sophisticated creditors. They may also be employed, as they were said to be in the United States during the Great Depression, as a device by which certain groups of corporate stakeholders could "squeeze" other groups, taking more of the enterprise's value for themselves.[2] On the other hand, when informal procedures are used to affect primarily the interests of lenders and other sophisticated creditors, those concerns are largely avoided and the benefits of the informal approach are more difficult to deny.

An informal workout probably would not be attempted unless a number of well-defined conditions were present; for example, a significant amount of debt should be owned by a number of bank or financial institution creditors, the debtor should be unable to service that debt, and it should be possible to carry out all the arrangements without the need for a formal moratorium. Further, it almost goes without saying, there should be agreement to carry out such discussions not only between the debtor and the creditors but also among creditors.

INSOL International, in a document endorsed by the World Bank, the Bank of England, and the British Bankers' Association, expressed considerable support for informal workout procedures in the following terms:[3]

> During the last thirty years there has been a growing recognition amongst the world's financial institutions that, as creditors, they can achieve better returns through supporting an orderly and expeditious rescue or workout of a business in financial difficulty than by forcing it into formal insolvency. This realization has coincided with efforts by certain regulatory and official authorities to encourage financial institutions to co-operate with each other when dealing with debtors to whom they are collectively exposed, particularly in cases of large exposures.

In their document, INSOL International identified eight principles to ensure the best practice in multi-creditor workouts. In brief, these principles would require that all relevant creditors should be prepared to

---

[2] *See generally*, United States Securities And Exchange Commission, Report on the Study and Investigation of the Work, Activities, Personnel, and Functions of Protective and Reorganization Committees (1936).

[3] *See e.g.*, *Statement of Principles for a Global Approach to Multi Creditor Workouts*, INSOL International 2000 at p. 4.

cooperate in avoiding any enforcement actions against the debtor for a period (the "standstill period") during which all relevant information as to the debtor might be obtained and evaluated. The debtor would help the creditors obtain such information and would also agree to take no action that would adversely affect the return to creditors. Information so obtained would be made available to all creditors but otherwise would remain confidential. The creditors would agree to coordinate their response to the debtor through selected representatives and appointed professional advisers. The creditors would conduct themselves in accordance with existing legal principles, and, finally, any funding of the debtor during the standstill period would have priority treatment *vis-à-vis* any other claims of the creditors.

INSOL International was quite explicitly addressing the issue of large-scale business failure and clearly restricted its comment to one group of creditors, namely financial institutions. In some circumstances, Small- and Medium-Sized ("SAM") enterprises should consider them as well.

Certain legal preconditions seem important to widespread use of informal rescue agreements. In particular, these agreements are facilitated where efficient legal procedures exist for enforcement of security interests and judgments as well as effective insolvency and reorganization laws. Also important are legal mechanisms for creation and enforcement of workout agreements outside a formal legal proceeding, including necessary "bridge" or temporary financing of operations.

5.1. *What is an Informal Rescue?*

An informal rescue arises within the concept of business rescue and presupposes a debtor either in or near serious default *vis-à-vis* its creditors. It is classed as informal because it is contemplated as being outside the legal institutions of insolvency, in particular the business rescue regime (which is more than likely to have been created by statute). The rescue may well seek to alter the rights of some or all of the creditors *vis-à-vis* the debtor in order to enable the latter to continue or renew trading with either no debt or a smaller burden of debt than it had before rescue. In principle, the alteration of these rights requires the consent of each creditor and therefore presupposes unanimous agreement among all the creditors to the informal rescue. In fact, as we shall see, in the large scale rescue in which a substantial part of the claims against the debtor is carried by financial institutions, there are mechanisms that will enable agreement to be achieved and made binding on dissenting creditors.[4]

The prize of achieving agreement for a workout in such circumstances is the avoidance of waste of time and money that inevitably attends contentious court processes. On the other hand, it must be remembered that a superficial agreement that later breaks down and is followed by contentious litigation, quite possibly in the context of the debtor's further depleted estate, may be a worse outcome than if formal procedures had initially been invoked. Thus it might be said that informal workouts and restructurings must never lack seriousness of consideration by all parties as well as genuine agreement. Apart from anything else, this genuine agreement may be an important positive contribution to the dynamic rescue process. Spurious or temporizing agreement must be seen as contrary to the spirit of the exercise.

5.2. Key Elements of a Rescue

In the case of a large-scale default, there will almost certainly be a large body of creditors with claims that are likely to be quite varied. Some will have preferential claims and others will have claims that are secured against assets owned by the debtor. Some may be able to assert a setoff against money that they in turn owe to the debtor. It is, thus, highly unlikely that anything like the necessary agreement will exist among the creditors to even contemplate informal rescue proceedings. If, however, a substantial part of the claims against the debtor is held by financial institutions—quite possible where the debtor is a large corporation or group of corporations—it has been shown that there may well be sufficient homogeneity to sustain a collective view while investigations are carried out to establish whether a viable plan for the debtor's rescue can be put to all the creditors.[5]

In this chapter, we discuss various approaches that seek to provide for the workout and restructuring of the debtor where the role of the court will, at most, be limited to conferring a public blessing on the parties' agreement but where, initially, one or more of the interested parties opposes the course of workout.

---

[4] See infra 5.4.8.
[5] Id.

Large business failure is, of course, also likely to impinge on many creditors other than financial institutions. The restriction implied by INSOL, however—and quite properly, in our view—reflects the fact that only groups of financial institutions possess the homogeneity that is decisive in achieving informally an agreed approach to the insolvent debtor's future.[6] Informal approaches to business failure are also employed in relation to small- and medium-sized business failure.

It needs to be stressed that for successful informal rescues and restructurings to take place a clear and comprehensive formal legal environment must be in place. Thus, the parties should be aware that any agreement properly and voluntarily reached may be enforced by the courts of the country concerned. Furthermore, it has to be appreciated that failure in the informal negotiations might well lead to formal, court-based, or otherwise enforceable insolvency procedures. It is this potential threat by dissatisfied creditors to utilize the formal corporate rescue process that serves as an important counterweight to holdout creditors that might otherwise disrupt the out-of-court process.

Ideally, the parties will have access to clear, comprehensive, and relevant information as to the debtor's past as well as sufficient information from which careful assessments may be made as to the debtor's prospects, if rescued. Here, too, formal processes may play a part in countries that have formal procedures for the gathering of information to assist the appropriate officer in formal insolvency processes. Any failure to provide relevant information in informal procedures might be met with the threat that the formal processes may be employed.

In addition, certain positive institutions should be in place. Thus, the legal system should enable the financing of the debtor, either positively by way of loan or investment or negatively by way of the writing off of part or all of the debt. There are many imaginative instruments by which this form of financing can be achieved—a debt/equity swap is but one example—and it is of considerable assistance if the tax system will support the enterprise of serious informal rescues. The legal system should include provisions that can effectively eliminate the destructive opposition of minority interests such as majority voting provisions to overcome the unreasonable opposition of a stubborn creditor. We

---

[6] See the discussions on the London Approach and Pre-packaged Bankruptcy, *infra* 5.5.2, 5.5.4.

would also argue, certainly in the case of large-scale debtors but also more widely, in favor of as wide representation as possible of all groups that have an interest in the debtor's business.

A successful reorganization also presupposes that one or more of those who are directly interested in the debtor's business believe that some form of rescue of the debtor is both possible and desirable. It is possible, although highly unusual, that all those who are interested in the debtor's business—employees, other senior creditors, other junior creditors, management, investors, possibly one or more public interests with legally enforceable powers *vis-à-vis* the debtor such as a relevant government department, the debtor itself—are in agreement as to the way forward for the debtor. Such might be described as a successful informal workout and, to the extent agreed, restructuring of the debtor. Any court involvement would be simply to provide an official imprimatur for the parties' agreement.

A further significant feature of an informal rescue is the absence of a moratorium on all claims and enforcement processes against the debtor; hence, the need for strong initial support for the informal process. It follows that an informal process is almost invariably restricted to cases where either: (1) there is substantial agreement among all the creditors as to the way forward for the debtor; or (2) the senior creditors have the will to seek agreement for a plan for the debtor's future and they carry the weight or authority to restrain other creditors from taking steps that might lead to the liquidation of the debtor or are able to provide the financing that will permit smaller creditors to be satisfied.

5.3. *Preventive Action*

There can be little doubt that early action in the form of consultation between a debtor that is insolvent, or nearing insolvency, and major creditors substantially increases the chances of a successful informal outcome for all who have an interest in the debtor's business. A recent development in the United Kingdom has been the increasing role for insolvency practitioners in acting as monitors and advisers in the debtor's business while the latter is a going concern, as opposed to carrying out what has so often been the provision of last rites and a decent burial for a business beyond rescue for failing to seek help early enough.

The fact that this has emerged especially in the United Kingdom may be connected with two important initiatives in the radical overhaul of the United Kingdom's insolvency principles by that country's Insolvency Act of 1986. The first of these was the creation of a jurisdiction, wrongful trading, discussed earlier.[7]

The second of the two major United Kingdom reforms was the creation of the insolvency practitioner profession. There had been, for many years leading up to 1986, a growing group of specialist accountants and lawyers, and the creation of a separate profession with its own qualification regime and principles for sound ethical practice has emphasized the public role of the insolvency practitioner. This may have enabled insolvency practitioners to escape from their popular images as servants of the senior (bank) creditors and undertakers of failed businesses and to replace these with the more wholesome one of business advisers.

With a more cooperative and less confrontational relationship between management and insolvency practitioners, earlier diagnosis of impending business failure is more likely as is the finding of a less radical remedy than liquidation or contested formal rescue proceedings. This more informal attitude might also assist in enabling management to be more open about its failures at a time when repair and rehabilitation is either easier or possible. It may also assist in seeing insolvency as a natural part of the business cycle and in reducing the stigma attached to business failure.

5.4. *The Main Aspects of an Informal Workout*

It may be important to assure the proper and meaningful participation of representatives of *all* interests in the debtor's business.[8] In the case of large debtors, this may well include separate employee representation as well as representation of all other classes of creditors and of investors and management.[9] In some cases, even representatives of the consuming public and of relevant public officers may be included. Although it is often the case in insolvency that creditors and, in particular, senior

---

[7] *See supra* 3.3.1.2.2.

[8] Consider the approach of the Corporate Debt Restructuring Committee in Malaysia, briefly described by Chris Wai Kit Lee in his presentation to the Forum for Asian Insolvency Reform, 7–8 February 2001 (*Relationship Between Informal Workouts and the Courts in Malaysia*), http://www.oecd.org/dataoecd/7/52/1873920.pdf.

[9] "In any restructuring, the support of all stakeholders is essential to reach a common goal, that is, to achieve a solution that is supported by creditors, shareholders and management." (Chris Wai Kit Lee, *op. cit.* p. 3).

creditors are the most powerful interests in the debtor's business, some jurisdictions give powerful voice to the public interest[10] and others grant blocking powers to organized labor.[11] Furthermore, it is possible that senior creditors themselves may favor a rescue. In that case the agreement of, or at least some compromise with, the most junior interests, such as management and investors, may need to be sought. However weak a hand the latter might have, they are quite likely to have the potential of wrecking a rescue attempt by carrying out a threat to put the business into liquidation.

5.4.1. *Commencing the Process*

Someone must bring together the debtor and creditors (at least the main creditors). There will rarely be any law to facilitate this and the debtor may not be willing to have a dialogue with creditors. Among creditors, some will be concerned for their own position and may not want a collective process. Well-established and widely used creditor remedy and insolvency law regimes can be used to influence the commencement and progression of an informal workout. In that case, if the debtor refuses the opportunity to engage in informal discussions, it will face the prospect that individual creditor remedies or formal insolvency proceedings will be pursued. Unwilling creditors face a similar sanction.

This threat is generally sufficient to initiate some type of dialogue. In countries where creditor remedy and formal insolvency regimes are suspect, it may be desirable to provide, in some semi-official way, for a facilitator to encourage the commencement of the process. This approach has been adopted, with some success, in some Asian countries. A forum must be selected in which the debtor and relevant creditors can come together to negotiate an arrangement to deal with the debtor's financial difficulty.

---

[10] This sentiment can be seen, for example, expressed by Robert Zafft (Senior Corporate Governance Specialist, OECD) and Lampros Vassiliou, in their presentation *Policy Implications from the Second Forum on Asian Insolvency Reform*, to the Second Forum of the OECD's regional overview on the form and substance of Asian Insolvency Reform, December 2002, at 9 ("While cutting up and selling off pieces of the business might fully satisfy secured creditors' claims, it is wasteful to the economy—and unfair to unsecured creditors, shareholders and employees—to do so where the claims of creditors can be satisfied in some other manner."), available at http://www.oecd.org/dataoecd/17/54/16211282.pdf.

[11] The best example may be France, although it should be added that the blocking mechanism has been somewhat watered down in recent years.

5.4.2. *Engaging Advisers*

Few if any attempts are made at a workout in the absence of independent advisers or experts. They provide expertise and a fresh, more detached view for debtors and the reassurance of independence for creditors. They may be accountants, finance officers, lawyers, business reorganization specialists, marketing executives, and so on. It is here where potentially divisive issues such as the cost of the process and the surrender of control will need to be resolved.

5.4.3. *Coordinating the Participants*

A lead creditor should be appointed to provide leadership, coordination, management, and administration. The lead creditor typically reports to a committee that is representative of creditors (a steering committee) to help the lead creditor and to act as a sounding board for proposals for the debtor and creditors.

5.4.4. *Stabilizing the Business*

As soon as possible, to allow business operations to continue, parties will need to provide for a negotiation period. This is generally accomplished by entering into a standstill agreement (a contractual agreement to suspend adverse actions by both the debtor and the main creditors) that endures for a defined, usually short, period. This is akin to the moratorium or stay under the formal rescue process.

5.4.5. *Ensuring Adequate Cash Flow*

This requirement imposes a need for financing and therefore is often a serious problem. The law of the jurisdiction under which the informal negotiations take place might not provide for the super priority of any funding during the informal standstill. It may be possible to provide for this under contract, but equally the law of the jurisdiction might invalidate such an agreement. What often results is an "intercreditor" agreement among major creditors that emergency funding by one or more will rank for repayment in advance of their other entitlements in the event of a formal insolvency administration of the debtor. Here as elsewhere, a senior creditor may be required to make some sacrifices to save the business. In particular, it may be crucial to find cash to satisfy smaller creditors and thus keep the negotiations to a manageable number of parties.

5.4.6. *Securing Access to Complete and Accurate Information on the Business*

This is essential for reaching a consensual agreement. The creditors will seek information about the debtor's business activities, current trading position, general financial position and assets and liabilities. This is akin to the statutory requirement for similar disclosure found in most formal rescue regimes. The provision of information is a key role for independent professionals, because it makes the information provided more credible.

5.4.7. *Negotiating, Agreeing to, and Implementing the Restructuring Plan*

The creditors should establish what majorities will be required for adoption of various aspects of the plan. Thus it is common for the following majorities to prevail: 75–90 percent for restructuring, 75 percent for moratoriums, 66 percent for capital spending, credit draws and asset sales, and 100 percent for new money. Many credit agreements or intercreditor agreements in syndicated lending arrangements will already have specified the level of approval required for making decisions and these should be respected to the extent possible. In the absence of such agreement, all decisions will have to be unanimous. The plan will also need to take account of creditors with valid security rights.

5.4.8. *Dealing with Outside and Dissenting Creditors*

In most cases, the number and diversity of the claims will make it impossible to include or involve every creditor in the workout process. Some creditors will be owed small amounts and others will have little or no commercial expertise, knowledge, or will to participate in the process in a constructive manner. But such creditors may be important to the continued business operations of the debtor. Moreover, given that this is an informal process, no creditors can be compelled to accept the decision of a majority of their number.

Often in an informal workout, trade and small creditors recover payment in full that is provided by the larger financial creditors. Although this smacks of inequality, it may make commercial sense to a group of major creditors. Alternatively, complete unanimity might be sought. Thus, where the major creditors have agreed on a rescue with the debtor, the plan is circulated to all creditors and their agreement is requested. The latter are advised that such a plan would be the likely result if the affairs of the debtor were to be dealt with under the formal rescue law and that if unanimity is not obtained, the debtor will volunteer itself under that law, with the likely result that the plan will be approved thereby binding all creditors. This highlights the desirability of an adequate formal rescue law.[12]

5.4.9. *The Restructuring Agreement must be Legally Binding on all Creditors*

The final restructuring agreement is made legally binding on a dissenting minority, provided it is party to an inter-creditor agreement that binds it to the majority decision. Parties who have not bound themselves contractually would not be bound by the decision of majority creditors thus raising a risk that the restructuring could be rendered meaningless by the independent action of minority and holdout creditors. In such a situation, one would have to revert to a formal process. In formal proceedings the statute creates the mechanism for binding minority creditors.

5.5. Some Well-Known Informal
Rescue and Restructuring Procedures

5.5.1. *Receivership*[13]

Despite the growing interest in multilateral approaches, the grand old lady of private workout and restructuring is a decidedly unilateral institution, namely Receivership, discussed earlier. It was developed by the Common Law in England and Wales and exported to several countries in the period of the British Empire. Although this institution may now be—at least in the United Kingdom—in serious decline,[14] its conception and efficacy is not without interest in the present discussion.

---

[12] Consider in this context the pre-packaged bankruptcy. *See infra* 5.5.4.
[13] For a fuller discussion of the operation of receivership, see Harry Rajak, COMPANY LIQUIDATIONS (2d ed., 2006) ch. 3.
[14] *See supra* 4.1.

Under the English[15] system of Receivership, a single creditor, almost invariably the major lending bank, was[16] enabled to take complete control of the debtor's management and all its assets. This not infrequently led to an effective rescue, most often through the receiver's exercise of the power to abandon the loss-making side of the business and the sale of the remainder as a going concern. The not-infrequent inefficiencies of democracy were thus avoided and remedial action quickly undertaken. Undoubtedly, the system of Receivership saved certain businesses (especially those where immediate and urgent action was vital) that the democratic process might well have further endangered. And, most relevant to this discussion: (a) the appointment of a receiver with all these powers was effected by a simple appointment by the creditor whose contract with the debtor conferred on that creditor this power to appoint a receiver; and (b) the receiver was deemed the agent of the company, not the secured creditor, thus limiting the potential liability of the latter. A more simple and informal process could hardly be envisaged.

The problem with an autocratic institution like Receivership is, of course, that the autocrat necessarily has sufficient power to deploy the process for its own ends to the detriment of all other interests, which the creditor has a right to do under such a system.

The United Kingdom reform is not without interest. By the Enterprise Act of 2002, it simultaneously drastically reduced the efficacy of Receivership and also reformed its court-driven business rescue process—Administration. The reform was designed to simplify the process in such a way as substantially to increase the role of the insolvency practitioner and to reduce the participation of the court.[17] These reforms may have the effect of informalizing Administration and at the same time making it more responsive to interests beyond those of the senior creditor. If significant advances are made by the United Kingdom's reformed Administration procedure, it may offer valuable lessons for other systems.

---

[15] Receivership evolved out of the principles of the *English* Common Law. Scotland, for example, which has a somewhat different legal system from England and Wales, only received the institution of receivership by statute, as recently as 1972 with the passing of the Companies (Floating Charges and Receivers) (Scotland) Act.

[16] This analysis is couched in the past tense, because, apart from a few very specialised exceptions, the institution of Administrative Receivership was abolished by the Enterprise Act 2002, *see supra* 4.2.1.

[17] This is described briefly above, see *id.*

5.5.2. *The London Approach*

The London Approach was, as its name suggests, developed in London, in fact by the Bank of England, which until 1998 had a supervisory role as the United Kingdom bank regulator. The substantial increase from the 1970s in the number of banks operating in England, the growth in the syndicated bank loan market, of which corporations in London took considerable use as they expanded through acquisitions, and the recessions in the 1970s and 1980s, created a very volatile situation. Large corporations with temporary liquidity problems were potentially at the mercy of one or only a few of their lenders, despite the fact that all other lenders might have wished to keep the corporation afloat.

Some agency was necessary to coordinate the actions of all lenders of a corporation and in 1990 the Bank of England circulated a letter to banking associations with the aim of ensuring that every bank in London would follow an informal code to support corporations in difficulty. This was designed to avoid the potentially catastrophic effects of an insolvent liquidation of a large corporation at the behest of one, quite possibly small, lender despite the fact that all other lenders were prepared to support the corporation through its liquidity crisis.

The London Approach has been described as existing on four major tenets. First, lending banks will be initially supportive and not seek to exercise their rights to open an official insolvency process. Second, any decision is made on the basis of reliable information that must be shared among all the lending banks. Third, banks and, where appropriate, other creditors should work together to try to form a collective view on whether support for the debtor should continue and, if so, in what form this should be. Finally, the burden of supporting the debtor should be shared equally by all lending banks.[18]

These four tenets are closely in line with the usual stages of a workout under the London Approach—a standstill, followed by an investigation into the debtor's affairs, followed by negotiations fronted by the selected lead bank and, finally, either the abandonment of the debtor or, where the investigation has revealed circumstances ripe for rescue, a monitored plan for new financing.

The London Approach has been able to operate on the basis of unanimity, and insiders speak of a great deal of market pressure that trans-

---

[18] *See* Alice Belcher, CORPORATE RESCUE: A CONCEPTUAL APPROACH TO INSOLVENCY LAW (1997) p. 118 ff.

lates into the comment that "[a] bank which frustrates an orderly work-out for a company may find that other banks are less likely to be construc-tive next time round when their roles are reversed."[19] It is also pointed out that with a now active distressed corporate debt market, dissenting finan-cial institutions can sell their debt and not incur the opprobrium of the other banks by breaking ranks.[20]

The procedure of the London Approach is, thus, essentially the agree-ment by all banks for voluntary restraint for a period to enable the debtor to seek to work out its difficulties. This voluntary procedure owes much to the strong support (and therefore authority) of the Bank of England, which in the early years of the London Approach took an active role in some of the major workouts. It is now content to leave the workout to the lending banks concerned. It cannot be denied that the success of the London Approach owes a great deal to the weighty authority of the Bank of England although there are clearly other factors that pull banks and other financial institutions into line in support of a multi-bank workout of a large corporation.[21]

The success of the London Approach—and quite possibly of the pre-packaged insolvency approach discussed in the next section—may also in a deeper and more indirect way owe much to the approach to corpo-rate and commercial activity in the common law world, in particular the United Kingdom and North America. These approaches may be related to a growing acceptance in the common law world of an informal and dereg-ulated environment as being best for business and of the corporation as an appropriate vehicle for purely private commercial arrangements.

In civil law countries, however—and perhaps here Germany is a sound example—the corporation may be perceived to a greater extent as a pub-lic institution. This may, in turn, suggest a more formal commercial and financial environment that is perhaps less ready to embrace informality in the approach to workouts and reconstructions.

---

[19] P. Kent, *The London Approach* (1993) 33 Bank of England Quarterly Bulletin 110, 112; *see also* John Armour and Simon Deakin, *Norms in Private Insolvency Procedure: The "London Approach" to the Resolution of Financial Distress* (ESRC Centre for Busi-ness Research, Univ. of Cambridge Working Paper No 173, 2000), pp. 3–4, and at http://www.cbr.cam.ac.uk/pdf/wp173.pdf.

[20] Belcher, *Ibid.*

[21] *Armour & Deakin, op. cit.*

5.5.3. *The Post-1997 Adaptation for Asia*

A significant advantage of out-of-court rescue procedures is that they can be put into place much more quickly than their formal legislative counterparts. This is especially important for jurisdictions in the midst of financial turmoil where law reform efforts will be too slow to save companies already in distress. And this clearly was the situation in Asia in the aftermath of the 1997 Asian Financial crisis. In jurisdiction after jurisdiction, the London Approach was adapted for local use—e.g., the Bangkok Approach, Malaysia's Corporate Debt Restructuring Committee (CDRC), the Hong Kong Approach, the Jakarta Initiative, and the Workout Accord in South Korea.[22] Some of these adaptations were premised on the need for government intervention to force the parties to the negotiating table. These procedures were implemented quickly and were responsible for many of the corporate rescue successes in Asia in the aftermath of the crisis. Through the use of these procedures, financial creditors were able to rescue some companies that would have languished in court for years—and likely have been liquidated—if recourse had been made to the formal corporate insolvency laws then applicable. Formal data is hard to come by because one of the advantages of out-of-court workouts is that it is able to preserve the secrecy of the process. However, an early study by the Asian Development Bank after the onset of the crisis (through mid-1999) highlighted the greater use of out-of-court rescue procedures in most countries in comparison to their formal legislative counterparts.[23]

A further advantage of the promulgation of out-of-court workout procedures is that their use is often the first important step on the path towards developing an effective corporate rescue culture. Banks that are able to work together and structure workouts out of court are more likely to be receptive to the use of formal corporate rescue legislative codes that are enacted at a later stage. Reforms that might have initially proved controversial when such laws were first proposed—e.g., a moratorium on the enforcement activities of secured creditors—will no longer be feared as much by such creditors.

---

[22] Douglas W. Arner, Charles D. Booth, Paul Lejot & Berry F. Hsu, *Property Rights, Collateral, Creditor Rights and Insolvency in East Asia*, 42 Tex. Int'l L.J. 515, 554 (2007).

[23] See ADB Office of the General Counsel, Insolvency Law Reforms in the Asian and Pacific Region, Report of the Office of the General Counsel on TA 5795-Reg: Insolvency Law Reforms, Law and Policy Reform at the ADB 10, 70–75 (2000). South Korea was the one jurisdiction that the study noted as an exception to this observation. *Id.*

5.5.4. *The Pre-Packaged Insolvency Procedure*

Pre-packaged insolvency emerged as a form of workout and reconstruction process in the United States in the early 1990s. It combines both the informality of private negotiations and the formality of the Chapter 11 process. The importance of the background of formal insolvency procedures, against which informal workouts are conducted, has already been noted. Here the formal process takes center stage together with the informal process. The central idea is to solicit support for a plan by which the debtor may go forward *before* any formal procedure is invoked and, when this is achieved, to then open a formal Chapter 11 procedure together with the plan.

One advantage is immediately apparent. The substantial agreement to the plan will reduce substantially the time and cost that might otherwise be expended in the Chapter 11 proceeding while opposition to the plan is whittled away. Given the spiraling legal costs, most would agree that this could well constitute considerable savings. On the other hand, the use of the formal procedure permits the majority to overrule a minority that may be uninformed or seeking preferred treatment. Perhaps the principal disadvantages to the process are that it is non-transparent and that smaller creditors and equity holders may be disadvantaged.

5.6. *Conclusion*

Formal and informal workout procedures are not mutually exclusive, and in both informal procedures discussed in this chapter, the London Approach and Pre-packaged Insolvency, the informal process gains much of its authority and success from the existence of the formal procedures. Indeed, in the case of the latter approach, the formal process is actually invoked.

We have also noted some of the features that have served to make these informal workout procedures successful. The authority of the Bank of England may be one contributing factor to the success of the London Approach (and its adaptations), but the fact that an uncooperative bank may, on account of its obduracy, suffer a retaliatory lack of cooperation on a subsequent occasion may also contribute to the success of that approach. The Pre-packaged Insolvency relies on cooperation in its solicitation of support for the plan prior to any formal process. Thereafter, it relies on the threat of formal procedures that, given the substantial support for the plan, are more than likely to defeat the stubborn holdout.

The success of these procedures will rest in large part on whether their supporting backgrounds—in one case the authority of the particular agency, in the other the formal procedures—are in place. Another possibility is to hope that through the establishment of such informal processes, the opportunity would arise to strengthen the authority of the agency chosen to be responsible for the implementation of the process.

The fiscal regime may be influential in underpinning or undermining a particular process. If a jurisdiction offers fiscal advantages as an incentive to encourage the employment of particular procedures, they may have a better opportunity to succeed.

Finally, it may be of some interest to consider very briefly the matter of informal workout procedures for small- and medium-sized debtors. This has not been addressed in the body of this chapter because it would seem that the discussion in the previous chapter that is concerned with formal procedures provides a perfectly good example of what is, in effect, an informal regime for small company debtors. Recent reforms to the United Kingdom's Corporate Voluntary Arrangement[24] enable this regime to be invoked by the debtor itself with a minimum of formality thus underlining an observation made in this chapter, namely that formal and informal workout procedures are not now—if they ever were—mutually exclusive.

---

[24] *See supra* 4.2.1.

CHAPTER SIX

EMPLOYEE RIGHTS IN INSOLVENCY

6.0. *Introduction*

Of the several types of contracts that are common in the commercial environment, one is of particular relevance in this chapter—the contract between employer and employee. The reader is referred generally to the most extensive survey ever done concerning insolvency law treatment of the employer-employee relationship, a report by Professor Janis Sarra of the University of British Columbia under the auspices of the International Insolvency Institute, among others.[1]

The interdependence between employers and employees in the commercial context is obvious. Where insolvency strikes an employer, there will almost invariably be employees to whom money is owed by way of unpaid salary or other obligations arising under the employer/employee contract that have not yet been paid by the employer. At this comparatively simple level, therefore, employees are a component of the category of creditors in the debtor's insolvency proceeding.

It would, however, be misleading to restrict the role of employees to that of creditors in the insolvency proceeding. It is the case that employees are very often much more closely integrated within the debtor's business than creditors whose claims against the debtor arise by way of goods supplied but not yet paid for or by way of loans to the debtor that are still outstanding. The role of employees is thus often perceived as being *within* the business by which they are employed as opposed to the arms length perception characteristic of most of the debtor's other creditors. Employees can justifiably claim to participate in the business and are thus to be consulted on business decisions and even to exercise constraints on proposed business decisions of which they—as a group—disapprove. That they may exercise such powers in practice cannot be doubted, but it is also the case that several legal systems confer rights such as these.

---

[1] Janis Sarra, EMPLOYEE AND PENSION CLAIMS DURING COMPANY INSOLVENCY: A COMPARATIVE STUDY OF 62 JURISDICTIONS (2008).

There is a strongly held view that insolvency law should, as far as possible, seek to protect the rights and obligations that existed during the debtor's solvency. Clearly this would provide the theoretical (and quite possibly the legal) justification for the continuation of employee contractual rights as well as any rights of the employees to participation and consultation in the management and governance of their employer when the latter is solvent and into the period of the employer's insolvency proceeding.

6.1. *Special Status of Employees*

Whether for these reasons or because of the political and economic strength of employees, or the necessarily integrated nature of their role within the business by which they are employed, they have achieved significant recognition at a public or macro level which, in turn, influences their role in an insolvency proceeding of their employer, both within the category of creditor and as a separate interest group. Within the category of the bankrupt's creditors, the significance of employees is recognized by many insolvency jurisdictions by an enhanced status *vis-à-vis* other creditors. This enhanced status, known generally as that of preferential creditor, ensures that the claims of employees are often met before those of some other creditors.

Furthermore, some jurisdictions go beyond the grant of preferential creditor status for employees and make available public funds for unpaid salary and other contractual benefits to which employees are entitled but which sometimes not even preferential status can command due to the seriously depleted nature of the bankrupt estate. The justification for this additional protection for employees, as against other creditors, is easy to appreciate. When their employer goes bankrupt, employees stand to lose their employment in addition to unpaid salary for work already performed. There can be little doubt that the overall effect on employees and their families is qualitatively far worse than it is on other creditors. This point has been expressed in financial terms by the observation that employees are unlike other creditors in that their investments are severely undiversified.

To this can be added a further serious setback suffered specifically by some employees on the insolvency of their employer. It is not uncommon for large corporate employers to provide employee pension arrangements linked to the corporation's fortunes. Pension funds—which in some measure will include money contributed by the employees themselves—may be invested in the employer corporation itself or in funds under the control of trustees who, while nominally independent, may be selected by the directors of the corporation and subject to their influence. In recent years, there has been a noticeable incidence of high-profile corporate collapse that has caused substantial pension fund losses for the employees.[2] Many of these collapses have involved the failure of huge multinational corporations and this has resulted not only in widespread unemployment but also in huge pension fund losses.

We discuss in Section 6.2 the status of preferential creditor for employees and the possibility of a public fund or some other guarantee to ensure that employees recover arrears in salary and other contractual entitlements even where there are insufficient funds in the bankrupt estate. In some countries under some circumstances, there may be an additional avenue for vindicating employee contractual rights: personal liability of officers and directors for unpaid compensation or pension contributions.

There is a further important feature of the position of employees as an interest group, separate from their status as creditors. Contemporary debates as to the management and governance of large corporations include a discussion of the role of the corporation's employees in influencing its management. This is not simply an academic or theoretical discussion. There are examples in several jurisdictions[3] of the right of employees to participate in and be consulted about matters relating to the running of the business of their employer. Even without the underpinning of legislative rights in this regard, there is the simple fact of the economic power that a large group of employees might wield in the fortunes of their employer.

This power alone might be of considerable importance in the search for a rescue plan of a large bankrupt corporate debtor. In addition, some jurisdictions have established a role for employees in the legislation that provides for business rescue and have done so with the expressed aim of encouraging the rescue of the debtor rather than its liquidation.

---

[2] Perhaps the most famous have been the Maxwell Companies in the United Kingdom, cite, and Enron in the United States.

[3] The most obvious is Germany, see *infra* 6.2.

In France, saving jobs is a main purpose of an insolvency proceeding. This has attracted some very interesting and innovative legislation in certain countries but its controversial nature cannot be underestimated.

Legislation of this kind tends to reduce the traditionally very powerful position of secured credit in the hierarchy of claims against the bankrupt estate, at least by limiting the circumstances under which the secured creditor might seek to realize the secured property in execution of the underlying claim.[4] Thus, where the encouragement of a business rescue is linked to the employees' preferential creditor status, secured creditors will feel doubly victimized. In the first place, the creation of the status of preferential creditor may have enabled employees to leapfrog above secured creditors in the hierarchy of claimants against the bankrupt estate.[5] This dispensation is now well-embedded in many jurisdictions,[6] but the added feature of encouraging business rescue, which is a very recent innovation, will inhibit, to a greater or lesser extent, the secured creditor's remedy of selling the secured property and recovering the loan out of the proceeds. This adds a further twist to the competition between preferential employee and secured creditors.[7]

Collective bargaining agreements are another aspect of the employees' role in the management of the insolvency and the future of the enterprise. In most countries these agreements remain effective in an insolvency proceeding, but the extent to which they continue to protect employee rights varies considerably. In the United States, for example, the provisions of such agreements are regularly modified in major respects in a Chapter 11 proceeding, almost always to the detriment of employee entitlements and control.

Employees are greatly concerned in the insolvency of their employers —in protecting their contractual rights and pensions on the one hand and in affecting management of the bankrupt debtor on the other. We will sample typical approaches to these two types of issues in the following sections.

---

[4] This opposition or tension was one reason the Chinese Bankruptcy Law took 12 years to prepare.

[5] The UK dispensation in this regard is especially interesting, see *infra* 6.2.1.

[6] See *infra* 6.2.

[7] See *infra* 6.2.1.

6.2. *Protecting Employees as Creditors*

6.2.1. *Wages and Benefits*

The principle that employees should have a superior claim as against other creditors is widely accepted in insolvency systems throughout the world. In the words of the influential UK Report on Insolvency Law and Practice:[8]

> The preferential treatment of employees in an insolvency in respect of their claims for unpaid wages was originally a social measure. It was introduced in an effort to ease the financial hardship caused to a relatively poor and defenseless section of the community by the insolvency of their employer. In the early days of the Bankruptcy Acts there was no welfare state, and wages were low.[9]

Even the establishment of a comprehensive welfare state in the United Kingdom has not dented the case for a system that prioritizes the payment of employee claims in an insolvency proceeding. Indeed, the Cork Committee recommended the further strengthening of employee claims, which at present are treated as preferential, by arguing that such claims should be paid with public funds.[10] This would have the effect not only of removing such claims from the bankrupt estate but also of guaranteeing their satisfaction. Obviously, where the estate is very small even preferential claims may not be met in full or even at all.

The Cork Committee's purpose in making this recommendation was, it has to be said, less to benefit the employees than to benefit the other non-preferential creditors (the ordinary creditors) who often recover little if anything from the bankrupt estate.[11] This was underlined by the further recommendation that in exercising its right of subrogation, the government department responsible for the administration of the public fund out of which employee claims would be met should not enjoy any priority as against other (ordinary) creditors in an insolvency proceeding. In a number of other jurisdictions, however, such public funds do have a priority.

---

[8] The Cork Report (so named after the chair of the review committee responsible for the report, Sir Kenneth Cork), 1982 (cmnd 8558).

[9] *Id.* ¶ 1428, p. 324.

[10] *Id.* ¶¶ 1428–1433, pp. 324–325, ¶ 1450(f), p. 329.

[11] *Id.* ¶ 1430, p. 325.

It is important to generalize this discussion. In the first place, there are many countries that do not enjoy the benefit of a comprehensive welfare state and where, therefore, a strong case exists for a system under which unpaid wages, if not guaranteed, are at least prioritized. However, it is also clear from the recommendations of the Cork Report that the existence of such a system does not depend on the absence of a welfare state. The case for the continued protection of employee wage payments has recently been made directly and eloquently in the following terms:

> There can be no doubt that employees do deserve special protection. Very often their wages or salaries are their sole source of income. The loss of employment can thus have a devastating effect on them and their families, an effect exacerbated by non-payment of their entitlement by their employer. The relationship between employee and employer is a continuing relationship requiring mutual trust and confidence and it is a relationship in which the employee is very clearly the subordinate. Moreover, without the work of the employees, the employer's business would not function and creditors would not get paid.[12]

A very helpful paper[13] alludes to the competition among creditors, especially that between lenders and employees,[14] and records in its annex the order in which creditors of a bankrupt entity are paid in 36 countries. This annex is summed up in the following terms:[15]

  a. Give the employees absolute priority protection, *i.e.* employee rights come prior to secured creditors' rights. Countries with such regulations are Brazil (this section is being modified in a new law), Chile, Columbia, Indonesia (specified in the New Labour Law in 2003), and Mexico.
  b. Provide absolute priority to employee creditors with certain restrictions. For example, employee creditors meeting certain requirements have priority over secured creditors within a certain period. Countries using this approach are the Czech Republic ... Russia and Mexico.

---

[12] Roy Goode, PRINCIPLES OF CORPORATE INSOLVENCY LAW (3d ed., 2005), p. 198.

[13] Wang Huaiyu, *An International Comparison of Insolvency Laws*, (OECD Fifth Forum for Asian Insolvency Reform, (27–28 April 2006), http://www.oecd.org/dataoecd/41/41/38182541.pdf.

[14] "It is very important for enterprises to maintain their banking relationships as a source of financing. But employees are necessary to actually run an enterprise." (*Id.* p. 2).

[15] *Id.* p. 3.

c. Secured creditors come prior to employee creditors while employee creditors come prior to floating security creditors. Examples are Australia; Bermuda; England; Hong Kong; China; Israel; Romania; Scotland; Singapore; Slovakia; and Wales.

d. All secured creditors' rights are prior to employee creditors' rights while employee creditors' rights are prior to common creditors' rights. See Austria, Canada, Hungary, Japan, Malaysia, Norway, South Africa, Sweden, Switzerland, Thailand, Venezuela, Viet Nam, [and] the US ....

Among the above, generally speaking, there are certain restrictions on employee creditors' rights in items c and d, including restrictions on time and amount.

e. Employee creditors do not enjoy any priority. They are repaid together with common creditors. Estonia, Germany and other countries have such regulations.[16]

An even more comprehensive survey of 62 jurisdictions has been made by Professor Janis Sarra.[17] It summarizes its priority findings as follows:

– Absolute priority, including over secured creditors, for a capped amount; examples include Brazil, Chile, Colombia, Malaysia.
– Restricted absolute priority, secured creditors and employees paid preferentially only for a percentage of assets; for example, Czech Republic.
– Split priority, distinguishing types of employees in ranking; for example, India.
– Priority as a Cost of Insolvency, with first priority as part of costs of administration; for example, Slovenia.
– Priority after secured creditors but prior to floating security creditors, Australia, Israel, Ghana, Slovakia.
– Priority by time frame, for example, France, with different priorities for different time frames.
– Priority over unsecured creditors, for example, Austria, Hungary, Japan, Norway, Thailand, and Switzerland.

There are at least three broad observations which may be made. First, very few countries afford the employee creditors no priority. Second, the

---

[16] Such an approach usually requires a strong Social Security System. In Germany, for instance, a non-bankruptcy employers fund compensates the employees.

[17] *See* Sarra, *supra* note 1, at 18.

Sarra survey makes it apparent that a wide variation in the nature and scope of the employee priority exists from country to country. The report of the survey contains a series of charts and country summaries that set forth these variations in detail. Claims by employees may stretch from unpaid wages or salary, to damages for unfair dismissal or termination of employment without cause or requisite notice, to unclaimed benefits such as holiday pay or maternity leave. And even within each of these categories there are further variations—for example, caps as to the amount or as to the period of employment for which a priority is granted.[18] It is also the case that in some of these countries, other provisions outside the insolvency system ensure that employees recover some, or even all, of salary or wage arrears.

Third, employee preferential claims generally cede priority to the claims of secured creditors, where the security is fixed or immovable. As we have seen above, only five countries—Brazil, Chile, Columbia, Indonesia, and Malaysia—resist this dominant position absolutely, and four more—the Czech Republic, France,[19] Russia, and Mexico—do so under certain conditions. This picture does, however, change considerably where the security is not fixed or immovable but consists of the tangible and intangible assets that the debtor uses, acquires, consumes, and disposes of in the course of the operation of the business. This type of security is described in the OECD Report discussed above as a "floating security." In 10 further countries—actually eight if one treats England, Scotland, and Wales as the single country of Great Britain—employee creditors have priority over secured creditors, whose claim is protected by a floating, as opposed to a fixed, security.

International and regional organizations have given much thought to the issue of the claims by employees in the event of their employer's insolvency. The International Labour Organization adopted the Protection of Wages Convention in 1949, Article 11 of which provides that:

> In the event of the bankruptcy or judicial liquidation of an undertaking, the workers employed therein shall be treated as privileged creditors either as regards wages due to them for service rendered during such a period prior to the bankruptcy or judicial liquidation as may be prescribed by

---

[18] *Id.* at 13–15.

[19] France appears in the Annex to Wang Huaiyu, *An International Comparison of Insolvency Laws*, as conferring priority, subject to certain conditions, to employee creditors over secured creditor claims, but is not identified as such in the summary quoted above (see *supra* note 14).

national laws or regulations, or as regards wages up to a prescribed amount as may be determined by national laws or regulations.

The European Union has not addressed the issue of priority for employee claims against an insolvent employer but it has addressed the issue of an employee payment guarantee. It issued a Directive in 1980,[20] the first preamble of which provided as follows: "Whereas it is necessary to provide for the protection of employees in the event of the insolvency of their employer, in particular in order to guarantee payment of their outstanding claims, while taking account of the need for balanced economic and social development in the Community; ...." Under Article 3.1 of this Directive, member states of the European Union were required to establish a guarantee institution that would pay employees any outstanding contractual claims they have against their employer that would not be paid on account of the employer's insolvency. Provision was made for member states to limit the extent of the guarantee institution's liability. Furthermore, under this Directive, member states were required to ensure that where prior to insolvency the employer had failed in its duty to make compulsory contributions on the employees' behalf to insurance institutions under national statutory social security schemes, the employees' benefit entitlement was not to be adversely affected. The point is made in this provision of the Directive that a deduction at source of income will have been made by the employer from the employees' salary or wages to fund the employees' social security contributions.[21]

The 1980 Directive was amended in 2002[22] essentially to take account of insolvency developments within the European Union. This amending Directive makes this clear in the following preamble:

> In order to ensure legal certainty for employees in the event of insolvency of undertakings pursuing their activities in a number of Member States, and to strengthen workers' rights in line with the established case law of the Court of Justice, provisions should be introduced which expressly state which institution is responsible for meeting pay claims in these cases and establishes as the aim of cooperation between the competent administrative authorities of the Member States the early settlement of employees' outstanding claims. Furthermore it is necessary to ensure that

---

[20] Council Directive of 20 October 1980 on the approximation of the laws of the Member States relating to the protection of employees in the event of the insolvency of their employer (80/987/EEC).

[21] Article 7, Directive 80/987/EEC.

[22] Directive 2002/74/EC of the European Parliament and of the Council, 23 September 2002.

the relevant arrangements are properly implemented by making provision for collaboration between the competent administrative authorities in the Member States.

The amending Directive inserted into the original Directive a provision[23] that declares that where an employer undertaking has activities in at least two member states the guarantee institution responsible for meeting any employee claims will be that of the member state in whose territory the employees "work or habitually work." The Directive also makes clear that the obligation to protect employees from the insolvency of their employer is not restricted to cases of liquidation. In defining insolvency for the purposes of this protection, the amending Directive adopts a formulation similar to that of the European Union's regulation on insolvency proceedings, namely:

> [A]n employer shall be deemed to be in a state of insolvency where a request has been made for the opening of collective proceedings based on insolvency of the employer, as provided for under the laws, regulations and administrative provisions of a Member State, and involving the partial or total divestment of the employer's assets and the appointment of a liquidator or a person performing a similar task . . . .

By way of example, the relevant United Kingdom legislation requires the Secretary of State to meet claims by employees to whom money is owed by an insolvent employer.[24] The payment will come from what is described as the National Insurance Fund and the actual amount paid to an employee will depend on a number of factors to do with the latter's employment, such as the length and continuity of that employment. It is also provided that any rights to which the employee might be entitled in relation to the money owed shall be transferred to the Secretary of State to enable the latter to recover whatever is recoverable from the employer's bankrupt estate. Thus, the Secretary of State will, where appropriate, succeed to the employee's preferential creditor status.[25]

The value of preferential status naturally depends upon its priority *vis à vis* other preferential creditors. Many countries retain a large number of categories of preferential creditors who will compete with employees, the most common one being fiscal and related state authorities.[26] In some

---

[23] Article 8a–8d.

[24] See §§ 166–169, Employment Rights Act 1996.

[25] See § 167(3)(a), Employment Rights Act 1996.

[26] The UK removed the preferential creditor status of tax and related state claimants; see the UK Enterprise Act 2002.

jurisdictions other preferential creditors may be superior to employees; but even where they rank equally with employees, they will reduce the employees' dividend from the bankrupt estate.

The most important threat to employee recovery, however, comes in the competition between secured creditors and employees (as well as other preferential creditors), which has long been recognized as one of the major points of tension in the resolution of claims in an insolvency proceeding. This tension was recognized by the recent World Bank's Principles and Guidelines for Effective Insolvency and Creditor Rights Systems in terms that made clear how it should be resolved.

> The rights of creditors and priorities of claims established prior to insolvency proceedings under commercial or other applicable laws should be upheld in an insolvency proceeding to preserve the legitimate expectations of creditors and encourage greater predictability in commercial relationships. Deviations from this general rule should occur only where necessary to promote other compelling policies, such as the policy supporting reorganization or to maximize the insolvency estate's value. Rules of priority should enable creditors to manage credit efficiently consistent with the following additional principles:
>
> The priority of secured creditors in their collateral should be upheld and, absent the secured creditor's consent, its interest in the collateral should not be subordinated to other priorities granted in the course of the insolvency proceeding. Distributions to secured creditors should be made as promptly as possible.[27]

Nonetheless, in the United Kingdom, and other common law countries like Australia, New Zealand, Singapore, and Ireland, which treat decisions of the United Kingdom courts as persuasive authority, a creditor whose claim is secured by a floating charge is entitled to the benefit of the realization of the company's assets that are the subject of the charge only after the employees' claims (and other preferential claims) have been accounted for.

By and large, developed societies have come to accept a responsibility for alleviating the crisis where employers go into an insolvency proceeding leaving unpaid arrears in employees' salaries or wages plus other contractual benefits to which employees are entitled. Priority status for such

---

[27] Annex C, 12.1–12.2, *World Bank's Principles and Guidelines for Effective Insolvency and Creditor Rights Systems*, accessible at http://www-wds.worldbank.org/external/default/main?pagePK=64193027&piPK=64187937&theSitePK=523679&menuPK=64187510&searchMenuPK=64187283&theSitePK=523679&entityID=000012009_20050701152900&searchMenuPK=64187283&theSitePK=523679. *See also* Legislative Guide at Two V ¶ 62.

claims against the bankrupt estate is common but, given the competition for funds out of this estate and the strong claims of secured creditors, such status will rarely be the complete solution.

The result has been adoption of the two-pronged approach of preferential creditor status and a state-administered guarantee fund to cover a reasonable part of the loss suffered by employees. While the guarantee fund is not as widespread as preferential creditor status, it is a legal requirement in all member states of the European Union and is also a feature of the legal systems of Australia and Japan. The introduction of such an institution is under active consideration in both China and India.

6.2.2. Pensions

The recovery of contractual entitlement to current wages and benefits is not the only or even necessarily the major concern of employees faced with a bankrupt employer. Many loyal, longstanding employees may have a substantial proportion of their overall income—perhaps between 5 percent and 15 percent—invested in a retirement pension and in many cases this pension investment will have been with the bankrupt employer.

In many instances the decline in the employer's financial health coupled with the control that the employer is able to exercise over the management of the pension fund has led to the pension being inadequately funded. In the worst cases, the employer has used the pension fund in a desperate attempt to shore up the business. The control by the employer over the pension fund, effected by the appointment of directors of the employer corporation as trustees of the pension fund, and the failure of the latter to act as independent trustees have enabled this gross conflict of interest and duty.

A lack of funding generally creates a claim against the insolvent company but the priority given to that claim varies considerably. Professor Sarra has summarized the results of her survey in this regard:

> Numerous jurisdictions of the 62 studied treat pension related claims on the same basis as wage claims in terms of priority or preference. They have created a statutory priority for pension claims, including claims for failure to make remittances to a pension or superannuation fund and for general underfunding of the pension promise....

> In contrast, other jurisdictions treat such claims as unsecured claims, even where wage claims are given a preference. However, these jurisdictions need to be assessed on the basis of whether or not employer-sponsored

pension plans form any, or a significant, part of their pension system. Where the system is exclusively state funded or state and industry funded, the impact of any failed contributions by the debtor company at the point of insolvency may not affect the actual pension that the employee will receive. However, where the pension promise is employer-sponsored, employees may face losses from outstanding contributions to the pension plan or from a serious underfunding of the plan ....[28]

This problem has been addressed in two other ways: legislation to try to ensure independence in the administration of pension funds and investment guarantee institutions established by the state to replace lost funds. As an illustration of the first approach, the United Kingdom moved swiftly in the wake of the Maxwell scandal, establishing a committee of enquiry[29] and acting on its report. In 1995, the United Kingdom legislature enacted the Pensions Act, which has since been replaced by the Pensions Act 2004. This provides for a Pensions Regulator with wide powers to oversee the administration of pension funds, including provision for the appointment of independent trustees and for the removal or suspension trustees. Among its many far-ranging provisions, the Pensions Act 2004 has what was described in its predecessor Act as a whistleblowing section:[30]

Duty to report breaches of the law

1. Subsection (2) imposes a reporting requirement on the following persons—
   a. a trustee or manager of an occupational or personal pension scheme;
   b. a person who is otherwise involved in the administration of such a scheme;
   c. the employer in relation to an occupational pension scheme;
   d. a professional adviser in relation to such a scheme;
   e. a person who is otherwise involved in advising the trustees or managers of an occupational or personal pension scheme in relation to the scheme.
2. Where the person has reasonable cause to believe that—
   a. a duty which is relevant to the administration of the scheme in question, and is imposed by or by virtue of an enactment or rule of law, has not been or is not being complied with, and

---

[28] *See* Sarra, *supra* note 18. Professor Sarra points out that general social insurance, as in China, may serve some of the same purposes as a guarantee fund.

[29] Pension Law Reform—The Report of the Pension Law Review Committee. The Committee was chaired by Professor Sir Roy Goode and the report was published in September 1993.

[30] Section 48 of the UK Pensions Act 1995.

b. the failure to comply is likely to be of material significance to the Regulator in the exercise of any of its functions, he must give a written report of the matter to the Regulator as soon as reasonably practicable.

Professor Sarra describes such institutions established in a number of other countries, including Sweden, Germany, Ontario (Canada), Japan, the United Kingdom, and the United States. There are, unsurprisingly, many variations, on such matters as eligibility, the capping of benefits, and whether the benefits are index-linked. In an ideal world, pensions will be doubly protected by both a vigilant authority and a state-backed guarantee.

6.3. *Personal Liability of Officers and Directors*

Professor Sarra reports that only a minority of jurisdictions establish direct liability against officers and directors for unpaid employee compensation, but a majority of the jurisdictions surveyed make them personally liable for violation of non-insolvency statutes relating to employee compensation.[31] For example, in many instances in Canada officers and directors may be personally liable for six months of unpaid wages under corporate law or employment standards legislation.

6.4. *Employees, Consultation, Participation, and Business Rescue*

In the previous section we discussed the employees as a sub-group within the group of creditors of the insolvent debtor. In this section, we consider the role of the employees in the management and governance of the employer. We will begin by reviewing briefly the current trends in employee participation in the governance of large corporations and we will consider the provision for the consultation of employees in cases where the corporate employer wishes to dismiss large sections of the workforce on the grounds of redundancy. Thereafter we will consider the role of the employees in the management of the insolvency proceeding.

---

[31] *See* Sarra, *supra* note 1, at 98–99, graph 9.

6.4.1. *Employee Participation in Large Corporations*

The role of employees in the governance and management of large corporations was often dominated by the capital versus labor divide. Common assumptions included, first, that employees were essentially outside the corporation engaged in collective bargaining negotiations with the corporation over traditional matters such as wages, hours of work, and so on. Second, it was assumed that the corporation was governed in the interests of the stockholders by a board of directors elected from among the stockholders. A serious and sustained challenge was mounted in the early 1930s by Berle and Means. They argued that the directors exercised power without property and that they governed the corporation in their own, rather than in the stockholders', interests.

There has been much debate around this thesis, but one tenet has emerged and been accepted in many countries: namely, that the board of directors is more than simply the agent of the stockholders.[32] This coincided with the acceptance by influential courts of the proposition that directors, having been elected, should be left to manage the corporation and should not be dictated to by the stockholders. If dissatisfied, the latter's remedy lay in voting out the board or some of its members and electing others. Another more or less coinciding development was the adoption by Germany of the principle of *Mitbestimmung* (co-determination)—the governance of large corporations by representatives of the investors and the employees.[33] Although this idea spread to a few neighboring European countries, as a formal principle of corporate governance, it remains a minority position. The attempt by the European community to have co-determination adopted as a formal principle for all corporations throughout the European community has failed. Nevertheless, consultations between employers and employees in large corporations on a wide variety of issues have become commonplace, and of particular relevance here is the formalization of such consultations on corporate proposals for the dismissal of employees on the grounds of redundancy.

It should be noted that even in countries without co-determination or other employee rights of governance or consultation, collective

---

[32] *But see* Henry Hu and Jay Lawrence Westbrook, *Abolition of the Corporate Duty to Creditors*, 107 COLUM. L. REV. 1321 (2007).

[33] This principle is addressed also in the EU Directive on Co-determination within a SE (= Societas Europea = European corporation) as one of the prerequisites for a SE.

bargaining agreements often give employee organizations some rights with respect to the operation of the business. In some countries, notably the United States, reorganization provisions include the opportunity for the debtor to weaken or eliminate those employee rights through modification of its collective bargaining agreements.[34] On the other hand, Professor Sarra has found that most countries have successor employer provisions that impose upon purchasers of an enterprise the obligation to continue to recognize existing employee contracts.

Dismissal on grounds of redundancy are likely to be closely associated with a downturn in the corporation's fortunes and might be part of a package to stave off insolvency. The principle, even the obligation, to consult on such proposals could be said to have been formalized at least by 1963 when international standards were agreed under the auspices of the International Labour Organization in the Termination of Employment Recommendation. This recommendation was further formalized by the ILO's Termination of Employment Convention, 1982.[35] This Convention has been ratified by 34 countries. In addition, the United Kingdom and the other European Union countries have enacted legislation implementing the European Union Directive on the approximation of the laws of the member states relating to collective redundancies, which also imposes an obligation on employers to consult with the workforce when contemplating mass dismissals on grounds of redundancy.[36]

The ILO's Termination of Employment Convention, 1982, provides:[37]

1. When the employer contemplates terminations for reasons of an economic, technological, structural or similar nature, the employer shall:
   a. provide the workers' representatives concerned in good time with relevant information including the reasons for the terminations contemplated, the number and categories of workers likely to be affected and the period over which the terminations are intended to be carried out;

---

[34] 11 U.S.C. § 1113–1114.

[35] C158 Termination of Employment Convention, 1982; for the text, see http://www.ilo.org/ilolex/english/convdisp1.htm.

[36] Council Directive 98/59/EC of 20 July 1998; for the text, see http://eur-lex.europa.eu / smartapi / cgi / sga-doc?smartapi!celexapi!prod!CELEXnumdoc&lg=EN&numdoc=31998L005a&model=guichett.

[37] Article 13.

b. give, in accordance with national law and practice, the workers' representatives concerned, as early as possible, an opportunity for consultation on measures to be taken to avert or
to minimize the terminations and measures to mitigate the
adverse effects of any terminations on the workers concerned
such as finding alternative employment.

The provisions of the European Union Directive have a like effect, as does
the implementing legislation in the member countries.[38]

6.4.2. *Employees in the Management of the Insolvency Proceeding*

There is a complex interrelationship between the protection of employee
interests and the encouragement of business rescue, as opposed to the
piecemeal liquidation of the debtor's property. Given that a business
rescue generally carries with it an automatic stay that has the effect of
temporarily neutralizing the secured creditors' power to sell the property
that comprises the security, the position of the employees who wish to
carry on the business is strengthened. There may be something of a
connection between countries that encourage business rescue and the
existence of pro-employee provisions in their insolvency laws.

Thus, in France, where there is a single gateway into formal insolvency,
under the previous law it was necessary after opening insolvency proceedings to begin an observation period with a view to a rescue before
thought could be given to the ordering of liquidation. However, in cases
of clear and outright failure, the courts developed the practice of ordering judicial administration (*redressement judiciaire*, the business rescue
regime) and then pronouncing the liquidation on the same day. This was
unnecessarily cumbersome. The Reform Law of 1994 simplified the procedure so that liquidation was the only viable option for an insolvent
company. Now, a court may order the liquidation of a company directly
without placing it under judicial administration.

A number of countries have undergone recent legislative changes that
have encouraged business rescue instead of liquidation. For example,
in Brazil, this seems to have been specifically linked to a strong pro-
employee provision.[39] In Sweden, the encouragement of business rescue
seems to have involved extending the employees' wage guarantee to the

---

[38] *See* s. 188, UK Trade Union and Labour Relations (Consolidation) Act 1992.
[39] *See* Sarra, op. cit. p. 305.

restructuring regime under which rescues are attempted. Previously the guarantee had existed only in the insolvency regime under which the business was liquidated.[40]

On the other hand, the reduction of employee rights is often seen as necessary to achieve reorganization. Perhaps the most aggressive reorganization regime in the world is found in the United States under Chapter 11, which has routinely been used to undo collective bargaining agreements on the argument that the enterprise can no longer support the wages and benefits that had been promised to the employees. Conversely, a standard criticism of the Mexican composition system prior to the adoption of its new insolvency law was that its generous treatment of workers made reorganization impossible.[41]

The tension between reorganization and employee rights is revealed by the history of the European Union Acquired Rights Directive originally enacted in 1977[42] and recently replaced by an updated Directive.[43] The purpose of this Directive is to protect employees in the circumstances where a business is sold and the sale is the cause of the dismissal of some or all of the employees. The original Directive provided that in such a case—unless the dismissal of the employees was for an economic, technical, or organizational reason—the claims that the dismissed employees might have against the seller of the business would be transferred to the purchaser of the business. This Directive applied irrespective of whether the sale of the business was by a bankrupt seller.

This Directive attracted much criticism from insolvency practitioners and others engaged in the attempted rescue of bankrupt businesses on the grounds that the transfer of employee liabilities to the purchaser made it difficult to sell such businesses and thus inhibited rescues to the detriment, among others, of the employees themselves. This criticism has been addressed in the new Directive, which, while reenacting the transfer of rights,[44] gives to member states the option of not applying this provision:

---

[40] *See* Nina Baecklund & Mathias Winge, *Wage Guarantee in Reconstructuring [sic] Proceedings in Sweden*, 2006 GLOBAL INSOLVENCY & RESTRUCTURING YEARBOOK 552, pp. 55–57.

[41] ALI Mexican Statement 51–52.

[42] Council Directive 77/187/EEC.

[43] Council Directive 2001/23/EC of 12 March 2001.

[44] Article 3.1 "The transferor's rights and obligations arising from a contract of employment or from an employment relationship existing on the date of a transfer shall, by reason of such transfer, be transferred to the transferee."

... to any transfer of an undertaking, business or part of an undertaking
or business where the transferor is the subject of bankruptcy proceedings
or any analogous insolvency proceedings which have been instituted with
a view to the liquidation of the assets of the transferor and are under the
supervision of a competent public authority (which may be an insolvency
practitioner authorized by a competent public authority).[45]

Thus the interests of employees are argued both to be served by reorganization and to make reorganization difficult or impossible.

---

[45] Article 5.1.

CHAPTER SEVEN

JUDICIAL AND ADMINISTRATIVE INSTITUTIONS

7.0. *Overview*

Any law—be it the best one—is of little use unless there are personnel who are willing and capable to transform the written rules into reality and daily practice.[1] If the current authors were forced to choose, we would opt for bad law and good personnel over good law and bad personnel. Any discrepancy between the law on the books and the law in action leads inevitably to some kind of implementation gap[2] that need not necessarily cause inefficiency but that in any case distorts to a higher or lesser degree the original intentions of the law. In the field of insolvency there are two actors whose integrity and expertise are central to the functioning of the insolvency system: judges and administrators. While lawyers, accountants, and other professionals are also important, these two actors perform the core tasks. Thus learning about the qualities of these actors is almost always more important to an understanding of an insolvency system than knowledge of its legal rules and procedures.[3] The key elements are their backgrounds—educational and practical—their expertise, and their roles in the system. Closely related is knowledge of the procedural systems in a given jurisdiction, systems that likely operate in insolvency among many other aspects of that country's legal institutions. We do not attempt a discussion of procedures in that broader sense.

---

[1] *See* Christoph Paulus, *Germany: Lessons to Learn from the Implementation of a New Insolvency Code*, 17 CONN. J. INT'L. L., p. 89 ff. (2001).

[2] Important observations about the problems leading to and resulting from such implementation gap are presented by Terence Halliday, *Closing the Implementation Gap: Why Good Laws Fail and We Can Help Them Succeed*, available at: http://www.worldbank .org/WBSITE/EXTERNAL/TOPICS/LAWANDJUSTICE/GILD/0,contentMDK: 21031904~ pagePK:64065425~piPK:455253~theSitePK:215006,00.html.

[3] Especially in this area it is important to view debt collection and enforcement of security outside of insolvency as part of the overall "insolvency" system. *See supra* 2.2.

A country's insolvency system is defined in large part by its allocation of functions between judges and administrators and by the legal and
organizational relationships between them. Some systems give administrators broad powers, subject to limited judicial oversight. In those systems, the courts serve almost entirely to adjudicate legal disputes that
arise in the course of the proceeding. In other systems, the courts are
closely involved in the proceeding and administrators are required much
more often to get judicial approval for their decisions.

Beyond these specifics, the student of insolvency systems will look for
three main characteristics in these institutions: efficiency, transparency,
and accountability. *Efficiency* encompasses a proceeding without undue
delays and an enforcement mechanism for decisions rendered by the
court that permits a swift handling of cases. Systems will strike different balances between the obvious importance of assuring that the parties
involved have an opportunity to be heard to the extent possible and the
need to avoid giving stakeholders the chance to abuse judicial remedies
to delay and distort the proceeding. The Mexican experience is an important example. Prior to the recent reforms, cases would be delayed for years
by an elaborate and formal process of reviewing claims. Creditors had little or no protection as long as the debtor could delay the completion of
that process. The new law in Mexico has a reasonable claims procedure
that avoids those delays.[4]

Transparency, in the present context, means in particular that procedural stages are foreseeable, that the court and administrator's staffs fulfill
their tasks in strict compliance with the legal prescripts, and that there are
safeguards against corruption. Related to transparency is *accountability*,
a tool for monitoring both the court and the legality of the procedure. The
files relevant for the proceeding should be accessible for the public. This
does not necessarily mean the public in general; in many legal systems
access will be restricted to those persons who can demonstrate a justified
interest in seeing the files—such as creditors, potential contracting parties, and others. Adequate notice to stakeholders and the availability of
regular reports of officials are important as well. The accountability factor
also embraces a meaningful right to appeal.

---

[4] *See* ALI Mexican Statement at 69.

7.1. *Judiciary*

Because the great majority of countries use their courts to supervise insolvency proceedings, we focus on courts and judges first of all, along with two broad structural points. We start with a general point often undiscussed. In many countries, particularly in developing or transition economies, much remains to be done to improve the social standing of the judges. Low income, bad reputations, and the general public's prejudices about their corruptness might well force them into exactly this sort of behavior and thus work as a kind of self-fulfilling prophecy. The details of a country's laws may be of limited relevance where these conditions exist.

Jurisdictions can be distinguished by three key variations: civil law or common law; full career judges or late career judges; and specialized or general courts supervising insolvency cases. This book is not the place to undertake a full discussion of the distinctions between the two great legal systems of the world, but it is worth noting that observers all too often err in both directions in considering the effects of the distinction between the civil law and the common law: they fail to recognize important intellectual and practical differences or they exaggerate those differences. The first mistake is illustrated by the person who expects a civil law judge to exercise the kind of wide-ranging discretion often given to common law judges. The second is illustrated by the person who imagines that common law judges do as they please and will not feel bound by the wording of a governing statute.

The second variation—the career paths of judges—is often ignored but is of crucial importance. In many countries, especially civil law jurisdictions, judges spend most if not all of their careers as government officials. Often they are trained as judges, not as advocates per se, and serve in judicial capacities throughout their professional lives. The result is often a high level of legal expertise but little commercial experience. In many other countries, especially common law jurisdictions, judges are typically appointed as judges after successful careers as lawyers. Many of them may have less judicial expertise but more commercial experience.

Relatively few countries have specialized insolvency courts (the United States is the leading example) but a number have commercial courts that deal with business disputes generally, including insolvency. The Commonwealth in general and the commercial division of the Ontario court in Toronto specifically are good examples of the latter approach.

Many other countries leave insolvency matters to be handled by the courts that exercise general civil jurisdiction. France, the Czech Republic, and Estonia exemplify this approach.

A related point is whether a particular system "attracts" all disputes concerning a debtor to the insolvency court or leaves many of them to be resolved in other courts despite the initiation of the insolvency proceeding. Some jurisdictions adopt a middle course, where some disputes go to the insolvency court and others do not. The system adopted can make an important difference in the evolution of commercial law. If there is a *vis attractiva concursus*, insolvency law may be a legal area of its own and definitely distinct from other areas. All disputes emerging in this context are seen and treated as specific insolvency matters irrespective of what they would be—e.g., commercial, tax, or administrative matters—outside the proceeding. Thus, there is the potential for developing a coherent body of insolvency law. This can be seen both as an advantage and as a disadvantage. It is an advantage since any coherence is to be welcomed as it aids the understanding of this body of law, yet at the same time it may isolate insolvency law from other areas of law in that it develops its own rules. There has long been a passionate debate in the United States as to the role of insolvency law as mere procedure or as a body of law that may alter the ordinary legal rules after a general default.[5]

To be sure, those jurisdictions that do not follow the concept of *vis attractiva concursus* create also their own body of insolvency law. However, they avoid the danger of a somewhat isolated development by seeing insolvency law as something like a template that is laid over the rest of the law; for them, insolvency law modifies other law but does not replace it. Again, there are pros and cons. On the positive side, since under this concept insolvency law tends to be adjusted to the rest of law in a more coherent way, there are no sharp changes in rights following default. On the other hand, different court competences might result in incompatible decisions and create tensions within this body of law. In addition, it is plausible to argue that a general default changes the social and economic context of a commercial law rule and may require a different result to achieve the desired goals.

---

[5] *See, e.g.,* Elizabeth Warren, *Bankruptcy Policy,* 54 U. Chi. L. Rev. 777 (1987); Douglas G. Baird, *Loss Distribution, Forum Shopping, and Bankruptcy: A Reply to Warren,* 54 U. Chi. L. Rev. 815 (1987).

7.2. *Administrators*

It is the prevalent pattern in most of the existing insolvency laws that administrators are entrusted with the central tasks of managing and handling insolvency proceedings; the success, speed, and efficiency of such proceedings depend primarily on the administrators' skills, knowledge, and experience. Therefore, an understanding of an insolvency regime depends upon knowing the rules of the process of selecting administrators and of the safeguards for the administrators' trustworthiness, ongoing qualification, and integrity.[6] After all, it is this person who deals with the debtor's assets in a way that promises the creditors the greatest return or serves other purposes inherent in the particular insolvency law. In fulfilling this task the administrator, depending on the particular circumstances, has to manage the continuation of the debtor's business or to sell it (as a whole or piecemeal)—thereby staying in contact with the debtor's employees and its creditors (each of whom might have different interests in this particular case) and fulfilling all kind of legal and contractual obligations—and has to be throughout as quick and efficient as possible. The risk of an "implementation gap" between the statute and the reality of practice is greatest here.

To be sure, the said distortion of the law in action as compared to the law on the books is less dangerously imminent in jurisdictions that place the main responsibility for the effectiveness of insolvency cases on the courts and have the administrators exercise more or less a mere executive role; this pattern is quite often found in transition countries that, for obvious historical reasons, tend to place their trust more in the courts than in independent professionals. However, even then it is to be considered that it is the administrator who is doing the "field work," who—unlike the court or the individual judges—is in direct contact with the debtor and its assets and maybe also the creditors. Because of that, at least the integrity requirement (as described below) is highly relevant for this type of administrator as well.

Being aware of the danger or problems resulting from such an implementation gap, an observer can look for some legislative devices that may serve to a certain degree as a bridge over this omnipresent separation between written rules and their practical application. These devices are

---

[6] See also Legislative Guide at 115–125.

not mutually exclusive and are exercised with varying emphasis. One is to develop and guarantee a certain level of constant high qualification, trustworthiness, and professional ethos among the administrators (*see* Section 7.4 below). Another complementary device is to make it financially attractive to follow the path of the statutory provisions (*see* Section 7.6 below).

A few jurisdictions from various backgrounds have been selected for the demonstration of the diversity with which these issues may be resolved in legislation (see Section 7.3 below). Needless to say that there is no abstract generalization intended (nor possible) as to which solution might be more preferable than the other. But it is noteworthy that all laws take at least some pain to make sure that the administrator displays special qualifications that make him suitable for this kind of fiduciary position between the debtor and the creditors and that justify special rules about its remuneration.

It should also be noted that jurisdictions vary as to the professional training usually expected of an administrator.[7] In the majority of jurisdictions, lawyers perform this function, but in a good number of jurisdictions (mostly common law countries) accountants are typically employed. In yet a third group of countries, the function is performed by public officials. The choice likely depends upon a mix of highest possible qualification, local tradition, controllability, and trustworthiness. Also to be considered is whether an administrator should be in every case an individual or whether a legal entity should be admissible for this position as well.

7.3. *Comparative Approaches*

7.3.1. *General Remarks*

For obvious reasons, admission to the body of administrators is not granted to everyone who happens to be interested in this job.[8] This is

---

[7] To the degree that the debtor's reorganization becomes increasingly an alternative to plain liquidation, it is worthwhile to reconsider the distrust in independent administrators. As reorganization is a highly economic undertaking, courts (and mere lawyers as such) might not be the ideal candidates for fulfilling this task.

[8] Yet some laws, such as the Moroccan one from 1996 (*Code de Commerce*), leave the selection to the judge alone without giving any indications as to necessary qualifications.

true, at least, for all those jurisdictions that entrust the administrator
with more power than just being a kind of executing arm of the court
or any other decisionmaker. It is a truism not only in times of economic
difficulties that insolvencies have an enormous impact on the overall
(macro) economy. The administration of these cases requires so much
economic, legal, organizational, and, quite often, psychological skills that
most jurisdictions put some effort into establishing a selection system
that attempts to ensure that only highly qualified persons in fact become
administrators.

The most common baseline requirements are education and a professional qualification or business experience. As discussed elsewhere, jurisdictions are divided between using lawyers or accountants as administrators. Generally, either type of professional must have satisfied the relevant
professional requirements, which usually include the necessary education. However, it is possible for business people to serve as well. Where
that is true, it is necessary to state education and experience requirements
for them.

The following examples from a few different jurisdictions demonstrate
that the selection, supervision and remuneration of administrators can be
done in quite a number of ways. To begin with the latter, remuneration
might be calculated either on a time basis or on a value basis whereby
the latter is capable of many specifications. Not least important is the
identity of the person who decides about the remuneration (court or
creditors or a supervising body). Depending on the choice, incentives for
efficiency can be given: the time-based remuneration model encourages
the administrator to really engage in the affairs rather than just ticking off
the various tasks. On the other side, the danger with this approach is that
proceedings might be dragged on endlessly,[9] a problem that is apparently
non-existent in Switzerland but is complained of, however, in numerous
other countries. In case of a value-based remuneration, the administrator
is induced to increase the estate to the greatest extent possible that, in
turn, is for the benefit of the common creditors. The disadvantage thereby
is the administrator's potential concentration on value increasing efforts
and, thus, a lesser interest in other topics in the proceeding.

---

[9] As just one example out of many possible, Colombia has developed such a system despite contradicting legal rules in its Reorganization Law 550 of December 30,
1999.

One has to distinguish selection[10] from supervision.[11] Selection reflects a two-step process: first, the creation of a pool of potential administrators and, second, the appointment of the individual who is to administer a given case. These two steps may be governed by a single authority or divided between two institutions, one to test and qualify the available pool and the second to make an appointment in a particular case. For example, a regional or national agency expert in the field might qualify applicants, but a court might choose the administrator for each case.

The appointment of an administrator is usually left to the courts—increasingly subject to subsequent approval by the creditors.[12] This works at the same time as a kind of supervision as the court is, after all, the institution with usually the closest contact to the administrator and that, therefore, can judge best its (initial and increasing/decreasing, respectively) abilities and performance. On the other hand, an insolvency proceeding serves, *inter alia*, the ultimate purpose of achieving the best possible outcome for the creditors; therefore, it is justifiable that they have the power to replace the original court-appointed administrator. However, given the realities of insolvency proceedings, this right of the creditors can easily be abused in that the most powerful creditors have someone acting as administrator who might not be entirely independent from these creditors.

Supervision of the administrator is of material relevance because it helps to reduce the mentioned perils. Supervision can be conducted in various ways. The most prevalent one is that the insolvency court exercises control over all acts of the administrator in the case at hand; however, one has to keep in mind that this form of control is primarily restricted to legal affairs rather than economic ones. However, since insolvency administration is in many respects economic activity, the control of this part of activity is very often left to the creditors.[13] They can

---

[10] Pursuant to §§ 53 and 55 of the Swiss *Schuldbetreibungs- und Konkursgesetz*, the competent administrator (a civil servant working in a public authority, *Konkursamt, see also* § 237) is determined by the domicile of the debtor. This is to say that the selection of the pool of administrators is done by the debtor itself.

[11] For an overview of jurisdictions that have established a formal system of supervision, *see* http://www.insolvencyreg.org.

[12] *See, e.g.*, § 702, 1104 U.S. BC; §§ 28, 37 Italian *Legge Fallimentare*; § 56, 57 German Insolvency Ordinance; § 22 Chinese Bankruptcy Statute. art. 35 in connection with art. 42 of OHADA's Uniform Act Organizing Collective Proceedings for Wiping Off Debts.

[13] It is noteworthy that China, in the course of drafting a new law, switched from an official-controlling system (2002) to a system where control of the administrator is entrusted to a creditors' committee.

sue the administrator who generally is personally liable for his administration if they think that something has been done less efficiently than
it could or should have been done.[14] Some jurisdictions, however, have,
apart from the two control mechanisms described so far, a third one: a
supervising authority independent from the insolvency courts and the
creditors in the given case.[15]

All these measures serve the purpose of safeguarding the best possible
outcome in each insolvency case and, at the same time, of strengthening
the general public's confidence in the administrators' qualification. It is
hard to overemphasize this task: Whereas neither commercial law nor
the overall economy usually demand any specific personal abilities or
particular qualifications from general business persons—as long as these
persons are acting successfully—the pattern changes when the enterprise
gets into financial difficulties and begins to threaten the credit given by
the creditors. If and when this is the case and an insolvency proceeding
is to be opened, there exists proof of a certain failure that is seen in most
jurisdictions as a justification for a change of the requirements. From
now on, the interests of the creditors need to be taken into stronger
(sometimes even exclusive) consideration.[16]

It is for this reason that the general scheme of activity changes once an
insolvency proceeding has been opened. The most evident indication of
this change is the appointment of the administrator who is now put in
charge over the debtor's estate. This is true also in most jurisdictions that
provide for the possibility of a debtor in possession (DIP)—that is, the
managing person is left in charge despite the opening of the insolvency
proceeding; they pay tribute to the new circumstances by establishing
a surveillance institution such as a trustee or examiner who supervises
all or certain acts and transactions (to be) done by the DIP.[17] In light

---

[14] Of course, a system that permits such suits too liberally will find that few are willing
to serve as administrators or that they demand very high fees.

[15] For an overview of jurisdictions that have established a formal system of supervision, see http://www.insolvencyreg.org.

[16] *See generally* Henry Hu and Jay Lawrence Westbrook, *Abolition of the Corporate
Duty to Creditors*, 107 COLUM. L. REV. 1321 (2007) (criticizing this trend).

[17] See IMF, Orderly & Effective Insolvency Procedures, 1999, p. 57 et seq., and World
Bank, Revised Principles for Insolvency and Creditor Rights Systems (Draft 2005), Principle C 6.2, Legislative Guide on Insolvency Law 174 (2004); available at: http://www
.uncitral.org/pdf/english/texts/insolven/05–80722_Ebook.pdf. As practical examples,
see, e.g., § 30 of the Vietnamese Bankruptcy Law (2004); § 274 f. German Insolvency
Ordinance.

of this almost dramatic change of responsibility it should be sufficiently evident that the administrator or trustee is highly dependent on the general public's and the individual creditors' confidence in his abilities and qualifications.

7.3.2. *Australia*

The Corporations Act 2001 (Cth) provides rules in Sections 410 *et seq.*, 448 *et seq.*, 1279, and 1282 *et seq.* as to how to become an administrator. These rules are specified by the Policy Statement 186 of the Australian Securities & Investments Commission (ASIC) from Sept. 30, 2005.[18] Accordingly, to become a "registered liquidator" a natural person residing in Australia must fulfill the following criteria: (s)he must either be a member of The Institute of Chartered Accountants in Australia (or another prescribed body) or hold a university degree (or diploma of an equivalent institution) that certifies that the candidate has attended three years of study in accountancy and two years in commercial law or can provide other qualifications equivalent to the two criteria mentioned before; furthermore, the candidate must have experience with the winding up of companies; and, finally, the ASIC must be satisfied that the applicant is capable of performing the duties and is otherwise fit and proper.

With respect to the appointment for a given insolvency case, Sections 448C and D establish standards that disqualify the respective person— namely having certain connections with the debtor or being themselves the subject of an administration proceeding. Once appointed, the administrator has to present to the creditors prior to the first meeting a statement of independence; this is supposed to be a safeguard against disproportionate friendliness towards the debtor.

Section 449E rules that the administrator's remuneration shall be determined by the debtor's creditors or by the court—in both cases based on the calculation offered by the administrator. The administrators are regulated and supervised by the ASIC.

---

[18] Policy Statement 186 External administration: liquidator registration. Part 9.2— Registration of auditors and liquidators, Issued 30/9/2005, available at http://www .services.thomson.com.au/asic/ps/ps186.pdf.

7.3.3. *Canada*

Pursuant to Section 5 of the Bankruptcy and Insolvency Act (1985), the Superintendent of Bankruptcy—a governmental authority—is in charge of licensing and supervising administrators. The requirements for receiving a license differ depending on whether an individual or a corporation applies. The details of the prerequisites are set down in a directive[19] that has been issued by the Superintendent on the basis of Section 5(4)(d) of the Act. Accordingly, an individual needs either a university degree,[20] a minimum of five years relevant work experience, or a relevant professional designation. Furthermore, the applicant must have completed the three-year National Insolvency Qualification Program by passing the final National Insolvency Examination successfully. Finally, the applicant must be of good reputation and character and he is supposed to be suitable—that is, he must demonstrate in an oral exam, apart from his skills and abilities, his ethical standards and so on.[21] If a corporation applies for a license, it is supposed to prove *inter alia*, its solvency and the majority of its directors and officeholders must hold a license as individuals.[22]

Section 34 *et seq.* of Appendix A of the Directive reserves investigation rights to the Superintendent in that he shall verify (and guarantee) that the licensed administrator meets at any time the requirements and qualifications necessary for obtaining a license.

For the specific case, the administrator has to be neutral towards the debtor and the secured creditors,[23] and in exercising his duties he shall "... comply with such code of ethics respecting the conduct of trustees...."[24] He may be replaced by the creditors at any time pursuant to Section 14. Creditors also decide the administrator's remuneration.[25]

7.3.4. *Finland*

Finland has no insolvency licensing system. Any member of the Finnish Bar Association may be chosen for a specific case to become adminis-

---

[19] Directive No. 13, Trustee Licensing, issued on March 31, 2000, available at: http://www.strategis.ic. gc.ca/epic/internet/inbsf-osb.nsf/en/br01057e.html.

[20] Not necessarily a degree in law.

[21] *See supra* n. 19, §§ 8–20.

[22] *See supra* n. 19, §§ 21–29 for details.

[23] §§ 13.3 and 13.4 of the Bankruptcy and Insolvency Act (1985).

[24] *See id.*, § 13.5.

[25] *See id.*, § 39.

trator. Pursuant to Section 1 of the Bankruptcy Law from September 1, 2004, the court selects and appoints the administrator after having given the main creditors the opportunity to be heard. The general suitability requirement for being appointed is specified in Section 5; it comprises, *inter alia*, possessing the "ability, skills and experience required for the duty" as well as neutrality, independence and impartiality.

Until 1995, the supervision of the administrator was left to the creditors in each given case and to the Bar Association in general. However, since this was felt to be insufficient, a new statute was enacted[26] that introduced the completely novel institution of a Bankruptcy Ombudsman. This is an independent authority that is organizationally affiliated with the Justice Department. The Ombudsman has to be impartial; that is, he is not the advocate of any group such as debtors or creditors and so on, but rather the advocate of the legality of the handling of insolvency proceedings. He shall help to develop proper practice of administering a bankrupt's estate.

His task is the supervision of any insolvency proceedings including those that have been closed because of lack of sufficient assets. The Ombudsman does not have the power to give any directions to an administrator or the court. Instead, he has quite a far-reaching right to acquire information and to inspect the minutes of any case. For this purpose, administrators have the duty to inform and to cooperate, even after a case has been closed. He is also in the position to supervise the decision-making of the creditors. If he finds any improperness or illegality, he shall point this out to the persons concerned. If this does not suffice, he shall turn to the court and demand adequate steps to be taken, such as fining that person, dismissing the administrator or reducing his fees, and so on.

7.3.5. *United Kingdom*

The United Kingdom has in its Insolvency Act 1986 a number of general rules, Section 388 *et seq.*, about Insolvency Practitioners and their qualification. They require, in order to be admitted to the group of administrators (or to be allowed to remain there), an authorization by either the Secretary of State, Section 392, (or another Competent Authority)[27] or by

---

[26] Law No. 109/1995 from Jan. 31, 1995.
[27] This option has so far not been utilized.

a recognized Professional Body.[28] There are presently seven such bodies and they are elected (directly or indirectly) by the Secretary of State pursuant to Section 391. They must have the capacity to control their "members" (Section 391(3)) with respect to their qualifications, their ongoing education, and their practical experience. The grant of admission (revocable under Section 393) is dependant on a showing that the applicant[29] is, and continues to be, "fit and proper." What this means is clarified in Regulations 6–8 of the Insolvency Practitioners Regulations 1990 (IPR).

The applicant must, according to Regulation 6(e), fulfill his duties "with the independence, integrity and the professional skills appropriate to the range and scale of the practice and the proper performance of the duties of an insolvency practitioner and in accordance with generally accepted professional standards, practices and principles." Moreover, the applicant must not only have a clean record with respect to convictions for offences involving fraud, dishonesty or violence[30] but he must, additionally, not even have appeared "to be deceitful or oppressive or otherwise unfair or improper, whether unlawful or not, or that otherwise cast doubt upon his probity or competence for discharging the duties of an insolvency practitioner." In sum, the applicant must have acted in all related matters—inside as well as outside the administration office—in a way that does not allow any doubts as to his integrity, his professional ethos,[31] and his lawfulness.

Apart from these personal requirements, an applicant has to deliver proof of his professional qualifications as set down in Regulations 7–8 of the IPR. They require good English language, the passing of the Joint Insolvency Examination, and a minimum time and case amount of practice respectively. The grant of admission is limited to three years pursuant to Regulation 10 of the IPR and needs, therefore, constant renewal.

Rule 2.106 of the Insolvency Rules 1986 entitles the administrator to receive remuneration "for his services as such." Its fixing can be done on the basis either of a "percentage of the value of the property with that he

---

[28] *See* Insolvency Practitioners (Recognised Professional Bodies) Order 1986.

[29] This must always be an individual, § 390 (1).

[30] *See*, in addition, § 390(4) of the Insolvency Act 1986.

[31] For this, *see Guidance to Professional Conduct and Ethics for persons authorised by the Secretary of State as insolvency practitioners* (available at: http://www.insolvency.gov.uk/guidanceleaflets/conductethics/conductethics.htm). In addition, the Insolvency Practices Council was established in 2000 for the investigation and examination of the professional and ethical standards of the insolvency profession.

has to deal" or of the time he has spent with the case. The determination of which of these alternatives is to be chosen in a specific case is left to the creditors or if they fail to do so, to the court.

7.3.6. *United States*

The Attorney General appoints 21 regional United States Trustees whose task, apart from, *inter alia*, exercising surveillance powers, pursuant to 28 U.S.C. Section 586(a)(1) (Judiciary and Judicial Procedure), is to "establish, maintain, and supervise a panel of private trustees." This panel constitutes the pool of potential candidates out of which the competent U.S. Trustee appoints the one to serve in a given case. The general qualification requirements for the private trustees in order to enter into and to remain within this pool are to be set down by the Attorney General pursuant to Section 586(d).[32] Section 321 of the United States Bankruptcy Code has some details about the eligibility for a particular case. They differ slightly depending on whether the appointee is an individual or a corporation. An individual need not necessarily be a lawyer.

The appointment is preliminary, however, in that this person is subject to replacement by another one through a vote of creditors.[33] As a warranty for proper treatment of the case, the "interim trustee" is generally bound to file a bond with the court "conditioned on the faithful performance of such official duties."[34] He acts as a representative of the estate and is entitled to remuneration that is determined by the Bankruptcy Court based on the "nature, the extent, and the value of such services, taking into account all relevant factors, including the time spent on such services, the rates charged for such services, whether the services were necessary to the administration ... etc."[35] Section 326 of the Bankruptcy Code puts, however, a cap on the amount of such remuneration.

---

[32] For the details, see 28 Code of Federal Regulation Part 58. § 58.3(b) makes as a condition, for example, that the candidate possesses "integrity and good moral character," "be courteous and accessible to all parties with reasonable inquiries," "be a member of good standing of the bar of the highest court," or be a certified public accountant, holding a certain bachelor's degree, and so on.

[33] *See* §§ 701 and 702 of the Bankruptcy Code.

[34] *See* § 322(a) of the Bankruptcy Code.

[35] *See* § 330 of the Bankruptcy Code.

7.3.7. *Slovakia*

In its newly enacted Insolvency Trustees Act (2005), Slovakia sets out the pre-conditions that a person (or legal entity) must fulfill in order to get into the administrator pool.[36] Thus, a prospective administrator—not necessarily a lawyer—must participate in a professional training and learning program, pass a professional exam, and register with the authorities. Furthermore, it is requested that this person has unrestricted legal capacity and a good reputation. The pool of administrators stands under the supervision of the Ministry of Justice, which is given broad powers, including the right to impose fines or even remove a person from the administrators' registry. For an individual case, the court selects "randomly;"[37] the creditors are given the opportunity, however, to replace this randomly selected administrator by another administrator through a vote in the first creditors' meeting.

7.3.8. *China*

The new Chinese Insolvency Statute from 2006 provides in Section 22 the selection and appointment process of the administrator. Accordingly, pursuant to Paragraph 3, it is up to the Supreme Court to determine the method for selection and remuneration of an administrator. In contrast, Paragraph 1 states that the insolvency court (peoples' court) appoints the administrator in the individual case. However, if the creditors are of the opinion that this particular administrator does not cope—legally and/or factually—with the tasks of this position the creditors' assembly can request an exchange.

A similar mechanism applies with respect to remuneration: it is the peoples' court that determines the amount. But the creditors' assembly is given the right to express its different view to this court.

---

[36] Like the present Slovakian law (but unlike its predecessor rules), the Estonian one has quite elaborate rules about the administrators' qualification, selection, and remuneration in§ 56 ff. of the Bankruptcy Act 2003.

[37] It should be noted that in some small countries, the neutrality requirement for an administrator sometimes poses problems because there are just not enough people who would not know each other. Random selection could be an escape from this trap.

7.4. Competence of Insolvency Administrators

The administrator's competence is crucial for the efficiency and success of any insolvency proceeding—where success means the optimal result in a given case (liquidation or reorganization).[38] Because of the complexity of the tasks—including completing agreements with employees, commencing proceedings against banks and tax authorities, commencing lawsuits, continuing the viability of economic units, finding prospective customers, and negotiating the sale of individual assets or the company itself—the necessary competence reaches beyond mere legal or business knowledge and experience. This is not something that can be learned either exclusively theoretically or practically but only (or at least best) through an education that combines both aspects.

Thus, the initial and continuous proof of this competence is a highly important aspect of an insolvency system. As already indicated, in this context it is helpful to (at least theoretically) differentiate between two stages of the selection process:

- At the first stage, a pool of potential candidates for exercising the job of an administrator has to be created. At this level it is usually sufficient to provide for more general capabilities such as certain professional requirements, good reputation, proof of ongoing education, and so on.[39]
- The second stage is the one on which an individual—be it a natural person or a legal entity—is to be selected from this pool for acting as the administrator in a given case. At this level more specific requirements can be requested, such as the administrator's neutrality or pre-existing experience in the debtor's economic surrounding.

This bifurcation is more or less visibly reflected in the described legislation. With respect to the creation of the pool, the legislation makes clear that the proof of the qualifications need not necessarily be proven

---

[38] See the General Commentary to the Principles of European Insolvency Law, 30 et seq. (W. McBryde, A. Flessner, & S. Kortmann, eds., 2003). See also UNCITRAL, LEGISLATIVE GUIDE ON INSOLVENCY LAW 174–175 (¶¶ 36–40) (2005).

[39] Note that the US law, for example, requires as a general attitude "being courteous," see supra n. 26; the new Brazilian Insolvency Law from 2005 states in art. 21 that "the administrator shall be a reputable professional, preferably a lawyer, economist, business manager or accountant …." Similarly, the UNCITRAL Legislative Guide states that it "may be desirable for the insolvency representative to possess certain personal qualities, such as integrity, impartiality, independence and good management skills." UNCITRAL, LEGISLATIVE GUIDE ON INSOLVENCY LAW 175–176 (¶ 41)(2005).

through performance on an examination, as in Canada, or through membership in a prescribed committee, as in Australia. The Finnish example of the Ombudsman shows that the constant possibility of unexpected control and the credible threat of considerable sanctions might also serve as a disciplining factor that pushes the administrators to "voluntarily" improve their skills and knowledge. Moreover, the Finnish example shows that the creation of a common pool of administrators need not be particularly specific.[40] The selection process is in such a case a sort of market behavior—only those who offer best services are taken and "survive" in that market.[41]

The problem with this approach—at least seen from a theoretical point of view—as well as a list solution (that is, where a judge has a list of potential candidates[42] from which the administrator is selected in any given case) is that it entrusts the court with the power to decide upon qualifications about which the deciding judges often have no personal experience.[43] As a rule of thumb, judges are experts in legal matters but in many systems have little economic (let alone, troubleshooting) experience. However, this theoretical deficit might be compensated to a certain degree by a judiciary that (alone or together with the creditors) has supervisory powers throughout the duration of the insolvency cases. If this is the case, the judges are in the position to correct their initial decision as to the qualification of the administrator in question.

The licensing system facilitates the ongoing control of the administrator's competence—provided that the license is granted not for a lifetime[44]

---

[40] In Austria, practically everyone interested is allowed to put their name on the general list on the internet from which judges are supposed to select the administrator for a given case. See § 15 of the *Insolvenzrechtseinführungsgesetz*. Such generality, however, looks more impressive on paper than it is when used in practice; there, an attitude similar to the Slovakian (or German) listing system prevails—that is, a given judge will in practically all cases appoint a person known to him as a qualified administrator so that it might be said that there is a "list" in the judge's mind.

[41] Sweden follows a similar approach by having a "supervisory authority" monitoring the administration under various aspects. See chapter 7, § 27 of the 1987 Bankruptcy Act.

[42] With respect of such lists, one has to distinguish between what might be called "closed lists"—that is, where the circle of candidates remains practically unchanged—and "open lists." Generally speaking, the latter appear to be more acceptable.

[43] Even though Finland and Slovakia are aligned on this point, the division line is most likely not that between common law and continental law. It might rather have to do with a different educational tradition: in England (and its "derivatives") the strong power of the Inns of Court and on the Continent the judge as the all-knowing jurist.

[44] As is the case, for example, according to art. 167 of the Bankruptcy and Insolvency Act 2001 of Barbados.

but for a certain period of time (for example, three years as is the case in the United Kingdom). However, such a system requires certain administrative costs that might appear to be superfluous because a person who falls behind the standard of professional administering will no longer be appointed as administrator in individual cases. This observation leads to the insight that the above-mentioned bifurcation continues to exist with respect to the control of the competence of a once-admitted administrator. It can be exercised, too, on two levels: first, on a general level—that is, the person in question becomes expelled from the pool of administrators; or, second, on an individual level—that is, he will no longer be entrusted with the administration of individual cases.[45] The latter is probably cheaper and the former more thorough in that it erases even the possibility of collusive actions between a judge and an unsuitable administrator.

7.5. *Integrity of Administrators*

The importance of the integrity of administrators has to be seen in close connection with what is said above about the eminently important confidence and trust in the actors in any insolvency proceeding.[46] The examples given stress the prerequisite of an administrator's good reputation—thereby emphasizing personal qualities that are beyond those required for most other legal or economic professions. This is justifiable only on the grounds that confidence in the insolvency system is crucial for its efficiency.

Integrity on the part of the administrator implies that he acts with impartiality. Even if a law like Australia's expressly states that the administrator is to be seen as the representative of the creditors, this does not permit the neglect of the justified interests of, for example, the debtor. This is particularly true in reorganization cases. Therefore, it is just another facet of said integrity that the administrator has to be independent, too, from the parties and the debtor's business involved.

---

[45] It is noteworthy in this context that the German Constitutional Court has decided that a once frequently appointed administrator has no claim whatsoever that he will be re-appointed in the future as well, see *Decision from May 23, 2006*, available at http://www.bundesverfassungsgericht.de/entscheidungen/rs20060523_1bvr253004.html.

[46] *See supra* 7.1.

It must, therefore, undoubtedly be of great concern if a businessman serves as administrator in the case of his competitor.[47]

Whereas the competitor example is self-evident, the independence issue becomes a bit more complicated when the question arises as to whether someone should be admitted to administer a reorganization proceeding who has advised the debtor before the opening of this proceeding —be it as accountant, lawyer, or consultant. The answer is dependent on the weight given either to the conflict of interest in which this person (possibly) is entangled or to the simple economic insight that a reorganization attempt is usually better and more promptly managed by a person who has gained previous insight into the debtor company and its functioning. If the latter shall be given priority, the question is whether safeguards have been established to exclude to the extent possible the threat of abusing this system—for example, the necessity to disclose all previous income from and connections with the debtor in order to put the judge (or other authorized institution) into the appropriate position to estimate that person's independence. Similar conflicts of interest can arise when a jurisdiction permits access to the administrators' pool not only by natural persons but also by legal entities. It might then happen that, for instance, the accounting branch of such an entity has previously worked for a debtor that, after the opening of the insolvency proceeding, stands to be rescued or liquidated by the insolvency branch of this very entity. Evidently, one must look for measures that assure—*ex ante* as well as *ex post*—that conflicts of interest are excluded. Depending on the respective jurisdiction's emphasis on this issue, the erection of "Chinese walls"[48] within that company might suffice; a harsher alternative would be the need to keep these branches legally distinct in different legal entities.[49]

Another protection for the administrators' integrity and, thus, another safeguard for ensuring the confidence in the system and its actors is the

---

[47] Explicitly regulated, for example, in art. 28, par. 3 of the Spanish Ley Concursal 22/2003, de 9 de Julio. In contrast, art. 41 of Cameroon's Uniform Act on Insolvency from 1998 excludes only the debtor's family members from appointment, whereas the new Chinese Bankruptcy Law from 2006 excludes, *inter alia*, those administrators "interested ... with this bankruptcy case."

[48] This term is used to describe temporary arrangements within a firm that are meant to ensure that information available to the firm in a certain capacity is not conveyed to other parts of the firm. It is sometimes extended to the idea that one part of the firm is acting independently so as not to be influenced by the interests of the rest of the firm.

[49] The expression "Chinese walls" is meant to express the idea of separation by effective but temporary partitions that can be erected or removed as needed.

more or less formalized control of the administrators. Apart from disciplining administrators by means of the credible threat of personal liability,[50] most jurisdictions have exercised this control through both the creditors' assembly and the courts—with the latter, however, acting usually not on their own but only upon the filing of a complaint or a specific request. To base this sort of control on solid ground, administrators are generally obliged to present reports and accounts in regular periods to the court and/or the creditors. As important as this particular task is with respect to an effective control system, it should be noted that this aspect should not be too exaggerated. A former draft of the Moldovian Insolvency Statute provided for a monthly report; taking into account that administrators, due to the remuneration system, needed dozens of cases in order to earn a living, this task turned into a serious hurdle for performing an administrator's daily tasks.

By contrast—and supplementing the topic of judicial oversight—a considerable number of jurisdictions have set up specific surveillance institutions like the ones grouped together in the International Association of Insolvency Regulators.[51] These countries have established independent institutions that exercise their monitoring function according to their internal or statutory rules. This is, so to speak, a third step of providing safeguards for the functioning and integrity of the insolvency system in general and its main actors in particular. Moreover, especially in times of increased numbers of insolvencies, the general public throughout the globe displays a certain tendency to grow irritated and blame, *inter alia*, administrators for the development. A surveillance institution is particularly valuable at such times as it absorbs such criticisms.

An alternative way of exercising such control functions exists, for example, in Germany: there the association of administrators relies on a kind of "soft law" by imposing certain behavioral rules on their members as a kind of code of conduct.[52] The sanction for an administrators transgression is (apart from other possible legally relevant repercussions) the lowered regard of his peers. One might call this approach a "Code of Ethics." Still another remarkable possibility of surveillance is realized

---

[50] One might call this control mechanism "internal control" in that it applies to the administrator's own sense of responsibility.

[51] *See supra* 4.4.1.

[52] *See* http://www.arbeitskreis-insolvenzverwalter.de under *Verhaltensrichtlinien*.

in Austria: the *Kreditschutzverein* (credit protection association)[53] which was founded in 1870 with the general purpose of protecting entrepreneurs from financial damage; part of this task is the representation of creditors (even beyond its members) in insolvency proceedings and the maintenance of their rights. In the course of time, this institution has gathered such an enormous amount of knowledge and insight that its judgment over each particular administrator, as a matter of fact, forms a credible threat to every administrator. This association has developed, thus, into something like a standard-setter in insolvency administration.

It deserves, however, to be mentioned that institutionalized controls, like those described here, are of lesser importance in those jurisdictions that entrust their administrators with mere executive functions within a court-driven proceeding.

7.6. *Rules of Compensation of Professionals*

The compensation of professionals (that is, of both administrators and judges) plays an essential role in developing a proper pool of insolvency personnel that fulfils the confidence requirements explained in the previous two sections. Compensation is the financial tool that helps give an incentive for creating the necessary professional ethos that is indispensable for any effective insolvency law.[54] Thus, as a starting point, an observer should look for a system of compensation that places professionals in a position to earn a decent living commensurate with their education and qualifications and that does not force them to look for other sources of income.

As the examples of the country descriptions discussed above show, there are different methods of remunerating administrators. The common thread through them all is that it is never left to the administrator alone to decide the matter. Instead, the decision is either entrusted to the

---

[53] For a description of the history, task, and success of this institution, see H.G. Kantner, *The Protection of Creditors in Austrian Insolvency Proceedings*, EUROFENIX 10 (Autumn 2006).

[54] As just one example, see Thomas Richter, *The New Czech Insolvency Act—New Insolvency Regime for Czech Corporate Debtors and Their Creditors*, BUTTERWORTH J. INTL. BANKING FIN. L.271 (2006) (discussing the law in force until June 30, 2006).

creditors[55] or to the court.[56] In both cases such a decision might be subject to further investigation upon application of either a party or a third person, such as is the case with the Ombudsman in Finland. The decision not only might be about the fixing of a certain sum to be paid to the administrator, but also can include the basis on which the sum is to be calculated—on the money received in the course of the proceedings,[57] on the value of the estate (United Kingdom), on the time spent on the case in question, or on a combination of all these criteria, as is the case in the United States.[58]

Evidently, there are several advantages to giving the decision about the administrator's remuneration to someone different from the one who receives it (that is, the administrator). Not only does this measure increase transparency, it also serves at the same time as a confidence-creating measure and functions thus as an incentive for the administrator to do "a good job." Nevertheless, there are also some caveats to be kept in mind: if it is the court that decides, then transparency can easily be lost if both sides work closely together in a collusive or corruptive manner. Therefore, such a regulation is conditional on a justified trust of the impartiality of the participants, particularly of the judiciary. If the decision is given to the creditors, however, the administrator might feel the need to give up (or reduce) his neutrality as to the parties at stake and support in a one-sided way the interests of all or a certain group of creditors.[59] In the worst case scenario, one creditor might blackmail the administrator—a fact that makes institutionalized surveillance all the more desirable.

Apart from the question of who decides about the amount of remuneration, there is the further question of how the amount of remuneration should be calculated. It has already been mentioned that one answer is

---

[55] See additionally, for example, art. 208 of the Bankruptcy and Insolvency Act 2001 of Barbados.

[56] See, e.g., the Chinese Bankruptcy Statute, § 28 par. 2. The Swiss example of a public authority acting as administrator (*Konkursamt*) demonstrates that the remuneration can also be fixed by means of legislation; *see* art. 43 ff. *Gebührenverordnung zum Bundesgesetz ueber Schuldbetreibung und Konkurs*—based on art. 16 of the *Schuldbetreibungs- und Konkursgesetz* (a combination of time- and value-based calculation).

[57] See, e.g., the example of Australia above. The same is found, for example, in § 65(2) of the Estonian Bankruptcy Act 2003.

[58] See also art. 34, par. 2 of the Spanish Bankruptcy Law, *supra* n. 40, that combines the complexity of the case with the assets and liabilities.

[59] This is less problematic in a jurisdiction such as Australia where the administrator explicitly acts as a "representative of the creditors."

to base this calculation on the time spent. Even though this is a fairly objective standard, it has its flaws[60] in that it might give an incentive for unnecessary prolongation of the proceeding. The alternative is to take the value of the estate as the basis for calculation. But here, a further distinction can be made: if the relevant value is that of the estate at the beginning of the proceeding, later efforts to increase the estate's value through, for example, the use of avoidance powers might be neglected. In contrast, if the relevant value is the estate as it is to be distributed to the creditors, then previous efforts to clarify which assets do and do not belong to it might be neglected. The examples show that there is, generally speaking, no "one size fits all" answer. Under such circumstances, it might be worthwhile to consider the use of a fixed amount to which can be added or from which can be deducted certain amounts depending on the particular case at hand. On the other hand, calculations based on the size of the dividends to creditors are also found in a number of systems.

7.7. Periodic Reports

Many systems require periodic reports and accounts from the administrator as an insolvency case proceeds.[61]

---

[60] See supra 7.1.
[61] See, e.g., 11 U.S.C. §704(a)(8) for the United States requirement. See Eberhard Braun, COMMENTARY ON THE GERMAN INSOLVENCY CODE 274–275 (2006).

CHAPTER EIGHT

CROSS-BORDER CONSIDERATIONS

8.0. *Overview*

As a consequence of the general rule that any state has the power to enact laws that are applicable and enforceable only on its own territory, problems necessarily arise when and if a debtor's insolvency stretches beyond the borders of a state. This is primarily the case when the debtor has assets in more than one jurisdiction. In such a case, the creditors will be interested in including assets from the other jurisdiction in "their" proceeding; the liquidation of these additional assets might increase the dividend. Also in case of an envisaged rescue of the debtor, the inclusion of assets located abroad might be essential for success or failure of the attempt. On the other hand, creditors in the other jurisdiction might have entered into contractual relationships with the debtor in reliance upon the location of assets in "their" jurisdiction. The question then arises as to whether or not this reliance on assets "at hand" deserves, or even needs, protection—a question that is all the more valid if and when these creditors are employees of the debtor. But reliance aside, some would question whether it can ever be legitimate that the insolvency law of one jurisdiction reaches out to assets positioned in another jurisdiction. As desirable as this result might be economically, can it be reconciled with the fundamentals of national sovereignty? On the other hand, does this very doctrine necessitate (at least) the formal recognition of the foreign proceeding? These are some of the questions that mark the initial problems of international insolvency law. Needless to say, innumerable further problems exist in this area. However, this chapter confines itself to describing and commenting upon only the more fundamental ones— those that have formed the starting point for national legislation.

Because of ever-growing multinational trade and investment, every jurisdiction—even smaller ones[1]—must consider regulating not only

---

[1] See, for example, Uganda, that has in its draft Insolvency Bill 2005 provisions dealing with trans-border issues. *See infra* 8.2.6.

purely domestic insolvencies but also cross-border insolvency cases. Even though the advent of cross-border cases reaches far back into history,[2] the common and worldwide need for regulating this phenomenon in some detail is becoming, more and more, an indispensable task for any legislator—with predictably increasing intensity as a consequence of constantly intensifying globalization. The key multinational legislation is found in the European Insolvency Regulation and the UNCITRAL Model Law on Cross-Border Insolvency.[3]

Before explaining the fundamentals of cross-border insolvency law, two caveats need to be made: (1) independent of the foregoing, the common understanding is that the treatment of foreign creditors is an issue for purely domestic regulation—the recommended rule being that of equal treatment;[4] (2) the international community has not yet found a satisfactory and widely accepted solution for the treatment of insolvencies involving more than one legal entity bound together as a group, despite its frequency and enormous practical importance. Such "group insolvencies" form statistically the predominant pattern of cross-border insolvencies, but there has not yet evolved something like a "best practice" for dealing with such situations.[5]

8.1. Fundamental Issues

Because this subject is so new, this discussion requires more theory and analysis than areas that are well-developed in all national legislation. As a matter of fact, any cross-border related insolvency legislation has to take into account a multiplicity of considerations resulting from, for example,

---

[2] See, for example, Friedrich Meili, *Die geschichtliche Entwicklung des internationalen Konkursrechtes*, Festschrift v. Bar (Orell Füssli 1908); Hans Hanisch, *Bemerkungen zur Geschichte des Internationalen Insolvenzrechts* in *Festschrift für Franz Merz*, 159 *et seq.* (W. Gerhardt et al. eds., RWS-Verlag 1992); Josef Kohler, *Lehrbuch des Konkursrechts*, 601 *et seq.* (F. Enke 1891).

[3] Council Regulation (EC) No 1346/2000 (available at: http://www.europa.eu/eur-lex/pri/en/oj/dat/2000/l_160/l_16020000630en00010018.pdf); UNCITRAL Model Law on Cross-Border Insolvency (available at: http://www.uncitral.org/uncitral/en/uncitral_texts/insolvency/1997Model.html). For an in-depth discussion of both, *see infra* 8.2.1., 8.2.4.

[4] The Model Law on Cross-Border Insolvency, discussed *infra* 8.2.1, specifically requires equal treatment of all creditors, whether domestic or foreign, although there is a special problem with foreign tax claims. *Id.* at ¶ 105.

[5] In December 2006, UNCITRAL started an initiative to elaborate such best practice. *See also infra* 8.1 (b).

the economic system of the respective country, the overall purpose of its insolvency law, the whole legislative body relating to the pre-insolvency situation (this might be called "turnaround or reorganization legislation"), its relationship with particular other countries, or the hoped-for treatment of its businesses abroad. After all, an effective cross-border law has far reaching implications including, for example, fostering informal workout attempts at the outset of a debtor's financial distress as it might help to prevent the possibly troublesome task of going through an insolvency proceeding.

Irrespective of this multi-dimensional task, however, there are a few fundamental issues[6] that more or less explicitly underlie practically all laws in the world on this subject. They require some brief listing and description.

8.1.1. *Basic Terminology and Concepts*

8.1.1.1. *Territoriality vs. Universality*

The most basic distinction of these concepts refers to the scope of the law's applicability. Since any cross-border case implies that assets of the debtor are located in a country other than the one in which the insolvency proceeding is commenced, the question arises as to whether these assets can be subjected to the present proceeding. Therefore, the alternatives are, generally speaking, that the scope is either restricted to the respective legislator's area of dominion or extended to all over the world.[7]

(a) The restrictive approach is called territoriality (or the territoriality principle). It designates a law that confines its applicability strictly to that physical area governed by the respective jurisdiction. It does not claim to reach out to assets located outside of this terri-

---

[6] See, for example, Philip Wood, PRINCIPLES OF INTERNATIONAL INSOLVENCY, (1995).

[7] See for a discussion of both approaches Jay L. Westbrook, *A Global Solution to Multinational Default*, 98 MICH. L. REV. 2276 (2000); Lynn LoPucki, *The Case for Cooperative Territoriality in International Bankruptcy*, 98 MICH. L. REV. 2216 (2000); Frederick Tung, *Fear of Commitment in International Bankruptcy*, 33 GEO. WASH. INTIL. L. REV. 555 (2001); Charles D. Booth, *Living in Uncertain Times: The Need to Strengthen Hong Kong Transnational Insolvency Law*, 34 COLUM. J. OF TRANSIT. L. 389, 393–396 (1996) [hereinafter Living in Uncertain Times]. *See* additionally Jay L. Westbrook, *Multinational Financial Distress: The Last Hurrah of Territorialism*, 41 TEX. INT'L L.J. 321 (2006).

tory.[8] Territoriality, thus, complies with the concept of sovereignty that was developed by the French philosopher Jean Bodin in the 16th century, that has guided public international law ever since, and that still exercises great influence today.[9] The territoriality principle, in its purest version, not only confines its own applicability overseas (outbound application), it additionally bars another state's claim to reach assets that happen to be located within the reach of such state's territory (inbound application).[10] Such a universalistic claim is blocked by a strict territorialism.

In this context, it is of more than just historical interest that the legislative power in insolvency matters always rested (and still rests) in at least most (if not all) national jurisdictions with the biggest relevant territorial (and economic) unit.[11] The most prominent example is, of course, the United States, which had in its Constitution right from the beginning a provision that entrusted the federation with the legislative power in insolvency matters; but this observation is true also for other states such as Argentina, Australia, Brazil, Canada, Germany, Russia, and Switzerland. Considering these examples and the increasing convergence of the world's economies, it seems likely insolvency law will expand in its scope to fit regional or even global markets.[12]

(b) By contrast, universality (or the universality principle) ignores such territorial restrictions and claims instead worldwide applicability of the law governing the case. This approach does not, as a matter of fact, ignore the other states' sovereignty; rather, it pays respect to it by leaving it to the foreign states whether or not they accept such outreaching claims. It is, therefore, consistent that the universality principle does not confine

---

[8] Note as an aside that the question of where assets are located deserves increasing attention due to the volatility of those "important" goods and financial assets that can be transferred very quickly from one jurisdiction to another.

[9] It should be noted that this concept of sovereignty that guarantees "the ruler" full authority over his territory (*see* Christian Tomuschat, *International Law: Ensuring the Survival of Mankind on the Eve of a New Century*, 161 *et seq.* (Martinus Nijhoff 2001)) has become in recent years less and less accepted in light of countervailing values advocating for the future togetherness of the people of this world. Suffice it to mention here the extension of public international criminal law that started with the Nuremberg Trials and that is now—after Rwanda, Pinochet, Milosevic, and so on—a solid and steady feature of modern international law; *see also* Christoph Paulus, *Some Thoughts on an Insolvency Procedure for Countries*, 50 Am. J. Comp. L. 531 (2002).

[10] Prominent examples for such an approach were Japan, until its new legislation came into operation in 2001, and China, before its new law came into operation in 2007.

[11] *See also* Westbrook, *supra* note 7, at 229.

[12] *See infra* 8.3.

itself to a one-way approach but includes acceptance of a respective claim from another state's insolvency law. It would be a consequence of a strict application of this approach that insolvency cases with cross-border implications would be governed by just one law—no matter where the assets might be located.

(c) However, these two principles have rarely existed in their purest versions; legislative practice quite often mixes or modifies them:

i. As to the mixture—a common version might be called a one-sided universality (or one-sided territoriality). Its characteristic is that a jurisdiction requests worldwide recognition (or at least expects it) of its own domestic trans-border cases but bars foreign cases with the same claim on its own territory.[13] One-sided universality is not only, shall we say, esthetically disturbing, it is obviously either arrogant or inconsistent. A somewhat softer version requests reciprocity in exchange for recognition of the foreign claim to universality.[14]

Under the present-day conditions, however, the justification for such distrust becomes more and more doubtful. Whereas in earlier times skepticism might have been understandable (or even appropriate) in light of the enormous differences among the various insolvency laws, today there exists a world-wide convergence in the area of these laws.[15] This is in large part because of the insolvency initiatives of the multilateral institutions such as the International Monetary Fund (IMF), World Bank, and UNCITRAL as a reaction to the

---

[13] A recent example is the interpretation given to the old Chinese bankruptcy law prior to the promulgation of the 2006 Chinese Enterprise Bankruptcy Law. *CCIC Finance Ltd., v. Guangdong Int'l Trust and Inv. Corp. and Guangdon Int'l Trust and Inv. Corp. Hong Kong (Holdings) Ltd., (In Liq.), HCA 15651 of 1999* (July 31, 2001), noted in Charles Booth, *Drafting Bankruptcy Laws in Socialist Market Economies: Recent Developments in China and Vietnam*, 18 COLUM. J. of ASIAN L. 93, 143, note 224 (2004).

[14] Article 5 of the new Chinese Enterprise Bankruptcy Law. Moreover, a few jurisdictions that have adopted the UNCITRAL model law make its applicability dependent upon reciprocity—for example, Argentina (draft), British Virgin Islands, Mexico, Romania, South Africa, or (prospectively) New Zealand. UNCITRAL, Status: 1997—Model Law on Cross-Border Insolvency. Look Chan Ho, *Overview, Cross-Border Insolvency: A Commentary on the UNCITRAL Model Law* 11, 12 (Look Chan Ho ed., 2006).

[15] *See* Christoph Paulus, *Rechtsvergleichung im nationalen wie internationalen Insolvenzrecht: Eine Erfolgsgeschichte*, in *Einheit und Vielfalt des Rechts*, Festschrift für R. Geimer, 795 *et seq.* (R. Schütze ed., 2002).

1997 Asian financial crisis and the subsequent creation of a Financial Stability Forum by the G7 States that spotted the effectiveness
and efficiency of insolvency laws as one of the decisive factors for
a state's financial stability.[16] Given this development towards a harmonization of the world's insolvency laws, territorial defense mechanisms lose much of their justification and tend to become somewhat outdated.[17] This is all the more true as a remedy of last resort
usually exists, so to speak, in that a foreign law's applicability might
be rejected (*in toto* or in a special respect) on grounds of the violation of domestic public policy (*ordre public*).[18]

ii. The modification of laws governing multinational cooperation may
consist in carving out certain fields of law (such as securities, treatment of labor contracts, secured transactions, tax law, or corporation law) in order to support the insolvency proceeding on a territorial level. This fact indicates that modifications are made because
of the great differences that still exist in the laws of different countries in the present world. The degree of modification forms part
of a second fundamental distinction—whether there should be just
one proceeding or several.

8.1.1.2. *Unitary vs. Multiple Proceedings*

(a) A more or less natural consequence of the universality principle is
that, ideally, there should be just one proceeding dealing with the debtor's
insolvency—no matter where in the world its assets are located: one case,
one law, and one proceeding. Seen from a purely theoretical perspective,
this solution would be the best in avoiding unnecessary costs such as
multiple administrators or exchange of information.

(b) However, it has already been mentioned that such a unitary approach
faces, at least for the time being, insurmountable practical obstacles
resulting from the still existing (or perceived) disparities of quite many
areas in the laws of the various countries of this world.[19] In order to over-

---

[16] *See* http://www.fsforum.org/compendium/key_standards_for_sound_financial_
system.html.

[17] *See* Jay Lawrence Westbrook, *Theory and Pragmatism in Global Insolvencies: Choice
of Law and Choice of Forum*, 65 AM. BANKR. L.J. 457 (1991).

[18] As just one example, see art. 311 of the Croatian Bankruptcy Law from 1996.

[19] There are few examples that document the possibility for providing unitary proceedings on a regional level. A prerequisite is that two (or more) countries have such a close
legal relationship that the differences are negligible. This was the case (at least to a certain

come these obstacles, two solutions have been developed in practice so far. The first one uses the private international law method of determining the applicability of a certain law; this method is used only for selected issues in the context of an insolvency proceeding. That means that even though the law of the main proceeding—commonly called *lex concursus*—governs the proceeding as a whole under the universality principle, more or less exactly defined areas might be governed by the law (or, narrower, the insolvency law) of another jurisdiction. Prominent examples for such exceptions are, *inter alia*, rights *in rem*, avoidance and setoff rules, or certain financial devices.

The second solution that has emerged is to split up the one, and ideally only, proceeding into several—potentially into as many as there are foreign jurisdictions involved. However, what looks like a fallback into the territoriality principle is avoided by providing for a ranking of the proceedings[20] and the coordination of them as well as the cooperation of the persons involved. This approach is commonly called "modified universalism." The degree to which such modification takes place allows for a further subdivision:[21]

i. Because the UNCITRAL Model Law on international insolvency is designed to assist and support the foreign proceeding on its own territory by reducing the applicability of the local insolvency law more or less to the degree necessary for the protection and fair treatment of the local creditors, the ancillary proceeding approach has gained prominence. Since an ancillary proceeding is not a full-fledged insolvency proceeding, it has the theoretical[22] advantage of

---

degree) for two countries like Austria and Germany with a long lasting common legal history and parallel developments; see Treaty between Germany and Austria on Bankruptcy, Winding-up, Arrangements and Compositions from 1979. *See infra* 8.2.6 and Scandinavian concord. However, the Peoples' Republic of China and Hong Kong have, even since 1997, not yet come to any agreement regarding the mutual recognition of their respective insolvency proceedings.

[20] It is crucial to designate thereby as precisely as possible the one and only main proceeding.

[21] See for what follows Jay. L. Westbrook, *Multinational Enterprises in General Default: The UNCITRAL Model Law and Related Regional Reforms* in: Aktuelle Entwicklungen des europäischen und internationalen Zivilverfahrensrechts 237 (2002), sub part II B.

[22] The example of Switzerland amplifies that a full local insolvency proceeding is not necessarily expensive and that it can be performed in great speed. Moreover, the protocol in the AIOC Resources, AG case (available at: http://www.iiiglobal.org/international/protocols/AIOC%20Resources%20AG%20Protocol.pdf) shows the flexibility of the Swiss authorities.

being cheaper, swifter, and more flexible. However, most existing ancillary proceedings provide for both procedural and substantive regulations; a supportive proceeding containing only procedural rules has not yet been developed.

ii. The alternative to an ancillary proceeding is a parallel proceeding. This is a regular insolvency proceeding with all its consequences as to time, effort, and costs, but it is restricted in its reach to the territory of the state in question (under the territoriality principle). The justification that is commonly given for this approach is the allegedly necessary protection of the local creditors.[23] A closer look, however, gives the impression in a great number of cases that the real reason might instead be the protection of the local law and its applicability.

The deference of a parallel proceeding to a main proceeding is of varying intensity. On the one side of the scale, it can be completely isolated in its performance, that is, there is no co-operation and no information exchange between the office holders of this proceeding and that of the main proceeding—with the only exception that any surplus will be handed over to the main proceedings; an informative example for this is Switzerland. The great disadvantage of this approach is the difficulty arising from such isolationism in case the debtor in question could be reorganized.[24] This is hardly possible under such a separatist attitude.

At the other end of this spectrum,[25] the parallel or concurrent proceeding can be employed in close cooperation with the main proceeding. This may be called the universality/plurality approach.[26] A secondary proceeding is a full insolvency brought in a jurisdiction other than the primary jurisdiction for that debtor. In contrast to an ancillary type of proceeding, it can exercise all of the usual powers of an insolvency court rather than merely assisting the primary court. Such a parallel proceed-

---

[23] For the value of this argument see John Pottow, *Greed and Pride in International Bankruptcy: The Problems of and Proposed Solutions to "Local Interests,"* 104 MICH. L. REV. 1899 (2006).

[24] It is noteworthy that Switzerland so far has not enacted a full-fledged reorganization proceeding; drafts are currently under discussion. Also, it should be noted that even in liquidation cases, cooperation may lead to a greater realization of value. *See supra* 3.6.1.

[25] Somewhere in the middle of this spectrum is the frequent rule that a parallel proceeding is not automatically initiated but only when and if certain conditions are fulfilled; *see* for example, the Croatian International Bankruptcy Law (described by Jasnica Garašić in INSOL Europe—9 International Case law-Alert II/2006, p. 5 *et seq.*) available at http://www.brsi.de/pdfs/international_caselaw_AlertNo9.pdf.

[26] It is also consistent with "Modified Universalism."

ing is secondary to the extent it fashions its actions in an effort to defer to and cooperate with the primary proceeding. In some forms there will even be mutual conformity between the concerned administrators and judges. The more intensive such coordination and cooperation is prescribed (or performed), the more similar becomes the parallel proceeding to an ancillary one. The European Union Regulation (discussed below) clarifies this deference and assistance of the parallel proceeding by calling it a secondary proceeding; however, it provides for a cooperation duty of just the administrators (and not the judges) and is therefore not as close to the ancillary proceeding as the UNCITRAL Model Law approach.[27]

8.1.2. *Jurisdiction*

The experience especially of the last 15 years has shown that the legislative as well as practical attempts to determine where the just-mentioned main proceeding is to be located is anything but an easy undertaking. These difficulties are particularly felt in the context of insolvencies of groups.[28] The formation of groups is today the predominant way of structuring businesses, especially multinational firms. Instead of having all activities bundled in one corporation, they are split up and attributed to several separate companies that are bound together under the roof of (usually) one company.

Practice teaches as a strong rule of thumb that, fairly often, if one company of such group goes bankrupt, the other ones will follow in a kind of domino effect. Such an event provokes a number of intricate questions, one of them being which jurisdiction shall be competent to open a main proceeding and which one a parallel or ancillary proceeding, respectively. This problem is currently probably one of the most intensely debated issues in international insolvency law. The background of this discussion is the need and desire to determine *ex ante* the competent jurisdiction and to exclude thereby forum shopping[29] to the extent possible.

---

[27] UNCITRAL MODEL LAW (1997) at Ch. 5 (arts. 28–32) (Concurrent Proceedings).

[28] See Neil Cooper, *Corporate Groups & Insolvency* (paper presented at the *Seminario internacional de insolvencia, insolvencia transfronteriza y contratación pública*, held in Bogota, Colombia, on March 29, 2006) at 101; Christoph Paulus, *Group Insolvencies— Some Thoughts About New Approaches*, 42 TEX. INT'L. L.J., 819 *et seq.* (2007).

[29] About forum shopping see A. Smits and I. O'Hearn, *Multinational Insolvency Forum Shopping* in: James R. Silkenat & Charles D. Schmerler, THE LAW OF INTERNATIONAL INSOLVENCIES AND DEBT RESTRUCTURINGS, 2006, 479 et seq.

8.1.2.1. *Determination of the Main Proceeding*

There are at least two options imaginable: Following the priority principle one could say that the jurisdiction in which to open a main proceeding shall be the court where the first filing of a petition has been lodged. However, such a rule could easily result in randomness when, for example, an obvious branch of the company gets the lead in the insolvency of the whole company or group; moreover, such a rule could easily be misused by creditors or debtors who were free to choose a jurisdiction for the main proceeding that is most favorable for them (forum shopping).[30] Therefore, it appears to be preferable to determine in advance which court has the jurisdiction to open a main proceeding and which court only a subordinated proceeding rather than leaving this decision to chance or strategic behavior.

Since there is some dispute among courts, practitioners, and scholars about the correct way of making such a determination within corporation law (should it be the statutory seat or the actual seat), international insolvency law is seeking its own solution. Under the lead of the European Union Regulation and the UNCITRAL Model Law it becomes nowadays increasingly accepted[31] that the correct place for opening the main proceeding should be the center of the debtor's main interests. As a consequence, jurisdiction to open a main proceeding is with that court where this center is located.[32] All other courts in the world, then, have just the competence to open a subordinated proceeding if the debtor has an "establishment" in the local jurisdiction (see below). If under such a rule two different courts, nevertheless, should be of the opinion that the debtor's center of main interests is located in their respective district, this conflict might be solved by the application of the aforementioned priority principle.

However, even though the European Union Regulation has been in force only since 2002, the experiences of the first years of application of this law have made quite obvious that the term "center of main interests"

---

[30] A vigorous dispute about these questions has arisen in the United States. *See* Symposium, William C. Whitford, *Courting Failure? The Effects of Venue Choice on Big Bankruptcies*, 54 BUFF. L. REV. 321, 322 (2006). *See generally* Elizabeth Warren and Jay Lawrence Westbrook, THE LAW OF DEBTORS AND CREDITORS 820 (5th ed., 2006).

[31] *See*, for example, art. 301 of the Croatian Bankruptcy Law from 1996.

[32] *In re Bear Stearns High-Grade Structured Credit Strategies Master Fund, Ltd.*, 374 B.R. 122 (Bankr. S.D.N.Y. 2007), *aff'd* 389 B.R. 325 (S.D.N.Y. 2008) (applying a strict reading of the center of main interests requirement).

is far from being sufficiently clear. Despite the additional specification that this center is to be presumed at that place where the legal person or the company has its registered office,[33] uncertainties exist as to whether an affiliate's center is where its own office is registered (that is, located) or where the parent company (so called "head office functions" or "mind of management") is registered.[34] This is where the jurisdictional question interacts with the unsolved problem of the treatment of insolvent groups. To find a more precise determination of the competent jurisdiction is certainly one of the most urgent challenges of the present-day international insolvency law.

8.1.2.2. *Minimum Requirements for a Non-Main Proceeding*

Closely related to the preceding remarks is the consequential question about which country should have jurisdiction to open a non-main proceeding or, respectively, under what conditions shall this possibility be granted. Does it suffice if only a few of the debtor's assets (or even just non-central interests) are located in the jurisdiction or should more than that be required, such as a branch (however this might be defined)? The decision for the one or the other alternative depends on the degree to which a country's law wants to protect its local insolvency policies. As a matter of fact, certain local creditors, who will be among the beneficiaries of a local proceeding, for various reasons (language, travel efforts, familiarity with local authorities, and so on), will be more comfortable with a domestic proceeding than a foreign one. On this basis, a number of countries establish, as a sufficient reason for opening a domestic proceeding, that the debtor has just a single asset located within this jurisdiction.[35]

However, such an approach opens avenues for fragmenting coherent trans-border cases and thus destroying the approach of the universality

---

[33] *See* art. 3(1) of the EU Regulation.

[34] For this, see (out of innumerable publications) Gabriel Moss & Christoph Paulus, *The European Insolvency Regulation—The Case for Urgent Reform*, 1 *et seq.*, 19 INSOLV. INT. 1 (2006); in contrast, however, see the European Court of Justice in the "Eurofood" case, available at: http://curia.eu.int/en/content/juris/index_form.htm. For comments on this decision by, e.g., Jay L. Westbrook, *Locating the Eye of the Financial Storm*, and Gabriel Moss, *Group Insolvency—Choice of Forum and Law: The European Experience Under the Influence of English Pragmatism*, (32 Brooklyn J. Int'l L. 2007); Christoph Paulus, *Group Insolvencies—Some Thoughts About New Approaches*, 42 TEX. INT'L L.J. (2007).

[35] An example is the United States. 11 U.S.C. § 109(a). If such a proceeding is limited to local assets and there is no other proceeding pending in the world, the problem is not

principle that strives to have, to the extent possible, one proceeding governed by just one law. This is all the more a realistic danger since, under the given economic circumstances, it becomes increasingly easy to transfer assets from one place to another. Therefore, the decision for establishing minimum requirements for the opening of a non-main proceeding should always bear in mind that the ultimate goal should be a unitary-universalistic proceeding. When and if this proposition is accepted, it is self-evident that the mere location of an asset should not be enough for opening a non-main proceeding. A prominent representative for such a "more than just an asset" approach is the requirement of an "establishment," a requirement found in both the European Union regulation and the Model Law. This is a term, however, that is not self-explanatory but rather that is apt to be defined in a way that might add to the existence of an asset, for example the presence of business activity;[36] further elements or different ones could easily be added for a more precise definition of what shall be understood by the term "establishment."[37]

8.1.3. *Choice of Law*

Since insolvency law is, in fact, a sort of meta level of any national law—meaning that it is related to and intertwined with virtually all areas of this law—it is obvious that not all rules of a given jurisdictional insolvency regime are equally adaptable to those of another. This statement presupposes, of course, that the jurisdiction in question adheres in one way or another to the universality principle since, by definition, the territoriality principle does not care about mutual adaptability. In some cases an adaptation is easier than in others so that in multi-jurisdictional cases the harmonization of the laws involved becomes a problem. Prominent examples for a particularly hard adaptability are the administrator's avoidance

---

one of cross-border law and may not be problematic at all. The point discussed in the text arises because there are also insolvency proceedings concerning the same debtor in other countries.

[36] This is what the European Insolvency Regulation and the UNCITRAL Model Law define as "establishment." UNCITRAL, MODEL LAW (1997) at Art. 2 (" 'Establishment' means any place of operations where the debtor carries out a nontransitory economic activity with human means and goods or services.").

[37] *In re Bear Stearns High-Grade Structured Credit Strategies Master Fund, Ltd.*, 374 B.R. 122 (Bankr. S.D.N.Y. 2007), aff'd 389 B.R. 325 (S.D.N.Y. 2008). That case rejected the idea that a jurisdiction of incorporation, with only formal contacts with the debtor, could be even a non-main jurisdiction.

powers or the treatment of secured rights; less hard (but still troublesome in many cases) is, for example, the scope of the administrator's powers or the granting of special privileges in insolvency proceedings. The problem is large and complex, and we introduce only the main elements in this brief treatment.

It is of central importance to distinguish between choice of insolvency law and choice of non-insolvency law. As to a given dispute, both choices may be necessary and it is crucial to see which choice a particular statute or court decision is making. For example, take a particular claim arising in contract and asserted to be entitled to priority in distribution. The law governing the validity of the contract, the amount of damages, and related issues are usually governed by non-insolvency law. Once those questions have been answered and the amount of the claim determined, then insolvency law will determine the proper priority in distribution.

The general rules of conflicts of law are usually not seen as *per se* applicable in cross-border insolvency cases but are said to need adjustment to the particular needs and peculiarities of these proceedings. The two cornerstones in between which this adjustment must be placed are, on the one hand, the above-mentioned ideal of one proceeding handling one case according to one law. On the other hand, there is the confidence of the people of other countries in the application of a law under which they have acted before and have performed legal transactions. Whereas the former principle would lead to an export of the whole body of the domestic insolvency law to all countries where the debtor might have assets, the latter approach tends toward a multiplicity of applicable laws: beyond the borders of the opening jurisdiction only those jurisdictions' laws are applicable where assets (or establishments)[38] of the debtor are located.

The contemporary compromise for the solution of these two conflicting approaches is that, as a general rule, the *lex fori concursus* shall be applicable, that is, the insolvency law of that jurisdiction where the insolvency proceeding in question has been commenced. However, there are exceptions to this unitary and universal approach: wherever the need is felt to protect nationals and their trust in "their" law, there are specific rules providing either for the exclusive applicability of this law or for at least mitigating the strict effects of the application of the *lex fori concursus*. Widely accepted examples for such exceptions are—apart from

---

[38] *See supra* 8.1.2.2.

the above-mentioned securities and avoidance powers—the treatment of lease and employment contracts, of setoff and netting rights, and of the exercise of the administrator's enforcement powers.

8.1.4. Recognition of Foreign Proceedings

8.1.4.1. Meaning of Recognition

The implementation of the universality principle results in the necessity to recognize a foreign country's insolvency proceedings. Recognition, therefore, is something like the other side of the universality coin or the threshold for reaching out beyond the borders of the opening jurisdiction. Such recognition, however, requires trust of that foreign country's legal system, such as its adherence to the rule of law and/or the comparability of that insolvency proceeding's policy goals. Accordingly, the intensity of this trust is crucial for the method of recognition and the speed at which a decision is made.

8.1.4.2. Forms of Recognition

8.1.4.2.1. No Trust, No Recognition
The most extreme result is no trust and no recognition. This was for a long time (and still is nowadays in many regions of this world) the prevailing attitude of those jurisdictions following the territoriality principle (or the one-sided universality approach).

8.1.4.2.2. General Trust
At the other end of the spectrum is general trust of the other jurisdictions' laws, with the consequence of an automatic recognition accordingly. This is the general rule underlying, for example, the European Union Regulation.[39] It is self-evident that such an approach usually requires a rather long-lasting common tradition plus a legal or economic interrelationship. However, if the future really belongs to the universality principle, the world as a whole has to come to this stage of development. This is facilitated to a certain degree by the above mentioned endeavors of the

---

[39] Described below in 8.2.4. For the trust requirement in particular, see Christoph Paulus & Marc Udink, *European Law and Trust*, EUROFENIX, 8 (2004).

multilateral institutions like IMF, World Bank and UNCITRAL to establish generally accepted (or at least acceptable) principles and standards in the world's insolvency laws.

8.1.4.2.3. *Mid-Ground Modifications*

Between these extremes, there are common alternatives. This midground is where the modifications of the universality principle come into play.[40] A general distrust can be mitigated by offering, for example, an ancillary or parallel proceeding, as described above. Another quite common modification is to make recognition dependent on an explicit decision by a court or agency. The granting of such an "exequatur," as it is usually called, can be subject to conditions; prominent examples are reciprocity of recognition, the conviction that the foreign proceeding fulfils the domestic functions and requirements of what an insolvency proceeding is; jurisdiction of the foreign court or institution to open the proceeding in question; and / or the compliance of the foreign proceeding with the domestic public policy (*ordre public*). The consequence of granting an exequatur generally is that the foreign administrator may, all or in part, act in this jurisdiction as he may in his home-jurisdiction or, alternatively, as a domestic counterpart would be allowed to act.

8.1.4.2.4. *Speed and Efficiency of Recognition*

Speed and efficiency are decisive for the outcome of any insolvency proceeding and, thus, as a matter of fact, for trans-border cases as well. This determination is true for liquidation proceedings but all the more for those that aim for the debtor's rehabilitation. Here, speed of the proceeding and the recognition is of utmost importance for efficiency.

Seen from a theoretical point of view, one might be tempted to believe that an exequatur approach is speedier than the necessity to initiate a separate proceeding. Practice, however, shows that promptness does not (or at least not totally) depend on either one of the concepts. The requirements for the granting of an exequatur can go on forever (and through several court instances) whereas the requirements for the opening of an ancillary proceeding can be highly specified and, therefore, expeditious. Given this insight, speed depends in large part on statutory conditions for recognition that are as precise as possible. This supports the attempt

---

[40] *See supra* 8.1.1.1.

to recognize quickly the foreign proceeding in the domestic jurisdiction and, thereby, to improve the law's efficiency. Lack of clarity will often lead to expensive litigation and delay at the very moment that the court needs to get control and protect assets.[41] The Model Law's provision in articles 15–17 is drawn in just that way.

8.1.4.2.5. *Access and Assistance (Effects of Recognition)*

One of the most important benefits of the approach of provisions permitting rapid recognition is that they enable a very rapid activation of a moratorium or stay against debtor and creditor activity—that is, a freeze that protects all concerned until the court can learn the facts. This point is illustrated by the Model Law because recognition of a main proceeding triggers an immediate moratorium with the same scope as that provided under the law of the local, recognizing jurisdiction.[42]

It has already been pointed out that the effects of recognition differ according to the approach that has been chosen. The extremes are, on the one side, that the foreign administrator has no access at all to the domestic institutions and/or proceeding; everything is handled by a local procedure (be it insolvency or any other form of execution) and its authorities, who may finally hand over any collected surplus to the administrator. The extreme on the other side is the permission to the foreign administrator to act domestically in the same way as he is allowed to act in the opening jurisdiction and/or as his domestic counterpart would do under domestic law. To be sure, such an approach pre-supposes usually a high degree of compliance with and confidence in the other jurisdiction's law.

Between these extremes there are, again, various alternatives that are possible and practiced. Thus, there is the possibility to restrict the effects of a foreign proceeding to those legal acts that do not require an administrator's intervention; examples would be the interruption of a pending domestic lawsuit because of the opening of a foreign insolvency proceeding or, for the same reason, the possibility to terminate contracts that are at the time of the proceeding's opening not yet fully performed from both

---

[41] As is the case in Hong Kong. Nevertheless, the Hong Kong Law Reform Commission has rejected recommendations for incorporating the common law jurisdictional criteria into detailed statutory provisions. *See The Law Reform Commission of Hong Kong, Report on the Winding-Up Provisions of the Companies Ordinance* (July 1999), at pp. 209–210, paras 26.9 to 26.11 & p. 212, ¶¶ 26.18.to 26.23.

[42] UNCITRAL, Model Law, art. 20.

sides. If, in contrast, the foreign administrator is permitted to act, this permission can reach from granting standing before local courts to collect assets to requesting support from the local authorities for support in enforcing the administrator's powers. It should be noted that the ideal of the universality principle would ask for granting the foreign administrator as much of the home jurisdiction's power as possible.

8.1.4.2.6. *International Cooperation*

8.1.4.2.6.1. *General Meaning* This term increasingly plays an essential role in international insolvency law today; it has already been mentioned above in the context of the prevalent modifications of the universality principle.[43] However, it has a history that goes back to the introduction of the universality principle in its double-sided appearance. This is so because when a jurisdiction is willing to accept another jurisdiction's claim for universality, such acceptance is justifiably called cooperation. Thus, all that is written above about recognition is a form of support for the foreign insolvency law.

8.1.4.2.6.2. *Modern Meaning* Today the term cooperation has a more specific meaning: the most important tool for coordination is cooperation among the main actors in a proceeding, that is, among the administrators and, according to recent (and not yet generally accepted) developments in international insolvency law, the judges.[44]

Cooperation implies, *inter alia*, that under these circumstances, the relevant actors communicate with each other.[45] Thereby, they follow the goal that the debtor's insolvency case is handled in a way that is in the best interest of all parties involved. Even though these actors deal with their respective cases according to their respective domestic law, they attempt to harmonize the results of their actions. It is self-evident

---

[43] *See supra* 8.1.

[44] For cooperation of the judges *see* Jay L. Westbrook, *International Judicial Negotiation*, 38 Tex. Int'l L. Rev. 567 (2003); *idem*, *The Duty to Seek Cooperation in Multinational Insolvency Cases* in *Annual Review of Insolvency Law* 187 (J. Sarra ed., 2004); Christoph Paulus, *Judicial Cooperation in Cross-Border Insolvencies* (2006), available at: http://siteresources.worldbank.org/GILD/Resources/GJF2006 Judicial Cooperationin-Insolvency_PaulusEN.pdf.

[45] For the attempt to proceduralize such communication and to put it in line with the requirements of a fair proceeding, see the IBA "Concordat" available at http://www .ibanet.org/ aboutiba/IBA_Resolutions.cfm.

that the intensity of such cooperation varies depending on whether a reorganization proceeding or a liquidation proceeding is at stake; in the former case, there is for obvious reasons greater demand for it than in the latter, although it will fairly often be true that cooperation will add value even in liquidation—as, for example, where a corporate division has factories in more than one country and will sell for a higher amount as a unit.

One of the mostly hidden problems of cooperation is the precise definition of what is in the best interest of all parties involved. This question need not come up as long as the jurisdictions involved in the actual case follow the same understanding of what the goals of insolvency law are. However, sometimes formidable differences exist hereby in the various insolvency laws. Whereas one jurisdiction designs insolvency law as a tool to satisfy the debtor's creditors to the fullest extent possible (which implies that insolvency law is understood as a qualified law of execution),[46] another one might shape insolvency law as a way to grant a debtor the possibility for a fresh start,[47] to save enterprises[48] or as many facilities and workers as possible,[49] or (sometimes) to save certain credits given to the debtor by the state.[50] Given these differences and assuming that in a given insolvency case cooperation is required of administrators or judges from such diverging approaches, there is a need for a common definition of what should be achieved through such cooperation.

However, such harmonization of the results creates a possible further problem: if the main proceeding pursues the liquidation of the debtor's estate, does that mean that all assets of the debtor wherever located shall be liquidated even if they form in some jurisdiction a viable enterprise?[51]

---

[46] This is traditionally the approach of, for example, Austria, Germany, or Switzerland.

[47] The main representative of this approach still is the US (even after the 2005 Bankruptcy Code amendments). However, even more rigid in protecting the debtor is the current bankruptcy law of Colombia (Law 550 of December 30, 1999), which was enacted in times of—then—serious economic difficulties for the Colombian economy as a whole.

[48] See, for example, Argentina.

[49] See, for example, France.

[50] See, for example, Italy with respect to its *Amministrazione Straordinaria di Grandi Imprese in Crisi*; for this proceeding see, for instance, Angelo Castagnola and Roberto Sacchi, LA NUOVA DISCIPLINA DELLA AMMINISTRAZIONE STRAORDINARIA DELLE GRANDI IMPRESE IN STATO DI INSOLVENZA (2000).

[51] This is the understanding of, for example, the European Insolvency Regulation, art. 3, par. 3§ 2; see Manfred Balz, *The European Union Convention on Insolvency Proceedings*, 70 AM. BANKR.L.J., 485, 523 f. (1996). For criticism see Gordon Johnson, *The European Union Convention on Insolvency Proceedings: A Critique of the Conventions Corporate Rescue Paradigm*, 5 INT. INSOLV. REV. 80, 96 (1996).

Or should it rather be possible for the other—non-main—proceeding to aim for a (locally confined) rehabilitation?

Finally, other considerable problems of cooperation result from historical differences in the approaches to the exercise of judges' powers and the judges' own perceived limitations as to their role.[52] Whereas especially in the common law world the judge has always been a law maker, his continental European colleague and the ones following this model have always been more or less a "servant of the statute" or even just its "mouth-piece." To be sure, this classification is just a very rough generalization, is historical, and is no longer as accurate as in years past. However, as a general phenomenon, these differences of the traditions are strong enough to establish great reluctance towards a judicial cooperation in an essential part of the world. The Model Law has great potential importance in this regard because it specifically mandates communication and cooperation with foreign courts.[53]

This deficit, however, is particularly troublesome with respect to a new stage of cooperation that is the result of quite a recent development. In the last 15 years or so, trans-border insolvency cases have emerged, starting with the *Maxwell* case,[54] that could not be resolved by the strict adherence to the respective national laws. These cases showed a complexity and complication for which the relevant laws did not offer any constructive solutions. The escape from this situation was to set up something new: both the administrators and judges who were involved in these cases acted together in drafting what they called a protocol that was in effect nothing less than a tailor-made law for the individual case.

Once the success of this new tool was discovered, its use has grown beyond the original idea.[55] Nowadays protocols are used, *inter alia*, to bundle the world-wide unsecured creditors' efforts to investigate into the debtor's directors' failures or to shift the place for the sale of the debtor's

---

[52] For these differences see generally, *Europäische und Amerikanische Richterbilder* (A. Gouron, L. Mayali, A. Padoa Schippoa & D. Simon eds., 1996).

[53] Model Law, arts. 26–27, 29.

[54] See for example, Evan Flaschen & Ronald J. Silverman, *The Role of the Examiner as Facilitator and Harmonizer in the Maxwell Communication Corporation Insolvency*, in CURRENT DEVELOPMENTS IN INTERNATIONAL AND COMPARATIVE CORPORATE INSOLVENCY LAW, at 621 *et seq.* (Jacob Ziegel ed., 1994); Jay L. Westbrook, *The Lessons of Maxwell Communications*, 64 FORDHAM L. REV. 2531 *et seq.* (1996); Burkhard Göpfert, *In Re Maxwell Communications—ein Beispiel einer "koordinierten" Insolvenzverwaltung* in *Parallelen Verfahren*, ZZP Int 1, 269 *et seq.* (1996).

[55] Numerous protocols are accessible under: http://www.iiiglobal.org/international/protocols.html. See ALI Principles.

assets to a country where the tax laws guarantee a better surplus. However, judicial consent is crucial; if the administrators alone were to agree on such protocols without the judges' consent, the risk of legal liability is extremely high. Therefore, international efforts should be increased to find a solution that allows bridging the different historical backgrounds.[56]

8.2. *International Initiatives*

The specific problem of any trans-border insolvency case results from the fact that different jurisdictions clash not only in a particular question of law (such as an issue of the laws of contract or copyright or succession) but in a whole bundle of such questions. Suffice it to repeat what has already been said about insolvency law as a meta-level of any domestic law: it is closely enmeshed in the whole body of that law and it forms even a kind of focal point for numerous fields of business law.[57] The problems resulting therefrom—problems that in earlier days led many countries to follow the territoriality principle—can be handled by at least three different approaches, all of which involve different degrees of harmonization of national laws. The first is to reduce the complexity of domestic insolvency law by distilling the underlying fundamental principles and, thereby, to encourage present and future legislators to follow a certain path of legal reform leading to the optimal result, with a consequent convergence of domestic laws.[58] This is more or less the approach of the multilateral institutions such as the IMF,[59] World Bank,[60] and UNCITRAL[61] in their respective texts. They serve, *inter alia*, to a certain degree as model for some regional efforts.[62]

---

[56] For this see Jay L. Westbrook, *International Judicial Negotiation, supra* note 44; for a guide as to how judge-to-judge communication can be established *see* http://www .iiiglobal.org/international/guidelines.html (available in various languages).

[57] As to the latter observation see Christoph Paulus, *Verbindungslinien des Modernen Insolvenzrechts*, 49 Zeitschrift Für Wirtschaftsrecht, 2189 *et seq.* (2000).

[58] *See infra* 8.3.

[59] *Orderly & Effective Insolvency Procedures*, (1999); available at: http://www.imf.org/ external/pubs/ft/orderly/index.htm.

[60] *Revised Principles on Insolvency and Creditor Rights Systems*, (Draft 2005); available at: http://www.worldbank.org/WBSITE/EXTERNAL/TOPICS/LAWANDJUSTICE/ GILD/0,,contentMDK:20774193~pagePK:64065425~piPK:162156~theSitePK:215006, 00.html.

[61] *Legislative Guide on Insolvency Law*, (2004); available at: http://www.uncitral.org/ pdf/ english/texts/insolven/05-80722_Ebook.pdf.

[62] See for example, *The General Commentary to the Principles of European Insolvency Law* (W. McBryde, A. Flessner & S. Kortmann, eds., Kluwer 2003).

The two other approaches are: (1) drafting a model law focused on procedure and cooperation that draws its strength from the authority of its author. This is the path of the UNCITRAL Model Law on International Insolvency;[63] or (2) reducing the complexity and multiplicity of the world's existing international insolvency laws by creating bigger units (regions) that share a common international insolvency law. This is what has been done by some South American States, by the European Union, and in Africa by OHADA.[64] A first step has been taken by the NAFTA states as well.

8.2.1. UNCITRAL Model Law on Cross-Border Insolvency

8.2.1.1. A Global Impact

In 1997, UNCITRAL adopted a Model Law on Cross-Border Insolvency that had been drafted by the Commission in close cooperation with INSOL and the IBA.[65] By definition, the model law has no binding force but tries to convince local (national as well as regional)[66] legislators by its quality and the authority of its authorship. In contrast to the regional attempts at harmonization,[67] the immediate impact of the model law is a global one. The Model Law is designed in such a way that it can be adopted without greater efforts by any legislator of this world (thus, bridging, *inter alia*, the dichotomy of Common Law and Civil Law), whereas the regional initiatives are quite deeply rooted into their specific surroundings in that they concentrate primarily (or even exclusively) on their inner relationships. Therefore, they hardly can be taken on without

---

[63] See *infra* 8.2.1 on the UNCITRAL model law.

[64] *See infra* 8.2.1.1, 8.2.1.2, 8.2.1.3, 8.2.1.4. For a similar recommendation concerning the region of Southern Africa *see* David Ailola, *Recognition of foreign proceedings, orders and officials in insolvency in Southern Africa: a call for a regional convention*, COMP. AND INT'L L.J. S. AFR., 54 *et seq.* (1999).

[65] For a discussion of the Model Law see especially Westbrook, *Multinational Enterprises in General Default, supra* note 21, at part III; K. Wimmer, *Die UNCITRAL-Modellbestimmungen über grenzüberschreitende Insolvenzverfahren*, in Zeitschrift für Wirtschaftsrecht 2220 *et seq.* (1997),; Claudia Tobler, *Managing Failure in the New Global Economy* The UNCITRAL Model Law on Cross-Border Insolvency, 22 B.C. INT'L & COMP. L. REV., 383 *et seq.* (1999): Bob Wessels, *Will UNCITRAL Bring Changes to Insolvency Proceedings Outside the USA and Great Britain? It Certainly Will!*, 3 Int. Corporate Rescue 200 *et seq.* (2006).

[66] The latter point is important. The regions described in 8.2.2, 8.2.3, 8.2.4, 8.2.5 below could use the model law as their international insolvency law insofar as the model law works on a higher level than these regional initiatives.

[67] Described in 8.2.1.1, 8.2.1.2, 8.2.1.3, 8.2.1.4 below.

many adaptations, corrections, and changes. However, this observation unveils a highly important development in the present cross-border insolvency law world: in a complementary way, regions are building on a closer network within these regions and the model law provides (possibly) for their connection. In summary terms, the regional initiatives are focused on the relations among nations in the region whereas the model law focuses outward to nations generally.

The global impact of the model law on cross-border insolvency has become more and more visible. Although at the outset there was not a "big run" on the national enactment of the model law—most countries adopted a wait-and-see attitude—the model law nevertheless influenced the national theoretical discussions right from its publication. And those discussions eventually did lead to enactment, with adoption in Australia (2008), British Virgin Islands; overseas territory of the United Kingdom of Great Britain and Northern Ireland (2005), Colombia (2006), Eritrea (1998), Great Britain (2006), Japan (2000), Mexico (2000), Montenegro (2002), New Zealand (2006), Poland (2003), Republic of Korea (2006), Romania (2003), Serbia (2004), South Africa (2000), and United States of America (2005). Various Asian countries are about to follow.[68]

8.2.1.2. The Basic Ideas

According to Article 1, the Model Law shall apply in any collective judicial or administrative proceeding in a foreign state, including an interim proceeding, for the purpose of reorganization or liquidation. The insolvencies of banks, insurance companies, or other institutions can be excluded from the Model Law's applicability if they are dealt with in special legislation. The Model Law is drafted on the assumption of the following considerations: first, there is just one main proceeding; second, the recognition of a foreign proceeding does not restrict the right to initiate a domestic proceeding; third, a domestic proceeding can be given local priority against the foreign proceeding, although not necessarily

---

[68] *See* http://www.uncitral.org/uncitral/en/uncitral_texts/insolvency/1997Model_status.html. *See also* Kazuhiko Yamamoto, *New Japanese Legislation on Cross-Border Insolvency—As Compared with the UNCITRAL Model Law*, 43 JAPANESE ANN. of INT. LAW, 83 et seq. (2000). For the peculiarities in South Africa, see Alistair Smith & Andre Boraine, *Crossing Borders into South African Insolvency Law: From the Roman-Dutch Jurists to the UNCITRAL Model Law*, AM. BANKR. INST. L. REV. 135 et seq. (2002).

so; whenever there are two or more proceedings pending they shall be coordinated by means of cooperation; fourth, such coordination may encompass support for the foreign administrator, provided that assets are at stake that "belong" to the foreign proceeding's estate; fifth, creditors are allowed to lodge their claims in any one of the proceedings, but their dividend in one proceeding will be recognized in another one; sixth, the court may turn over local assets for distribution in the main proceeding; and seventh, a surplus in a non-main proceeding shall be handed over to the main proceeding.

8.2.1.3. *Universality Principle*

Building on these premises, the Model Law approaches the universality principle by allowing several proceedings under the lead of one main proceeding. According to Article 2, this is the proceeding in that state "where the debtor has the center of its main interests." In contrast, a foreign non-main proceeding is in a state "where the debtor has an establishment," meaning any place where the debtor carries out a non-transitory economic activity with human means and goods or services. The goal of the Model Law, according to Article 1, is to supply assistance for any of these foreign proceedings. Article 6, however, has the general proviso that no court is required to grant such assistance where the action in question would be manifestly contrary to the public policy (*ordre public*) of this state.

(a) As a general rule, Chapter II of the Model Law, pursuant to Article 9, entitles a foreign representative to apply directly to a court in this state; thereby, the otherwise indispensable diplomatic support is eliminated. Thus, a foreign representative is in the position to file a petition to open a (parallel) proceeding in this state, pursuant to Article 11.

(b) A foreign proceeding, however, will not be recognized automatically. The application of a foreign representative shall be based on, for example, "a certified copy of the decision commencing the foreign proceeding and appointing the foreign representative" whereby a translation of the respective documents may be requested. If these requirements are met, the recognition (exequatur) shall be granted if the domestic court comes to the conclusion that within the meaning of Article 2: (a) the foreign proceeding is a (main or non-main) insolvency proceeding; and (b) the person applying for recognition is a proper representative. Since the recognition procedure may take some time, despite the aids to expedition in Articles 15–17, Article 19 provides for possible interim relief that may granted in order to protect the debtor's assets or the creditors' interests.

(c) The effects of such recognition are, *inter alia*, that the foreign representative is entitled to participate in the domestic proceedings;[69] the foreign creditors will be notified whenever necessary according to the domestic law;[70] and the foreign representative has standing pursuant to Article 23, to initiate a lawsuit before the local courts regarding his avoidance powers. The main effect, however, is put down in Article 20: subject to the law of the recognizing state, the "commencement or continuation of individual actions or individual proceedings concerning the debtor's assets, rights, obligations, or liabilities is stayed; execution against the debtor's assets is stayed; and the right to transfer, encumber or otherwise dispose of any assets of the debtor is suspended." This adds up to a moratorium that is, in terms of efficiency, particularly essential for any rescue attempt, especially if it is granted promptly. Article 21 lists further relief that may be granted upon the representative's request, including gathering information and empowering the foreign administrator to administer the local assets or to turn over those assets for distribution through the main proceeding.

(d) In Chapter IV, the Model Law describes in more detail how the coordination and cooperation of the multiple proceedings shall be performed. It is especially noteworthy that it entitles not just the representatives but also the judges to communicate with each other directly, without any diplomatic intermediaries.[71]

8.2.1.4. *Incompleteness of the Model Law*

The Model Law contains necessarily only partial and rather abstract provisions. This is the inescapable consequence of its global approach. Therefore, it is self-evident that it cannot go too deeply into details and that important features are just left aside. However, this may add some attractiveness to it since it leaves the interested countries much space to fill the gaps individually. In any case it is a grand step forward in

---

[69] *See* UNCITRAL Model Law at Art. 12.
[70] *See id.*, Art. 14.
[71] *See id.*, Art. 25. *See, e.g.*, ALI Principles, Appendix B.

the development of international insolvency law that such a Model Law has been accepted at all by the world's people represented by the United Nations.

8.2.2. *Latin American States*

As early as 1889 some Latin American states entered into a Treaty that is called the "Montevideo Treaty on Commercial International Law;" the ratifying states were Argentina, Bolivia, Colombia, Paraguay, Peru, and Uruguay. This treaty was updated in 1940 but was then ratified only by three states: Argentina, Paraguay, and Uruguay. Independently, and therefore additionally, another treaty with regulations concerning cross-border insolvency law—called the Bustamante Code from 1928[72]—was entered into by more states: Brazil, Bolivia, Chile, Costa Rica, Cuba, Dominican Republic, El Salvador, Ecuador, Guatemala, Haiti, Honduras, Nicaragua, Panama, Peru, and Venezuela. These lists reveal that there are only few overlapping memberships. Moreover, the development of the Montevideo Treaty shows a tendency of diminishing acceptance. Finally, as remarkable as it is that these countries have developed treaties on this subject at a time when other countries did not even think of the possibility—let alone the need—for this kind of cooperation, the date of their origin makes clear that they, being "children of their time," are not aligned with the needs of modern insolvency law in that they concentrate solely on liquidation proceedings.

8.2.2.1. *Contents*

(a) The Montevideo Treaty of 1889 deals with "Bankruptcies" in Articles 35–48. This title of the treaty is applicable when a debtor has assets not just in one jurisdiction but also abroad. Competence to commence a proceeding is with the court where the debtor has its "commercial domicile."[73] Once such a proceeding has been opened it shall have universal effect; it does not, however, become totally clear from the text's wording how the recognition in the other member states is supposed to work. Article 37 states, only with respect to provisional remedies in the opening jurisdiction, that they shall be enforceable in the other states as well; and Article 45 provides that the administrator's authority will be recognized.

---

[72] The Havana Convention on Private International Law, February 20, 1928.
[73] See art. 35 of the Montevideo Treaty of 1889.

There are modifications to this universalistic approach. They concern at first certain secured creditors as well as priority creditors and allow them the realization of their rights even though the assets in question are located in another jurisdiction or have been transferred thereto.[74] Second, Article 39 permits local creditors to initiate a parallel proceeding restricted in its applicability to the respective member state (territoriality principle) where the debtor has one "economically autonomous business" (out of at least two).[75] If there is a surplus in any one of the multiple proceedings after the distribution of proceeds, it has to be handed over to the other ongoing proceedings.

(b) The updated Montevideo Treaty from 1940 rephrases the predecessor treaty without adding substantially[76] new regulations.

(c) Compared with these treaties, the Bustamante Code impresses with more clarity and precision. Chapter I of Title IX of the Convention is titled "Unity of Bankruptcy or Insolvency." Accordingly, Article 414 declares that the opening of a proceeding encompasses all assets of the debtor wherever located within the realm of the contracting states. The universality principle underlying this approach is specified in Article 416 *et seq.*; thus, there is automatic recognition with respect to the administrator's powers,[77] and the opening decision is, pursuant to Article 417, to be deemed *res judicata* also in the other contracting states—provided that contingent publicity requirements, set out in Article 416, have been fulfilled in the other states. The out-reaching effect of such universalistic proceeding is extended also to agreements between debtor and creditors as well as "the rehabilitation of the bankrupt."[78]

The Code also arranges exceptions to the universality approach. Article 415 allows parallel proceedings in the other contracting states if the debtor has "in more than one contracting State various commercial establishments entirely separate economically." Article 420 declares the *lex rei sitae* applicable for certain rights *in rem*—irrespective of the insolvency proceeding that has been opened in another contracting state and that has the above-mentioned extraterritorial effect.

---

[74] *See id.*, arts. 43 and 44.

[75] *See id.*, art. 36.

[76] There is, for example, an extension of the treaty's applicability to related proceedings such as judicial liquidations, suspension of payments, and so on.

[77] *See supra* note 72, art. 418.

[78] *See id.*, arts. 421 and 422.

8.2.2.2. *Deficiencies*

Seen from a perspective as of today, the omissions and deficiencies are obvious: all three sets of rules concentrate on a liquidation proceeding; they neglect the quite fundamental insolvency principle of equal treatment of creditors but rather care explicitly for the protection of local creditors; and they coordinate the parallel proceedings in an insufficient way.[79] With respect to the Montevideo Treaties, it might be added that they lack the necessary legislative clarity to limit differing interpretations in different member states. Nevertheless, it should be emphasized once more that the mere fact of the existence of such early international agreements is noteworthy and that they already apply a number of features that are described as the modern standard.

8.2.3. *Nordic European States*

In 1933, Denmark, Finland, Iceland, Norway, and Sweden signed an agreement, called "Nordic Bankruptcy Convention,"[80] that forms the basis for insolvency proceedings that are commenced in one of the member states and whose estates comprise assets situated in more than one of the member states.[81] With its 17 articles it is a remarkably short body of law whose effectiveness for now more than 70 years has demonstrated the close ties and the common ground of the Scandinavian countries.

8.2.3.1. *Contents*

The Convention is based on the principle of a modified universality. Any insolvency proceeding within a member state is automatically recognized in all other member states; no exequatur is necessary or admissible. This

---

[79] Article 41 of the Montevideo Treaty excludes explicitly a judicial cooperation.

[80] Available at: http://www.iiiglobal.org/international/treaties/nordic_treaties.pdf; for a discussion see Michael Bogdan, *International Bankruptcy Law in Scandinavia*, 34 Int'l & Comp. L.Q. 49, 84 ff. (1985); Ian Fletcher, INSOLVENCY IN PRIVATE INTERNATIONAL LAW (2d ed. 2005), p. 290; C.H. Parment, *The Nordic Bankruptcy Convention—An Introduction*, available at http://www.iiiglobal.org/country/netherlands/Nordic_Bankruptcy.pdf.

[81] Certain restrictions apply with respect to Sweden and Finland after the enactment of the European Insolvency Regulation; see, for example, Odd Swarting & Ulrika Malmberg Livijn, *The European Council Regulation of 29 May 2000 on Insolvency Proceedings— the First Year From a Swedish Perspective* (2000), available at http://www.iiiglobal.org/country/netherlands/ Nordic_Bankruptcy.pdf.

is true both for liquidation and for composition proceedings.[82] The out-reaching effect comprises, *inter alia*, the seizure of property abroad as well as the automatic stay; as a general rule of thumb, the insolvency law of the opening state (*lex concursus*)[83] is applicable throughout the area covered by the territory of the member states.[84] However, primarily in order to protect the interests of the domestic creditors, many exceptions are provided for those assets situated in a member state where the insolvency proceeding has not been opened, such as those in Article 7.

It is left to the member states to determine the criteria for opening a proceeding. However, Article 13 influences this free choice insofar as it excludes from the Convention's applicability all those proceedings that are not based on the ground of the debtor's residence or registered office.[85] With respect to privileged claims, Articles 1, 7, and 8 present a rather complicated (albeit apparently functioning) diagram that dis-tinguishes between privileged claims against particular assets—that is, primarily secured claims—and those of a general nature. With respect to the latter category, a further distinction is drawn between tax claims and other privileged claims such as labor related ones. Whereas the for-mer may receive satisfaction only out of the sale of assets located in the respective member state, the authorities of which do have such claim, the other privileged creditors are entitled to their privileged satisfaction out of all assets wherever situated.

8.2.3.2. *Achievements and Deficiencies*

Despite its age, the Convention is a remarkably modern piece of leg-islation. In abstaining from almost any substantive rules, it proved to be sufficiently flexible. Further flexibility arises from its broad coverage, extending to both liquidation and reorganization proceedings. However, the Convention governs proceedings exclusively within its member states without the slightest indication as to how to proceed in cases where other jurisdictions might be involved. Like the European Union Regulation,

---

[82] *See* Nordic Bankruptcy Convention, art. 10 par.2.

[83] This includes the avoidance powers; but art. 9 excludes them from the rules about contracts that have not yet been fully performed by both parties as of the opening of the case.

[84] *See supra* n. 127, art. 1.

[85] The main alternative would be the mere presence of assets in the opening state; for this approach see Bogdan, *supra* n. 80, at 54 f.

described in the following section, the Convention creates a kind of artificial insular unit (a territory on a somewhat higher level) that in an increasing number of instances is bound to fail in correspondence with the economic realities.

The almost complete omission of substantive rules is a strong indication for the mutual trust of the member states in the soundness of their respective statutes. Thus, even though the Convention seems to be working smoothly and efficiently, it can serve as a model only to a limited degree as there are not too many regions on this globe of a comparable intense cross-relationship. The rather complicated rules about the treatment of privileged claims, for example, would under other conditions very likely lead to problems that could easily undermine the applicability of such Treaty.

8.2.4. *European Union Regulation on Cross-Border Insolvency*

Among the more recent endeavors, the European Union Regulation[86] has exercised quite intense influence on other efforts at reform, including the Model Law.

8.2.4.1. *Basic Elements*

The European Union Regulation is a good example of a quite common sort of cherry picking from the above-mentioned fundamental issues. Like the Latin American Treaties, it contains elements of territoriality and universality as well as those of unity and multiplicity, and it also provides for cooperation and coordination of the parallel proceedings. It is to be applied to all collective insolvency proceedings (listed in an Annex to the Regulation) with the exception of insolvency proceedings concerning insurance undertakings, credit institutions, and certain investment undertakings.[87] It entered into force on May

---

[86] For a profound discussion of its legislative history and its contents see Balz, *supra* note 51, at 485 et seq. Moreover, see Gabriel Moss, Ian Fletcher & Stuart Isaacs, THE EC REGULATION ON INSOLVENCY PROCEEDINGS, (2002): Miguel Virgòs & Francisco Garcimartín, THE EUROPEAN INSOLVENCY REGULATION: LAW AND PRACTICE, (2004); Paul Omar, EUROPEAN INSOLVENCY LAW, (2004); Christoph Paulus, EUROPÄISCHE IN-SOLVENZVERORDNUNG, (2006); Bob Wessels, INTERNATIONAL INSOLVENCY LAW, (2006), p. 263 et seq.

[87] For these institutions, there exist special Directives.

31, 2002;[88] it needs no intermediary legislative adoption steps from the member states—the Regulation is directly applicable.

8.2.4.2. *Universality Principle*

The Regulation's starting point is the ideal of a unitary proceeding with a universalistic approach. It tries to achieve this goal by three sets of rulings.[89]

(a) First, in Article 3(1), the Regulation grants jurisdiction to open a main proceeding to that court where the debtor's center of its main interests is situated.[90] This jurisdiction is binding for all member states and cannot be overridden. If, however, two states or courts claim to have such jurisdiction, the main proceeding shall be under that law where the first petition has been filed.[91]

(b) Second, once a proceeding has been opened it will automatically be recognized in all member states; there are no further requirements. The only admissible objection according to Article 26 is that the recognition results in a violation of the domestic *ordre public*. This automatic recognition means that the judgment opening the main proceeding shall "produce the same effects in any other Member State as under the law of the State of the opening of the proceeding unless the Regulation provides otherwise."[92] Thus, if an insolvency proceeding has been opened for a private consumer in, for example, Austria, this proceeding will automatically be recognized in France or Belgium irrespective of the fact that these countries' insolvency laws are applicable only to merchants and legal entities and, therefore, not applicable to other individuals' insolvencies. This means that an administrator may generally act in all member states as he may do in his "home country" and under that insolvency law.

---

[88] As to preceding attempts to reach common ground in international insolvency law cf. Harry Rajak, *European Cross Border Insolvency Developments*, EUROPEAN CORPORATE INSOLVENCY LAW: A PRACTICAL GUIDE (Rajak et al. eds., 1995), p. 3 et seq.

[89] *See* Christoph Paulus, *A Theoretical Approach to Cooperation in Transnational Insolvencies: A European Perspective*, 11 EUR. BUS. L. REV. 435 et seq. (2000).

[90] For the determination of this center see European Court of Justice in its Eurofood decision (*see supra* note 34).

[91] *See* Recital 20 of the Regulation.

[92] *See id.*, art. 17.

(c) Third, according to Article 4 "the law of the State of the opening of proceeding shall determine the conditions for the opening of those proceedings, their conduct and their closure." The second paragraph of this article contains a rather elaborate and still not exclusive list of what is to be seen as belonging to the *lex concursus*: for example, that debtors can be subjected to an insolvency proceeding; that assets form part of the estate; the respective powers of both administrator and debtor; the effect of the proceeding's opening on current contracts of the debtor; the admissible claims to be lodged against the debtor's estate; the ranking of claims; the creditors' rights after the closure of the proceeding; and so on.

8.2.4.3. *Restrictions of the Universality Principle*

What has been described so far is a remarkably close approximation to the universality and unitary principle. However, even though the Regulation's Europe is an area with a strong and rather long-lasting common history, a highly interrelated economy, and a common legal root (Roman law),[93] it is not yet ready for such a purist approach. Therefore, the Regulation contains mainly two sets of provisions that bring the ideal back to political reality.

(a) First, there is the possibility to open parallel proceedings. This is dependent on the existence of an establishment in that member state— establishment meaning "any place of operations where the debtor carries out a non-transitory economic activity with human means and goods."[94] Such parallel proceedings are dealt with under the domestic insolvency law. They follow a strict territorialistic approach, that is, neither the main proceeding may reach into this member state nor may this state extend its actions or effects beyond its borders. In order to mitigate the effects of this breach with the universality principle, Article 31 provides for a cooperation duty of the respective administrators but fails to include the respective judges as well.

(b) Second, partly because of the enormous differences in their respective laws, and partly due to the wish to protect domestic creditors, the Regula-

---

[93] This is true also for England; *see* Reinhard Zimmermann, THE LAW OF OBLIGA-TIONS—ROMAN FOUNDATIONS OF THE CIVILIAN TRADITION (1996); Reinhard Zimmermann, ROMAN LAW, CONTEMPORARY LAW, EUROPEAN LAW: THE CIVILIAN TRADITION TODAY (2001).

[94] EU Regulation, Art. 2.

tion lists a number of exceptions to the applicability of the *lex concursus*.[95]
Probably the most important exception is found in Article 5, which states
that the opening of an insolvency proceeding "shall not affect the rights
in rem of creditors or third parties in respect of tangible or intangible,
moveable or immoveable assets belonging to the debtor that are situated
within the territory of another Member State at the time of the opening of
the proceedings." In light of the well-known fact that many debtor's assets
are subject to such rights *in rem* and that primarily security rights tend
to occupy most of the debtor's assets without leaving very much for the
common creditors, this is a fundamental restriction of the *lex concursus*
concept.

Other exceptions refer to employment contracts or contracts relating
to immovables, to the right of setoff, to payment systems and financial
markets, and so on. Even though Article 4 has in its long list also the
applicability of the opening state's avoidance powers, this *lex fori concursus* becomes softened by Article 13: if the person in question is able to
prove that "the said act is subject to the law of a Member State other than
the State of the opening of proceedings, and that law does not allow any
means of challenging that act in the relevant case," then the action (or
transaction) in question is avoidance-proof. However, the effect may be
to make transactions unavoidable that would be avoided by the law of
each of the relevant countries because of the need to satisfy the differing
requirements of both. To that extent, an important insolvency policy may
be undermined.

8.2.4.4. *Deficiencies of the Regulation*

(a) The Regulation has a number of deficiencies. Taking into account the
newest development of international cooperation, as described above, it
is surprising that Article 31 addresses only the administrators as parties
to the mutual cooperation and information duty, leaving the judges aside.
The historical reasons for such an omission have already been addressed
supra; but it would have been time to dare a new step.

(b) Another lacuna in the Regulation is its complete silence about matters
of highest practical importance, namely group insolvencies. To be sure,
this is probably, at least for the time being, the most complex and difficult

---

[95] *See id.*, arts. 5–14.

problem in international insolvency law at all and a commonly accepted solution is not yet in sight.[96] The Regulation however, does not even provide for a joint administration or the pulling together of parallel proceedings. Instead, it explicitly states in Article 3(3) that any secondary proceeding has to be a liquidation proceeding; as almost any trans-border insolvency cases of some significance plainly demonstrate, such an inflexible order is counter productive in cases where a complete or partial reorganization appears to be feasible.

(c) Another deficiency of the Regulation is its complete neglect of the world outside its member states. There is no indication as to how cases shall be treated with respect to non-EU member states. It is left to each member state to decide on these problems so that the respective international insolvency laws of each of these members remain of great importance. It is for this reason that the Regulation excites the impression that it creates, irrespective of its internationality, something like a territoriality principle on a larger, European scale.

8.2.5. American Law Institute's Transnational Insolvency Project

8.2.5.1. The Approach

In May 2000, the American Law Institute approved a project called *American Law Institute, Transnational Insolvency Project, Principles of Cooperation in Transnational Insolvency Cases Among the Members of the North American Free Trade Agreement*.[97] After the European Union Regulation, this is a further regional step forward to a closer cooperation and harmonization of a number of trans-border insolvency laws. However, unlike the EU Regulation these Principles are just recommendations, although backed by the prestige of the initiating institution.[98]

This project is remarkable for several reasons, one being the way the members of the project proceeded: each one of the three involved countries—the United States, Canada, and Mexico—appointed reporters

---

[96] However, UNCITRAL started to work on this topic in late 2006.

[97] Available at: http://www.ali.org, under "ALI Projects online."

[98] For an authoritative report about the process and the contents *see* Jay Lawrence Westbrook, *Managing Defaulting Multinationals Within NAFTA* in FOUNDATION AND PERSPECTIVES OF INTERNATIONAL LAW 465–479 (2001).

who had, in a first step, to produce statements of their respective insolvency laws and, after having distributed them to the others, to comment on the statements of the other two countries involved. This enabled the reporters to familiarize themselves with, *inter alia*, the laws of the other countries. On this basis, the reporters then produced in a second step a statement with a set of agreed principles governing multinational insolvency cases that would offer useful approaches to managing such cases.

It is quite obvious that such a project becomes all the more complicated the more countries or insolvency laws, respectively, are involved. However, if there are just three as in the present case, the problem of different legal traditions (common law and continental law) is obviously surmountable.

8.2.5.2. *Basic Considerations*

The statement is based on three central ideas that form its fundament. First, that the law of these three NAFTA countries reflects fundamentally similar purposes despite their considerable dogmatic and methodological differences. Second, the ideal is to have a unified proceeding with a universalistic approach; this would be the best way to serve fully the purposes of insolvency law. Third, since this ideal is at the time being not yet achievable, the second best solution is to have a close co-operation between the stakeholders of the national proceedings in order to get as close as possible to the result of the ideal unitary proceedings, called "modified universalism." The statement explicitly identifies the benefits of that ideal: namely, maximizing the value of the enterprise and its assets; providing equality of treatment for creditors and other interested parties with similar legal rights; preventing and undoing fraud; and providing commercially predictable results and transparent legal procedures.

8.2.5.3. *Universality Principle*

Between the NAFTA countries, there is a long-lasting tradition of economic and legal cooperation that includes mutual recognition of the other countries' insolvency cases.

(a) Even though the statement does not grant an automatic recognition, but follows the UNCITRAL Model Law approach of an exequatur, it comes in fact to a virtually automatic result because of speedy issuance of recognition.[99] In addition, a moratorium (or a stay on any creditors' actions) may be granted.

(b) One of the consequences of the recognition is that the foreign administrator has direct access to the local courts, including the right of the foreign administrator to intervene in civil actions pending by or against the debtor and the right to initiate such civil actions or insolvency proceedings. If there is more than one proceeding, the Principles provide for communication between administrators and courts. In an annex it is recommended, *inter alia*, to make use of modern multi-media devices for such communication. The administrators are also encouraged to seek agreements of cooperation, that is, protocols. Unlike the European Union Regulation, the Principles do not eliminate the choice of how a secondary proceeding shall be dealt with if the main proceeding strives for the debtor's reorganization. Instead, it recommends that in the non-main proceeding everything should be attempted to assist the efforts of the main proceeding.

(c) With respect to group insolvencies, Principles 23 and 24 try to encourage coordination and cooperation among proceedings involving affiliated debtors to the maximum extent consistent with honoring the corporate form under applicable law.

(d) Principles 26 and 27 make a plan adopted in a main proceeding binding on all creditors who participated in the proceeding or who were subject to its jurisdiction, even if they dissented from the plan.

(e) Finally, the Principles present recommendations to the legislators of the three countries that state how further improvements could be achieved in the trans-border insolvency field. Most importantly, they refer to a desirable harmonization of the different priority systems among the three countries.

---

[99] Adoption of the Model Law, which the Principles recommend, largely moots this point. It has been adopted in Mexico and the United States and will become effective in Canada in the near future.

8.2.6. *OHADA*

8.2.6.1. *The Project*

In 1997, 16 African states founded an organization for the harmonization of their commercial laws, called *Organisation pour l'harmonisation en Afrique du droit des affaires* or OHADA,[100] that has developed a number of common legislative acts. One of them is the Uniform Act on Collective Proceedings for Wiping off Debts from 1998, which deals in Part VI (Sections 247–256) with International Collective Proceedings. Its approach is also that of one proceeding at the place where the debtor has its main place of business (*principal établissement*) or where the corporate body is registered.[101] However, this unitary proceeding can be subdivided into several in any other member state. If this happens, coordination shall be guaranteed by a mutual information duty of the administrators.

8.2.6.2. *Coordination of Several Proceedings*

Article 251 distinguishes between principal and secondary collective proceedings; the latter ones are applicable where the debtor does *not* have its main place of business or where the corporate body does *not* have its registered office. This distinction is important insofar as the administrators of any secondary proceeding shall enable the administrator of the principal proceeding to present proposals about the way to deal with the debtor's assets in that secondary proceeding (liquidation or reorganization).[102] In addition, the closure of a secondary proceeding shall be done only with the consent of the principal administrator's consent pursuant to Article 254.

8.2.6.3. *Recognition and its Consequences*

The opening or closure of a collective proceeding in one of the contracting states is in any other of the contracting states to be treated as a *res*

---

[100] For details see http://www.ohada.com/traite.php; *see also*, Boris Martor et al., Business Law in Africa—OHADA and the Harmonization Process (2d ed. 2007); in particular, on the international insolvency rules, see Filiga Michel Sawadogo, *OHADA—Droit des Enterprises en Difficulté*, 359 *et seq.* (2002).

[101] *See* Uniform Act on Collective Proceedings for Wiping off Debts, art. 251.

[102] *See id.*, art. 252.

judicata,[103] once the competent court's decision has become irrevocable.[104] Thus, there is a quasi-automatic recognition that has as the following consequences:

a. It does not bar the commencement of another collective proceeding in another contracting state.[105] This possibility leads to the aforementioned plurality of proceedings.

b. The administrator, pursuant to Article 249, if appointed by the competent court, has in all contracting states the powers conferred on him by the Uniform Act as long as no other collective proceeding has been commenced in that state.

c. If it comes to such plurality of proceedings, Article 252 provides that the administrators shall exchange all necessary information about their proceedings that might be useful for the other ones, especially the statement of production and verification of claims and measures aimed at completing the proceedings for which they are appointed.

d. The administrators of any proceeding (as well as any creditor) are entitled to lodge the claims of "their" proceeding at any other proceeding as well. In that case, however, it is to be guaranteed that creditors of the same rank do get an equal share.[106]

8.2.6.4. *Incompleteness of the Act*

The rules are not very detailed[107] even though the Uniform Act shares the main features of modern trans-border insolvency legislation, namely the division of parallel proceedings into one main and one or more secondary proceedings as well as automatic recognition in combination with mutual information duties. However, here (like in the European Union Regulation) this duty is confined to the administrators and, thereby, excludes the judges. However, in the Act the way in which the proceedings are to be harmonized is regulated in a fairly flexible manner by giving the administrator of the main proceeding the decisive word.

However, what is missing here as in the two other aforementioned regional harmonization attempts is a showing of how these regions could one day possibly grow together. For the Act, as for the European Union Regulation, the adoption of the UNCITRAL Model Law could serve as

---

[103] *See id.*, art. 247.
[104] *See id.*, art. 251.
[105] *See id.*
[106] *See id.*, arts. 253 and 255. *See also* art. 250, that contains a hotch-pot rule.
[107] *See* Sawadogo, *supra* note 100, at 372.

the connecting link. A second best alternative would be to incorporate third countries or regions by means of treaties into the applicability scope of the regional initiative.

8.3. *Possible Future Developments*

Even though the terminology of international insolvency law does not, strictly speaking, cover this development, the efforts of the multilateral institutions (in particular the IMF, World Bank, UNCITRAL) in creating standardized principles of worldwide applicable insolvency laws is leading already to a certain convergence of the insolvency laws in this world. One striking example makes the point: whereas the insolvency law of the United States developed reorganization procedures over a period of more than 100 years without leading to any significant number of imitators, the development of effective, formal reorganization regimes is nowadays becoming the centerpiece of law reform efforts. These efforts have been at the heart of most major corporate insolvency law reforms over the last decade—not least due to the fact that all those multilaterals' insolvency guides demonstrate a strong favor towards this type of proceeding.[108]

This global convergence among regional approaches may foster greater acceptance (or acceptability) of cross-border cooperation. Such dual action might strike a balance between globalization and localism respectively. Be that as it may, it is a fair guess that the law of cross-border insolvencies will increase in importance as the economic world grows more and more integrated.

Irrespective of these observations or speculations, one development must be observed with great attention and concern. As a consequence of the increasing economic globalization, some of the bigger enterprises might feel the wish (or need) to have insolvency laws not applied to them. One example is the Cape Town Protocol as developed by UNIDROIT[109] that offers the possibility to provide certain industries with a worldwide applicable super-priority under any national insolvency law. Even though these existing Protocols currently have only a strictly limited range of applicability, it seems to be a fair assumption that any successful attempt

---

[108] *See* for example, Thomas Felsberg, Steven Kargman, & Andrea Acerbi, *Brazil overhauls restructuring regime*, Int'l Fin. L. Rev. 40 (Jan. 2006).

[109] *See* http://www.unidroit.org/english/conventions/mobile-equipment/main.htm# NR1.

to opt out of regular insolvency regimes nurtures the temptation of other industries or institutions to seek an analogous privilege. If such arrangements spread, insolvency law would apply only for small creditors and those who do not have a respective lobby at their disposal. There is a trend in this direction already in the United States. Needless to say, the present authors believe this development has to be tamed.[110]

---

[110] *See* Christoph Paulus, *The Global Insolvency Law and the Role of Multinational Institutions*, 33 BROOK. J. INT. L. 755 (2007). Elsewhere in globally applicable treaties and agreements one finds similar trumping of national laws; for example, art. 54 of the Convention on the Settlement of Investment Disputes between States and Nationals of Other States (ICSID) provides for an award that has to be recognized by all states; for this see Guiliana Cane, *Enforcement of ICSID Awards: Revolutionary or Ineffective?* 15 AM. REV. OF INT. ARB., 439 ff. (2006).

BIBLIOGRAPHY

1. Articles

David A. Ailola, *Recognition of Foreign Proceedings, Orders and Officials in Insolvency in Southern Africa: A Call for a Regional Convention*, 32 Comp. & Int'l L. J. S. Afr. 54 (1999).

John Armour & Simon Deakin, *Norms in Private Insolvency Procedure: The "London Approach" to the Resolution of Financial Distress* (ESRC Ctr. for Bus. Research, Univ. of Cambridge Working Paper No. 173, 2000).

Douglas W. Arner, et al., *Property Rights, Collateral, Creditor Rights and Insolvency in East Asia*, 42 Tex. Int'l L. J. 515 (2007).

Douglas W. Arner, Charles D. Booth, Berry F.C. Hsu, Paul Lejot, Qiao Liu & Frederick Pretorius, *Property Rights, Collateral and Creditor Rights in East Asia*, in East Asian Finance: Selected Issues Part III.B (Ismail Dalla ed., World Bank 2006).

Douglas G. Baird, *Loss Distribution, Forum Shopping, and Bankruptcy: A Reply to Warren*, 54 U. Chi. L. Rev. 815 (1987).

Nina Baecklund & Mathias Winge, *Wage Guarantee in Reconstructuring [sic] Proceedings in Sweden*, 2006 Global Insolvency & Restructuring Yearbook 552.

Manfred Balz, *The European Union Convention on Insolvency Proceedings*, 70 Am. Bankr. L. J. 485 (1996).

Clifford Billig, *Corporate Reorganization: Equity vs. Bankruptcy*, 17 Minn. L. Rev. 237 (1933).

Régis Blazy, Bertrand Chopard, Agnès Fimayer, Jean-Daniel Guigou, *Financial Versus Social Efficiency of Corporate Bankruptcy Law: the French Dilemma?*, 3d Annual Conference on Empirical Legal Studies Papers (2007).

Michael Bogdan, *International Bankruptcy Law in Scandinavia*, 34 Int'l & Comp. L.Q. 49 (1985).

Charles D. Booth, *The Race of Two Tortoises: Insolvency Law Reform in Hong Kong and China*, 2 ABA China Law Reporter 3 (2006).

Charles D. Booth, *Drafting Bankruptcy Laws in Socialist Market Economies: Recent Developments in China and Vietnam*, 18 Colum. J. Asian L. 93 (2004).

Charles D. Booth, *When Government Intervenes: Winding Up Fraudulent Companies in Hong Kong*, 29 H.K.L. J. 368 (1999).

Charles D. Booth, *A Report on the Proceedings of the Joint Symposium on Insolvency and Secured Transactions*, Asian Development Bank (1999), http://www.adb.org/documents/others/insolvency/report_joint_symposium.pdf.

Charles D. Booth, *Living in Uncertain Times: The Need to Strengthen Hong Kong Transnational Insolvency Law*, 34 Colum. J. Transnat'l L. 389 (1996).

Charles D. Booth, *The Cramdown on Secured Creditors: An Impetus Toward Settlement*, 60 Am. Bankr. L.J. 69 (1986).

Christel Bourbon-Seclet, *Cross-Border Security Interests in Movable Property: An Attempt at Rationalizing the International Patchwork: Part 1*, 20 J.I.B.L.R. 419 (2005).

Giuliana Canè, *Enforcement of ICSID Awards: Revolutionary or Ineffective?*, 15 Am. Rev. Int'l Arb. 439 (2006).

Neil Cooper, *Corporate Groups & Insolvency*, presented at the seminario internacional de insolvencia, insolvencia transfronteriza y contratación pública, March 29, 2006.

Oscar Couwenberg, *Survival Rates in Bankruptcy Systems: Overlooking the Evidence*, 12 Eur. J.L. & Econ. 253 (2001).

Frédérique Dahan & John Simpson, *The European Bank for Reconstruction and Development's Secured Transaction Project: A Model Law and Ten Core Principles for a Modern Secured Transaction Law in Countries of Central and Eastern Europe*, in Security Rights in Movable Property in European Private Law, 98 (Eva-Maria Kieninger ed., 2004).

Ulrich Drobnig, *Present and Future of Real and Personal Security*, 2003(5) Eur. Rev. Priv. L. 623 (2003).

Ulrich Drobnig, *Recent Legislative Trends in the Field of Personal Security*, 2 Eur. Bus. Org. L. Rev. 511 (2001).

J.O. Fabunmi, *Contract Registration and Perfection: The Legal Basis for Issuing and Using a Warehouse Receipt (negotiable/non-negotiable) as Security for Trade Finance-Issues under the Nigerian System*, 14 Lesotho L.J. 175 (2001).

Thomas B. Felsberg, Steven Kargman & Andrea Acerbi, *Brazil Overhauls Restructuring Regime*, 25(1) Int'l Fin. L. Rev. 40 (Jan. 2006).

Vanessa Finch, *Pre-Packaged Administrations: Bargains in the Shadow of Insolvency or Shadowy Bargains?*, 2006 J.B.L. 568.

Evan D. Flaschen & Ronald J. Silverman, *The Role of the Examiner as Facilitator and Harmonizer in the Maxwell Communication Corporation Insolvency*, in Current Developments in International and Comparative Corporate Insolvency Law, 621 (Jacob Ziegel ed., 1994).

Jasnica Garašić, INSOL Europe—an International Case Law—Alert II / 2006, available at http://www.brsi.de/pdfs/international_caselaw_alertNo9.pdf.

Stuart C. Gilson & Mike Vetsuypens, *CEO Compensation in Financially Distressed Firm: An Empirical Analysis*, 48 J. Fin. 425 (1993).

Roy Goode, *Harmonized Modernization of the Law Governing Secured Transactions: General-Sectorial, Global-Regional—An Overview*, 2003 Unif. L. Rev. 342.

Roy Goode, *The Protection of Interests in Movables in Transnational Commerical Law*, 1998 Unif. L. Rev. 453.

Burkhard Göpfert, *In Re Maxwell Communications—ein Beispiel einer "Koordinierten" Insolvenzverwaltung* in Parallelen Verfahren, Zeitschrift fur Zivilprozessrecht (ZZP, 1996).

Terence C. Halliday, *Closing the Implementation Gap: Why Good Laws Fail and We Can Help Them Succeed*, World Bank ICR Seminar (2007), http://www.worldbank.org/wbsite/external/topics/lawandjustice/gild/0,,contentMDK: 21031904~pagePK:64065425~piPK:455253~theSitePK:215006,00.html.

Hans Hanisch, *Bemerkungen zur Geschichte des Internationalen Insolvenzrechts*, in Festschrift für Franz Merz, 159 et seq. (W. Gerhardt et al. eds., RWS-Verlag 1992).

Ronald Winston Harmer & Clare Wee, *The Need for an Integrated Approach to Secured Transactions and Insolvency Law Reforms*, Law and Policy Reform at the Asian Development Bank, Vol. I (2000).

Wang Huaiyu, *An International Comparison of Insolvency Laws*, OECD Fifth Forum for Asian Insolvency Reform (27–28 Apr. 2006), http://www.oecd.org/dataoecd/41/41/38182541.pdf.

Ronald Winston Harmer & Clare Wee, *The Need for an Integrated Approach to Secured Transactions and Insolvency Law Reforms*, Law & Policy Reform at the Asian Development Bank, Vol. 1 (2000), http://www.adb.org/documents/others/insolvency/integ_approach_secured_trans.pdf.

Nigel J. Howcroft & Hugh Gillespie, *Remedies under Security Interests (Bermuda)*, in Remedies Under Security Interests, 37 (Ian M. Fletcher & Odd Swarting eds., 2002).

Henry Hu & Jay Lawrence Westbrook, *Abolition of the Corporate Duty to Creditors*, 107 Colum. L. Rev. 1321 (2007).

Burkhard Jakel, *Outlines of Security Interests Under German Law*, in Cross-Border Security and Insolvency (Michael Bridge and Robery Stevens eds., 2001).

Gordon W. Johnson, *The European Union Convention on Insolvency Proceedings: A Critique on the Convention's Corporate Rescue Paradigm*, 5 Int'l Insolv. Rev. 80 (1996).

H.G. Kantner, *The Protection of Creditors in Austrian Insolvency Proceedings*, 2006 Eurofenix 10.

Andrew Keay & Michael Murray, *Making Company Directors Liable: A Comparative Analysis of Wrongful Trading in the United Kingdom and Insolvent Trading in Australia*, 14 Int'l Insolv. Rev. 27 (2005).

P. Kent, *The London Approach*, 33 Bank of Eng. Q. Bull. 110 (1993).

Eva-Maria Kieninger, *Evaluation: A Common Core? Convergence, Subsisting Differences and Possible Ways for Harmonization*, in Security Rights in Movable Property in European Private Law, 647 (Eva-Maria Kieninger ed., 2004).

Boris Kozolchyk, *Law and the Credit Structure in Latin American*, 7 Va. J. Int'l L. 1 (1967).

Chris Wai Kit Lee, *Relationship Between Informal Workouts and the Courts in Malaysia*, Presentation to the Forum for Asian Insolvency Reform (Feb. 7–8 2001), http://www.oecd.org/dataoecd/7/52/1873920.pdf.

Pablo Lerner, *The Chief Enforcement Officer and Insolvency in Israeli Law*, 7 Theoretical Inquires in L. 565 (2006).

Sulette Lombard, *Directors' Liability in Cases of Insolvency from a South African Perspective*, Presentation at INSOL, London (July 2001).

Lynn M. LoPucki, *The Case for Cooperative Territoriality in International Bankruptcy*, 98 Mich. L. Rev. 2216 (2000).

Lynn M. LoPucki & William C. Whitford, *Corporate Governance in the Bankruptcy Reorganization of Large Publicly Held Corporations*, 141 U. Pa. L. Rev. 669 (1993).

Stephn J. Lubben, *The "New and Improved" Chapter 11*, 93 Ky. L.J. 839 (2004).

Sarah McBride & Phillip Day, *Asia Looks Immune to "Enronitis"—Region's Investors Long Ago Learned Not to Expect Transparency*, Asian Wall St. J. (Feb. 2, 2002).

Gerard McCormack, *Reforming the Law of Security Intersts: National and International Perspectives*, 2003 Sing. J. Legal Stud. 1 (2003).

Andrew McKnight, *The Reform of Corporate Insolvency Laws in Great Britain*, 17 J.I.B.L. 324 (2002).

Gabriel Moss, *Group Insolvency—Choice of Forum and Choice of Law: The European Experience Under the Influence of English Pragmatism*, 32 Brook. J. Int'l L. 1005 (2007).

Gabriel Moss & Christoph Paulus, *The European Insolvency Regulation—The Case for Urgent Reform*, 19 Insolv. Int. 1 (2006).

C.H. Parment, *The Nordic Bankruptcy Convention—An Introduction* (2004), http://www.iiiglobal.org/country/netherlands/Nordic_Bankruptcy.pdf.

Christoph Paulus, *Group Insolvencies—Some Thoughts about New Approaches*, 42 Tex. Int'l L. J. 819 (2007).

Christoph Paulus, *The Global Insolvency Law and the Role of Multinational Institutions*, 32 Brook. J. Int'l L. 755 (2007).

Christoph Paulus, *Judicial Cooperation in Cross-Border Insolvencies* (2006), http://siteresources.worldbank.org/GILD/Resources/GJF2006JudicialCooperationinInsolvency_PaulusEN.pdf.

Christoph Paulus & Marc Udink, *European Law and Trust*, 2004 Eurofenix 8 (2004).

Christoph Paulus, *Some Thoughts on an Insolvency Procedure for Countries*, 50. Am. J. Comp. L. 531 (2002).

Christoph Paulus, *Rechtsvergleichung im nationalen wie internationalen Insolvenzrecht: Eine Erfolgsgeschichte*, in Einheit Und Vielfalt Des Rechts: Festschrift Für Reinhold Geimer Zum Geburtstag 65 (Rolf A. Schutze ed., 2002).

Christoph Paulus, *Germany: Lessons to Learn from the Implementation of a New Insolvency Code*, 17 Conn. J. Int'l L. 89 (2001).

Christoph Paulus, *A Theoretical Approach to Cooperation in Transnational Insolvencies: A European Perspective*, 11 Eur. Bus. L. Rev. 435 (2000).

Christoph Paulus, *Verbindungslinien des Modernen Insolvenzrechts*, 49 Zeitschrift für Wirtschaftsrecht 2189 (2000).

Nuria de la Peña & Heywood W. Fleisig, *Romania: Law on Security Interests in Personal Property and Commentaries*, 29 Rev. of Cent. & East Eur. L. 133 (2004).

John Pottow, *Greed and Pride in International Bankruptcy: The Problems of and Proposed Solutions to Local Interests*, 104 Mich. L. Rev. 1899 (2006).

Harry Rajak, *Director and Officer Liability in the Zone of Insolvency: A Comparative Analysis*, 11 Potchefstroom Elec. L.J. 32 (2008).

Harry Rajak, *Can a Receiver be Negligent?*, in The Corporate Dimension, 129 (Barry AK Rider ed., 1998).

Harry Rajak, *Rescue Versus Liquidation in Central and Eastern Europe*, 33 Tex. Int'l L.J. 157 (1998).

Harry Rajak & Johan Henning, *Business Rescue for South Africa*, 116 S. Afr. L.J. 262 (1999).

Thomas Richter, *The New Czech Insolvency Act—New Insolvency Regime for Czech Corporate Debtors and Their Creditors*, Butterworths Journal of International Banking and Financial Law, June 2006.

Alfredo L. Rovira, Alejandro I. Lubinski, Gonzalo Rovira, *Security Interests Under Argentine Law*, in Remedies Under Security Interests, 1 (Ian M. Fletcher & Odd Swarting eds., 2002).

Janis Sarra, *The Oppression Remedy: The People's Choice*, in Annual Review of Insolvency Law, 133 (Janis P. Sarra ed., 2005).

Janis Sarra, *Taking the Corporation Past the "Plimsoll Line": Director and Officer Liability When the Corporation Founders*, 10 Int'l Insolv. Rev. 229 (2001).

Meghan M. Sercombe, *Good Technology and Bad Law: How Computerization Threatens Notice Filing Under Revised Article 9*, 84 Tex. L. Rev. 1065 (2006).

David A. Skeel, Jr., *Creditors' Ball: The "New" New Corporate Governance in Chapter 11*, 152 U. Pa. L. Rev. 917 (2003).

Philip Smart & Charles D. Booth, *Provisional Supervision and Workers' Wages: An Alternative Proposal*, 31 H.K.L.J. 188 (2001).

Philip Smart & Charles D. Booth, *Reforming Corporate Rescue Procedures in Hong Kong*, 1 J. Corp. L. Studies 485 (2001).

Alastair Smith & Andre Boraine, *Crossing Borders into South African Insolvency Law: From the Roman-Dutch Jurists to the UNCITRAL Model Law*, 10 Am. Bankr. Inst. L. Rev. 135 (2002).

Christoph Stäubli & Nicole Battistini-Kohler, *Swiss Insolvency and Restructuring Law—A Short Overview and Some Issues of Debate in Corporate Restructurings in Switzerland*, 15 J. Bankr. L. & Prac. 5 (2006).

Stacey Steele, *Insolvency Law in Japan*, in Insolvency Law in East Asia, 50 (Roman Tomasic ed., 2006).

Peter Straub, *Remedies under Securities Interests—Switzerland*, in Remedies Under Securities Interests, 219 (Ian Fletcher & Odd Swarting eds., 2002).

Odd Swarting & Ulrika Malmberg Livjin, *The European Council Regulation of 29 May 2000 on Insolvency Proceedings—the First Year from a Swedish Perspective* (2000), http://www.iiiglobal.org/component/jdownloads/?task=view. download&cid=387.

Dr. Shinjiro Takagi, *Restructuring in Japan*, 12 Int'l Insolv. Rev. 1 (2003).

Claudia Tobler, *Managing Failure in the New Global Economy: The UNCITRAL Model Law on Cross-Border Insolvency*, 22 B.C. Int'l & Comp. L. Rev. 383 (1999).

Alexander Trunk, *German International Insolvency Law Under the New Insolvency Code: Continuity and Evolution*, in Legal Aspects of Globalization (Jürgen Basedow & Toshiyuki Kono eds., 2000).

Frederick Tung, *Fear of Commitment in International Bankruptcy*, 33 Geo. Wash. Int'l L. Rev. 555 (2001).

Lampros Vassiliou, *Legal Issues: Thailand*, in Siam Premiere's Guide to Restructuring in Asia, Asian Development Bank 126 (2001), http://www.adb.org/Documents/reports/restructuring_asia/Thailand.pdf.

Aparna Viswanathan, *Banking and Financial Reform in India: Will it Improve Lenders' Rights and Recovery?*, 18 J.I.B.L.R. 257 (2003).

Elizabeth Warren, *Bankruptcy Policy*, 54 U. Chi. L. Rev. 777 (1987).

Elizabeth Warren & Jay Westbrook, *The Success of Chapter 11: A Challenge to the Critics*, 107 Mich. L. Rev. 603 (2009).

Bob Wessels, *Will UNCITRAL Bring Changes to Insolvency Proceedings Outside the USA and Great Britain? It Certainly Will!*, 3 Int'l Corp. Rescue 200 (2006).

Jay Lawrence Westbrook, *Locating the Eye of the Financial Storm*, 32 Brook. J. Int'l L. 1019 (2007).

Jay Lawrence Westbrook, *Multinational Financial Distress: The Last Hurrah of Territorialism*, 41 Tex. Int'l L.J. 321 (2006).

Jay Lawrence Westbrook, *The Control of Wealth in Bankruptcy*, 82 Tex. L. Rev. 795 (2004).

Jay Lawrence Westbrook, *The Duty to Seek Cooperation in Multinational Insolvency Cases*, in Annual Review of Insolvency Law 187 (Janis Sarra ed., 2004).

Jay Lawrence Westbrook, *International Judicial Negotiation*, 38 Tex. Int'l L.J. 567 (2003).

Jay Lawrence Westbrook, *Multinational Enterprises in General Default: The UNCITRAL Model Law and Related Regional Reforms* in Aktuelle Entwicklungen des europäischen und internationalen Zivilverfahrensrechts 237 (Peter Gottwald, ed., 2002).

Jay Lawrence Westbrook, *Managing Defaulting Multinationals Within NAFTA*, in Foundation and Perspectives of International Law, 465 (Ian F. Fletcher, Loukas Mistelis, Marise Cremona eds., Sweet & Maxwell, 2001).

Jay Lawrence Westbrook, *A Global Solution to Multinational Default*, 98 Mich. L. Rev. 2276 (2000).

Jay Lawrence Westbrook, *The Lessons of Maxwell Communications*, 64 Fordham L. Rev. 2531 (1996).

Jay Lawrence Westbrook, *Theory and Pragmatism in Global Insolvencies: Choice of Law and Choice of Forum*, 65 Am. Bankr. L. J. 457 (1991).

Jay Lawrence Westbrook, *A Functional Analysis of Executory Contracts*, 74 Minn. L. Rev. 227 (1989).

William C. Whitford, *Venue Choice: Where the Action Is*, 54 Buff. L. Rev. 321 (2006).

James Q. Whitman, *The Moral Menace of Roman Law and the Making of Commerce: Some Dutch Evidence*, 105 Yale L.J. 1841 (1996).

Philip Wood, *Overview*, Directors in the Twilight Zone II, 4, Presented at INSOL (Mar. 13–16, 2005).

Klaus Wimmer, *Die UNCITRAL-Modellbestimmungen über Grenzüberschreitende Insolvenzverfahrn*, in Zeitschrift für Wirtschaftsrecht (1997).

Kazuhiko Yamamoto, *New Japanese Legislation on Cross-Border Insolvency— As Compared with the UNCITRAL Model Law*, 43 Japanese Ann. Int'l L. 83 (2000).

Nicola Yeomans, *UNCITRAL Convention on Assignment of Receivables: Toward a Uniform International Law of Bulk Assignments?*, 20 J.I.B.L.R. 411 (2005).

Arthur Anyuan Yuan, *Enforcing and Collecting Money Judgments in China from a U.S. Judgment Creditor's Perspective*, 36 Geo. Wash. Int'l L. Rev. 757 (2004).

Robert Zafft & Lampros Vassiliou, *Policy Implications from the Second Forum on Asian Insolvency Reform*, in Informal Workouts, Restructuring and the Future of Asian Insolvency Reform 7 (OECD ed., 2002), http://www.oecd.org/dataoecd/17/54/16211282.pdf.

Jacob S. Ziegel, *The EBRD Model Law on Secured Transactions—Some Canadian Observations*, in Festschrift für Ulrich Drobnig zum siebzigsten Geburtstag, 209 (Jürgen Basedow ed., 1998).

2. *Books*

Douglas G. Baird, The Elements of Bankruptcy (1992).

Jochen Beckmann, Internationales Insolvenzrecht im Mercosur (2000).

Alice Belcher, Corporate Rescue: A Conceptual Approach to Insolvency Law (1997).

Steven W. Bender, et al., Modern Real Estate Finance and Land Transfer: A Transactional Approach (3d ed. 2004).

Stephen V. Berti, Swiss Debt Enforcement and Bankruptcy Law (1997).

Gary Born, International Civil Litigation in United States Courts (3d ed. 1996).

Gilberto Boutin, La Faillite en Droit International Privé Panamien et Comparé (2005).

Richard F. Broude, Insolvency and Finance in the Transportation Industry (1993).

Eberhard Braun, Commentary on the German Insolvency Code (2006).

Michael G. Bridge & Robert H. Stevens, Cross-Border Security and Insolvency (2001).

Angelo Castagnola and Roberto Sacchi, La Nuova Disciplina della Amministrazione Straordinaria delle Grandi Imprese in Stato di Insolvenza (2000).

Neil Cooper & Rebecca E. Jarvis, Recognition and Enforcement of Cross-Border Insolvency: A Guide to International Practice (1996).

J.H. Dalhuisen, Dalhuisen on International Insolvency and Bankruptcy (M. Bender, 1980–1986).

J.H. Dalhuisen, Dalhuisen on Transnational and Comparative Commercial, Financial and Trade Law (2007).

Hernando de Soto, The Mystery of Capital: Why Capitalism Triumphs in the West and Fails Everywhere Else (2000).

Ian F. Fletcher, Insolvency in Private International Law (2d ed. 2005).

Ian F. Fletcher, Insolvency in Private International Law (1st ed. 1999).

Ian F. Fletcher, The Law of Insolvency (2d ed. 1996).

Grant Gilmore, Security Interests in Personal Property (1965).

Roy Goode, Principles of Corporate Insolvency Law (3d ed. 2005).

Roy Goode, Commercial Law (3d ed.).

Roy Goode, Principles of Corporate Insolvency Law (2d ed. 1997).

Peter Gottwald, Grenzüberschreitende Insolvenzen: Europäische und Weltweite Tendenzen und Lösungen (1997).

Europaische und Amerikanische Richterbilder (Andre Gouron, et al., eds., 1996).

Edgar J. Habscheid, Grenzüberschreitendes (Internationales) Insolvenzrecht der Vereinigten Staaten von Amerika und der Bundesrepublik Deutschland (1998).

Look Chan Ho, Cross-border insolvency: a commentary on the UNCITRAL model law (1st ed., 2006).

Margaret C. Jasper, Individual Bankruptcy and Restructuring (2006).

Andrew Keay, McPherson's Law of Company Liquidation (2001).

Hans Kohler, Lehrbuch des Konkursrechts, 601 et seq. (F. Enke 1891).

Boris Kozolchyk, La Contratación Comercial en el Derecho Comparado (2006).

Thomas Laut, Universalität und Sanierung im Internationalen Insolvenzrecht (1997).

Current Issues in Cross-Border Insolvency and Reorganizations (E. Bruce Leonard & Christopher W. Besant eds., 1994).

Oliver Liersch, Grenzüberschreitendes Insolvenzrecht (2004).

Lynn M. LoPucki & Elizabeth Warren, Secured Credit: A Systems Approach (5th ed., 2006).

Boris Martor, et al., Business Law in Africa: OHADA and the Harmonization Process (2d ed., 2007).

W.W. McBryde, A. Flessner, S.C.J.J. Kortmann, Principles of European insolvency law (2003).

Michael J.Y. McMillen, et al., "Shari'ah-Compliant Equivalents to Western Mortgage-Based Financings: Structures and Primary and Secondary Markets," The Common Core of European Law: Laws of Mortgage (forthcoming).

Friedrich Meili, Die Geschichtliche Entwicklung des Internationalen Konkursrechtes (1908).

François Mélin, La faillite internationale (2004).

Michael Moritz & Barrett Seaman, Going for Broke: The Chrysler Story (1981).

Gabriel Moss, Ian Fletcher & Stuart Isaacs, The EC Regulation on Insolvency Proceedings (2002).

Paul J. Omar, European Insolvency Law (2004).

Christoph Paulus, Europäische Insolvenzverordnung (2006).

Harry Rajak, Company Liquidations (2d ed. 2006).

Harry Rajak, Peter Horrocks, and Joe Bannister, European Corporate Insolvency: A Practical Guide (1993).

European Corporate Insolvency Law: A Practical Guide (Harry Rajak, Peter Horrocks & Joe Bannister eds., 2d ed. 1995).

Miquel Angel Hernadez Romo & Carlos Sanchez-Mejorda Y Velasco, ALI, International Statement of Mexican Bankruptcy Law (2003).

Carlos Sánchez-Mejorada y Velasco (2000).

Janis Sarra, Employee Pension Claims During Company Insolvency: A Comparative Study Of 62 Jurisdictions (2008).

Filiga Michel Sawadogo, OHADA: Droit des Entreprises en Difficulté (2002).

The law of international insolvencies and debt restructurings (James R. Silkenat & Charles D. Schmerler eds., 2006).

David A. Skeel, Jr., Debt's Dominion—A History of Bankruptcy Law in America (2001).

Philip Smart & Charles D. Booth, Hong Kong Receivership and Corporate Liquidation Manual (2001).

Philip Smart, Charles D. Booth & Stephen Briscoe, Hong Kong Corporate Insolvency Manual (2002).

Anker Sorenson & Paul J. Omar, Corporate Rescue Procedures in France (1996).

Benny S. Tabalujan, Indonesian Insolvency Law (1998).

Tibor Tajti, Comparative Secured Transactions Law (2002).

Christian Tomuschat, International Law Ensuring the Survival of Mankind on the Eve of a New Century (1999).

Alexander Trunk, Internationales Insolvenzrecht (1998).

Miguel Virgós & Francisco Garcimartín, The European Insolvency Regulation: Law and Practice (2004).

Elizabeth Warren & Jay Lawrence Westbrook, The Law of Debtors and Creditors (5th ed. 2006).

Bob Wessels, International Insolvency Law (2006).

Bob Wessels, Current Topics of International Insolvency Law (2004).

James J. White & Robert Summers, Uniform Commercial Code (5th ed. 2000).

Tom Wolfe, A Man in Full (Bantam 1998).

Philip R. Wood, Comparative Law of Security Interests and Title Finance (2d ed. 2007).

Philip R. Wood, Principles of International Insolvency (2d ed. 2007).

Philip R. Wood, Principles of International Insolvency (1995).

Philip R. Wood, Comparative Law of Security and Guarantees (1995).

Current Developments in International and Comparative Corporate Insolvency Law (Joseph S. Ziegel ed., 1994).

Reinhard Zimmermann, Roman Law, Contemporary Law, European Law: The Civilian Tradition Today (2001).

Reinhard Zimmermann, The Law of Obligations—Roman Foundations of the Civilian Tradition (1996).

3. Institutional Authors

R. Gitlin & R. Mears, International Loan Workouts And Bankruptcies (1989).

American Law Institute, Statements of Canadian, Mexican, United States bankruptcy laws (2003).

Asian Development Bank, Report on RETA 5795: Insolvency Law Reforms in the Asian and Pacific Region, Law and Policy Reform at the Asian Development Bank (Vol. I, 2000).

Asian Development Bank, The Need for an Integrated Approach to Secured Transactions and Insolvency Reforms, Law and Policy Reform at the Asian Development Bank (Vol. I, 2000).

Australian Law Reform Commission, The Harmer Report (1992).

European Financial Market Lawyers Group, Proposal for an EU Directive on Collateralisation (2000), http://www.efmlg.org/Docs/efmlg_proposal.pdf.

The Insolvency Service, Company Directors Disqualification Act 1986 and Disqualified Directors: Effect of Disqualification Orders and Disqualification Un-

dertaking (2004), www.insolvency.gov.uk/pdfs/guidanceleafletspdf/cddadd. pdf.

UNCITRAL, *Legislative Guide on Insolvency Law* (2005), http://www.uncitral. org/pdf/english/texts/insolven/05–80722_Ebook.pdf.

UNCITRAL, U.N. Model Law on Cross-Border Insolvency (1997), http://www .uncitral.org/pdf/english/texts/insolven/insolvency-e.pdf.

United Nations, United Nations Convention on the Assignment of Receivables in International Trade (2004), http://www.uncitral.org/pdf/english/texts/pay ments/receivables/ctc-assignment-convention-e.pdf.

World Bank, *Principles for Effective Insolvency and Creditor Rights Systems* (2005), http://www.siteresources.worldbank.org / GILD / Resources / FINAL-ICRPrinciples-March2009.pdf.

INDEX

Access issues
  automatic access, 129, 129n21,
    131, 141, 162–163
  discretionary access, 71, 129, 130,
    131, 147
  information access, 140–141,
    146–151, 162, 167, 169, 174,
    204
  rehabilitation statutes and, 129–
    135
  single vs. dual gateway, 127–129
Accountability in insolvency
  systems, 204
Accountants as insolvency administrators, 208, 209
Account debtors, 42
Accounts receivable, 31, 41–42,
  45
Ackermann, Judge, 150
Acquired Rights Directive (EU),
  200–201
Administrators. *See* Insolvency
  administrators; Judicial and
  administrative institutions
AMCs (Asset management companies), 63
American Law Institute, Principles
  for law reform, 2
Ancillary proceeding approach,
  233–234, 235, 241
Anti-assignment clauses, 34, 95,
  95n78, 99–100
Appeal, right to, 204
Approval rights, 80–81
Article 9. *See* Uniform Commercial
  Code
Asia. *See also specific countries*
  corporate governance in, 59–60
  debt collection and insolvency
    laws in, 8
  financial crisis of 1997 in, 8n2, 60,
    63, 163, 179, 232

informal workouts and restructuring in, 172, 179
law reform in, 163–164
London Approach adopted in, 72
Asian Development Bank, 179
Asian Wall Street Journal on Enron
  collapse, 60
ASIC (Australian Securities &
  Investments Commission), 212
Asset management companies
  (AMCs), 63
Assets
  abandonment of, 91
  administered in insolvency, 68–
    69
  asset constraint, 23
  concealment of, 15, 161
  disposing of debtor's, 90–91
  post-default control of, 24–26
  preservation and collection of, 84
  structural security and, 20
Associates, transfers to, 115,
  115n116
Attachment, enforceability against
  debtor as, 23
Attorney General (US), 216
Auctions, 36
Australia
  access issues in, 129–130
  employees' rights in, 194
  fraudulent trading in, 54
  information disclosure in, 151
  judicial and administrative
    institutions in, 212, 220
  rescue regimes in, 122
  secured creditor protection in, 71,
    137–138
  tax claims in, 89
  wrongful/insolvent trading in,
    55–56
Australian Securities & Investments
  Commission (ASIC), 212